The Pastor-Evangelist
in the Parish

Also by Richard Stoll Armstrong

Faithful Witnesses
   A Course in Evangelism for Presbyterian Laity
   Leader's Guide
   Participant's Book

The Pastor-Evangelist in Worship

The Pastor as Evangelist

Service Evangelism

The Pastor-Evangelist in the Parish

Richard Stoll Armstrong

Westminster/John Knox Press
Louisville, Kentucky

Book design by Gene Harris

First edition

Published by Westminster/John Knox Press
Louisville, Kentucky

PRINTED IN THE UNITED STATES OF AMERICA

9 8 7 6 5 4 3 2 1

Library of Congress Cataloging-in-Publication Data

Armstrong, Richard Stoll, 1924–
    The pastor-evangelist in the parish / Richard Stoll Armstrong. —
1st ed.
         p.   cm.
    Includes bibliographical references.
    ISBN 0-664-25131-5

    1. Evangelistic work. 2. Clergy—Office. I. Title.
BV3793.A753 1990
253—dc20
                                                              90-32388

This book is dedicated to
the Oak Lane Presbyterian Church
of Philadelphia, Pennsylvania,
where I first learned
what it means for a pastor
to do the work of an evangelist.

Contents

Preface

The preface of a book, as everyone knows, is the place for credits, acknowledgments, and thank-yous. In each of my previous books the last person to be thanked was my wife, Margie, to whom I have always been the most indebted. This time the last shall be first, for without her patience, understanding, and encouragement this book would never have been completed. More than any other human being, she has been my constant support and inspiration, the only one who really knows and understands the interruptions and competing obligations that seem to be my nemesis as a writer.

There are many others to whom I am also indebted, including my daughter Elsie Armstrong Olsen, a Certified Christian Educator, whose comments on Part Three were most helpful; my daughter Ellen Armstrong Kanarek, whose indispensable help with the index enabled me to meet the publisher's deadline; the students in my Pastor as Evangelist course at Princeton Theological Seminary, who were the first recipients of many of the ideas and suggestions in this book and whose feedback has been invaluable; the faculty colleagues who have responded to my concerns from their various academic perspectives; and the many pastors with whom I have interacted and reflected on what it means for a clergyperson to do the work of an evangelist. I am immensely grateful to all these persons, not just for being intelligent sounding boards but for being willing to take seriously the questions I have raised and to recognize the implications of those questions for their own ministries.

The preface is also the place for expressed intentions and disclaimers. Discerning readers need to know the author's intentions in regard to any topic that is greater than the scope of his or her inquiry. For this reason I must disclaim any intention of presenting an in-depth treatment of the various professional roles of a pastor. I do not pretend to be an expert in any of these areas, nor could I deal with them adequately in one volume if I were, for each is a major topic in itself, with many different subtopics, each with its own huge body of literature. Nor is this a book on the theology and practice of pastoral ministry. There are many good books in that category, and I have not attempted to add another to the collection.[1] Nor is it, except for a brief discussion in the introductory chapter, a book on the theology of evangelism, or on the meaning and importance of evangelism.[2] Nor is it about motivating and equipping others for evangelism, or about organizing for evangelism in the local church. I have already addressed these last-mentioned topics in my other writings.

This book has a very specific and, in a sense, narrow focus: the pastor's ministry of evangelism. It attempts to examine in very specific ways how a pastor does the work of an evangelist. Its focus is narrow in that the pastor's professional roles are viewed from an evangelistic perspective. How does a pastor fulfill her or his ministry as a teacher, a counselor, an administrator, a public figure, or in any other role, with evangelistic sensitivity?

This is the third in a series of books I have devoted to this general theme. With the exception of some of the material in chapters 1 and 2, this book does not repeat or review what was covered in the first two volumes;[3] rather, it moves on from where the second book ended.

The first book, *The Pastor as Evangelist,* considers the pastor's ministry of evangelism in terms of personal relationships and the various factors that determine the context and shape the style of that ministry. Pastors' concerns about the meaning and purpose of evangelism, along with a theology of evangelism, the nature and role of faith, and an evangelistic style, are discussed at length.

The second book, *The Pastor-Evangelist in Worship,* examines two of the pastor's professional roles through evangelistic glasses. Because there is no discussion of the meaning or theology of evangelism per se in this second book, my inaugural address as Professor of Ministry and Evangelism at Princeton Seminary is included as an appendix in that book.[4] The first half of the book is devoted to the pastor-evangelist as worship leader; the second half looks at the pastor-evangelist as preacher.

This third book in the series has been too long in the making. My excuse for the delay is that another major writing project intervened. I must confess, however, that I have also been guilty of procrastination, largely because of uncertainty about how to approach the topic. I finally decided that instead of treating the various roles theoretically and objectively, I would reflect on my own experience as a pastor-evangelist. My intention in so doing is to be not merely anecdotal but analytical, not simply biographical but personal. I want to talk honestly and openly about what it means to me to do the work of an evangelist and about the challenges and difficulties that oft-quoted exhortation to Timothy (2 Tim. 4:5) presents.

I believe that it behooves a pastor to face forthrightly and honestly the question, Am I fulfilling my personal ministry of evangelism? One must answer that question for oneself. The question this book addresses is, How does a pastor go about doing the work of an evangelist? What follows reflects my own continuing struggle with that question.

R.S.A.

Princeton, New Jersey

Introduction

I believe the gospel is (or should be) the unifying theme and the integrative principle for all ministry. To the extent that what we do as pastors[1] is not related to, reflective of, consistent with, guided by, focused on, or directed toward the gospel, it ceases to be Christian ministry. That is the premise on which I have based this three-volume study of the pastor as evangelist, viewing the pastor's personal relationships and professional roles from an evangelistic perspective.

Evangelism is not just one thing among many that a pastor does. It is the heart of *everything* a pastor does! If we have no concern about, no interest in, no sense of responsibility for sharing the good news, what are we doing in the ministry? How can we fulfill our ministry if we are not doing the work of an evangelist?

Lest there be any confusion about what I mean by the term, let me state my textbook definition of evangelism:

> Evangelism is proclaiming in word and deed the good news of the kingdom of God, and calling people to repentance, to personal faith in Jesus Christ as Lord and Savior, to active membership in the church, and to obedient service in the world.[2]

I say "textbook" because what I mean when I say doing evangelism does not always include everything in that definition. It describes for me what holistic evangelism should be striving to accomplish, but it does not define or limit the ways of reaching that goal.

For that reason, doing the work of an evangelist may call for different responses in different situations. Pastor-evangelists may differ in their ideas about what a proper response may be. For me, doing the work of an evangelist means acting with evangelistic sensitivity in a given situation. To be evangelistically sensitive is to know when to speak up and when to be silent, when to confront and when to console, when to proclaim and when to provide, when to exhort and when to explain. We sometimes think the only time we are doing evangelism is when we are the ones doing the talking. But a good witness knows she or he must win the right to be heard. We have not failed to do the work of an evangelist when, as caring listeners, we delay our presentation of the gospel until a more favorable time. The ultimate goal is to bear witness to Jesus Christ, and there are times when we do that better by listening than by talking. Sensitivity also means knowing the appropriate thing to say when we do speak.

Having defined the term, I want to say that my ideas about evangelism are not distillations of what I have read on the subject or theoretical conclusions drawn from my own academic research. They are personal convictions rooted in my own experience, and they represent the result of much theological reflection on my years as a pastor. I was never taught in seminary what it means to be or how to do the work of an evangelist. If there was an elective course in the theology and practice of evangelism, I was not aware of it. My understanding of evangelism, therefore, is the result of a kind of "progressive revelation," and the pilgrimage continues as the ever-changing world presents new challenges each day.

It was in seminary, nevertheless, that I had my first experience of any form of evangelism. It occurred in the context of the field education program. As one of the requirements of that department the director had arranged with a church in the area for every student to participate one evening in that church's visitation program. With some curiosity and much trepidation, I reported with a group of other students on the scheduled night. Each of us was assigned to a lay member of the church, who was to be the team leader as we called on people who had visited the church. Each team received a packet of five or six "prospect cards" and some literature about the church. After a few instructions and a brief prayer, we dispersed two-by-two into the community.

My partner and I had delightful visits in four homes that night, and I was pleasantly surprised by both the warmth of the reception accorded us and by the genuine appreciation of those we visited. I was also impressed by the natural manner of my partner, whose disarming friendliness gained us entry every time, despite the fact that we were calling without an appointment. My positive feelings about the experience were reinforced during the debriefing back at the church, as the various teams reported on their calls.

Sitting among those enthusiastic church members, the light dawned within me. This kind of outreach was something every church could and should do! Driving back to seminary, I resolved that I would strive to make such a program a priority for any congregation I was called to serve. Shortly thereafter I read Tom

Allan's book *The Face of My Parish* and became even more excited, as I saw that such a program need not be limited to calls only on those who had visited the church.[3]

That idea appealed to the members of the Pulpit Nominating Committee from the Oak Lane Presbyterian Church of Philadelphia, when they interviewed me as a candidate for the position of pastor. The congregation also responded to the vision and voted to call me as their pastor. They were eager to get started on their well-conceived and far-reaching self-renewal plan, dubbed "Operation Bootstrap," by which they hoped to reverse the downhill slide that the church had been on for the past twenty-five years. They viewed the idea of reaching out to the community as a natural extension of their rejuvenation effort, and soon Operation Bootstrap became "Operation Doorbell."

Little did I know, fresh out of seminary, about training people to do visitation evangelism—something I myself had done only once! Nor had my theological education included any instruction in how to do evangelism in a predominantly Jewish community. We realized, however, that if we wanted the church to grow, we were going to have to reach out to the unchurched people in the neighborhood. We did not have the luxury of a list of prospective members on whom to call. We would need to find new prospects, and that meant calling on strangers.

Many of the doors on which we knocked would be opened by our Jewish and Roman Catholic neighbors. Would they be offended by our doorbell-ringing? They would have every right to be offended or annoyed if our visitors were pushy, insensitive, or rude. But we were calling to win friends, not converts, and to offer our help in any appropriate and acceptable way to those who needed it, whether or not they joined our church. We were not out to steal sheep from other flocks. Ours was service-oriented evangelism.

The response was overwhelmingly positive. We soon discovered we had a mission field right in our own backyard. We began finding unchurched persons. Some of them we referred to other churches and synagogues in the community, some of them, of course, remained unchurched, and some of them eventually did join our church. When Oak Lane began to change racially, our membership reflected the demographics of the community, as every congregation should.

Our church was experiencing a remarkable rebirth. Attendance at worship and Sunday school increased dramatically. Mission giving soared. The various church committees and organizations were busier than ever as they geared themselves to minister to the needs of the community.

The human catalysts for this turnabout were the faithful visitors who were out ringing doorbells every Monday night. We were over-joyed by but not proud of our church's numerical growth. We knew we were only the seed planters and waterers; God was giving the growth. Our Monday night callers were themselves the principal beneficiaries of their own ministry, as they became more confident and competent ambassadors for Christ.[4]

Evangelistic calling is a spiritual discipline that a busy pastor can easily be tempted to neglect. Moreover, pastors can rationalize their noninvolvement on the grounds that their task is not to do evangelism but to train others to do it. My conscience would not let me off the hook so easily. So every Monday night I did my share of visiting, and when the callers returned for the reporting period, I was there with them to reflect upon and learn from our faith-sharing experiences. These were precious times for all of us, as together we were learning to be more faithful disciples and more effective witnesses.

Before long we were being asked to share with others what we had learned. That is when I began to do some serious theological reflection on our evangelistic ministry, in order to be able to con-ceptualize, articulate, and communicate whatever teachable princi-ples could be discerned from our experience. The foundational principle for our evangelistic outreach was the biblical image of the church as the servant people of God. As those who were called to follow in the footsteps of one who came as a Suffering Servant, we believed our mission was to minister to the needs of people within and beyond our church walls.

But how could we minister to people's needs unless we knew what their needs were? And how could we know people's needs unless we reached out to them? That is the best rationale I know for visitation evangelism. A servant church can do no less. The question is not whether to do it but *how!* Our answer was what I have called "service evangelism," described as "reaching out to others in Christian love, listening to them, identifying with them, caring for them, and sharing faith with them in such a way that they will freely respond and want to commit themselves to trust, love, and obey God as a disciple of Jesus Christ and a member of his servant community, the church."[5]

Making a case for Christ has been for me the focus of years of theological ruminating. It is an apologetic task, the complexities of which were multiplied for me by graduate studies at Temple Univer-sity, where my Christian beliefs were confronted head-on by the truth claims of other religions and philosophical systems. I had to understand why I believe what I believe, or I could no longer preach with integrity. I struggled with the paradoxical nature of faith and finally concluded that, ultimately, faith has to be a gift of God, not something we can make ourselves have but something we find ourselves with.

To take seriously the givenness of faith is to realize that we cannot answer the *why* question without finally having to resort to statements that are tautological and subjective. Our reasons are themselves faith statements. Our conclusions are assumptions. Our truth claims are not self-evident to someone who does not share our assumptions. Our dogmatic assertions from the pulpit and our propositional arguments in the living room are affirmations of faith, not facts provable to an unbeliever.

That reality has tremendous implications for the way we do evangelism, calling for a more confessional approach. I came to realize that our task as Christian witnesses is not to prove that Jesus Christ is the son of God. That we can never do. Our role as witnesses is to show by the way we speak and act that we really *believe* he is. That, *by God's grace,* we can do!

In such an enterprise, religious experience is indispensable. As a teacher of evangelism I realized that I had to make a rational case for an experiential faith.[6] Our references to personal experience are crucial and powerfully effective when offered not as proof that what we say is true but as the confirming evidence of our own faith assumptions. We cannot use our experience as the basis for making normative truth claims, but it is perfectly legitimate to show, when asked, how our experience reinforces our own faith. I can't speak or preach with conviction about a Savior I don't know personally. If I have no experience of God, what can I say about God?

Being convinced of the validity of experience as a basis for one's personal conviction of the reality of God, I have tried to develop ways of teaching people to share their faith. To do that, they must first win the right to be heard. Such an approach requires that a witness first be a good listener, someone who can free other people to identify and name their own experiences of God. It also requires a high degree of sensitivity to be able to relate to people "where they are."

The principles are as relevant for pastors as they are for lay people. The idea that because of their theological training pastors are more highly skilled at interpersonal evangelism than lay people is a false impression. Their theological training may be for some pastors more a liability than an asset in interpersonal evangelism. Mainline pastors especially may be averse to or intimidated by the "E" word (evangelism). Some have admitted to me that they are terrified by the thought of having a one-on-one faith-sharing conversation with an unchurched stranger. They confess they have no idea where to begin or how to go about it. Nor have they the slightest notion of what it means for a pastor to do the work of an evangelist.

Suspecting that not a few readers may harbor some of these feelings, at least to a degree, I have chosen to discuss first the pastor-evangelist as visitor, a role in which the pastor's interpersonal evangelism skills are most obviously employed.[7]

PART ONE

**The Pastor-Evangelist
as Visitor**

1

Pastoral Visitation as Evangelism

If visitation evangelism were defined strictly in relation to the intended recipients of the message, some pastors would insist that the term applies only to calls on those who are unchurched, be they unbelievers, adherents of other faiths, backsliding Christians, or even unbaptized believers. The distinction between an evangelistic call and an "ordinary" pastoral call, in other words, would hinge on the relationship of the recipient to the church. Pastors who hold this view, it is safe to say, do not think of pastoral visitation as evangelism. It is a plausible argument, for there is a legitimate conceptual distinction to be made between evangelism and pastoral care, even though all would agree that the distinction is sometimes blurred.

If, however, evangelism is more broadly conceived than merely as the proclamation of the gospel to the unchurched, all pastoral visitation can be viewed as an opportunity for evangelism. That is, every pastoral visit can be, and in my opinion should be, approached with evangelistic sensitivity. It is not a matter of labeling certain calls "evangelistic" and others "pastoral." It is a matter of being pastoral and evangelistically sensitive on any and every call. That is how I understand the pastor-evangelist's role as visitor.

Indeed, perhaps more than any other professional role, the ministry of visitation involves the pastor-evangelist directly in interpersonal evangelism. That includes what some call "ordinary pastoral calling." Since the goal of my evangelistic witness among church members is to face seriously with them what it means to be Christ's woman or Christ's man in the world today and to take the next logical step of faith in obedience to the Lordship of Christ, I view every pastoral visit as an evangelistic opportunity.

Among unchurched persons, however, I hope to help them discover the God who is already at work in their lives. When I have earned the right to be heard, I want to bear witness to the Christ who has shown the world what God has done, is doing, and can do for those who love, trust, and obey God. I want them to discover by grace through faith that Jesus Christ makes possible a relationship with God that is both personal and spiritual, present and eternal.

Some pastors and laypersons assume there are different sets of rules for calling on people in each of these categories. That is an unfortunate misconception. Although it is true that an active member acts regarding the church on a set of assumptions different from those of a totally unchurched person, the basic principles of interpersonal communication are the same in either case. The application of those principles varies with the individual, but the general rules cover the variations. That's why I make a distinction between "method" and "style." Methods may vary to suit the situation, but one's style of relating to people should be consistent with one's own faith commitment and theological beliefs.

Thus, to speak of an incarnational approach is to refer to a style that applies to any evangelistic situation. To say that a witness must first be a listener is to state a rule that is basic to effective interpersonal witnessing. To understand faith sharing as two-way rather than one-way communication defines a style that is relevant for relating to saints and sinners alike. To appeal for evangelistic sensitivity is to recognize that one's approach should be appropriate to the situation and relevant to the individual. That is a universally applicable principle, not a method.

There are, it is true, unique considerations regarding various kinds of visits. There are special rules pertaining to hospital calls, for example, that have no bearing on home visits. There are a few ways in which calling in the home of a stranger is different from visiting a member of the church. Some of these distinctions will be pointed out. Methods may vary, but the need for evangelistic sensitivity is constant. It is our evangelistic sensitivity that informs our method.

I have structured the contents of Part One on a vertical basis rather than a horizontal one. That is, the role of the pastor-evangelist as visitor will be discussed in relation to where the visit takes place, instead of in terms of the various types of individuals encountered. I have chosen this approach because of my conviction that the principles of evangelism and the interpersonal witnessing style described in the following pages apply no matter what the human situation may be. It is much easier to distinguish between a few locations where our pastoral visitation occurs than between the countless types of people we encounter.[1]

One other important distinction needs to be made. Someone might ask why I have chosen to discuss visitation and counseling in separate sections, rather than include these two subjects under the single heading of pastoral care, of which they are related aspects. The distinction is a functional one. Pastoral care is a nonspecific term, referring to the purpose or the intended effect (or at least one of the effects) of all pastoral ministry.[2] Pastoral care is provided not only through pastoral visitation and counseling but also through other ministerial practices, such as preaching, teaching, worship leadership (for example, funerals and weddings), and administration (for example, pastoral correspondence).[3]

One cannot correctly speak of "doing" pastoral care the way one speaks of "doing" pastoral visitation or counseling, which are identifiable functions. You may have an idea of what someone means by "visiting," but you have no idea of what I might have done to provide pastoral care unless I say more about it. I would have to describe what I did in functional terms. For example: "I called on Julio several times in the hospital before he died and visited his widow, Maria, at home, before and after the memorial service, which we planned together. She has joined a grief-healing group at our church." If I said something like that, you would have at least some idea of the form of pastoral care Julio and Maria received. One provides pastoral care *through* the ministry of counseling, pastoral visitation, preaching, and so forth.

It is legitimate to speak of the ministry of pastoral care when that expression is intended to mean everything we do to provide for the spiritual and general well-being of the recipient of that ministry. The ministry of preaching is a very important part of the overall pastoral care of a congregation and therefore ties in directly or indirectly with the pastor's counseling ministry. An example of a direct tie-in might be a discussion with a shut-in relating to the subject of your sermon, which the person has received in the mail or heard on tape. An indirect tie-in might be your sermon series on death and dying and your visit with a family grieving over the loss of a loved one. Although no direct reference is made to your sermons, your messages have already been helping the family to cope and have paved the way for your visit.

Since the focus of this book is not pastoral care but evangelism, it is helpful to make the functional distinction between visiting and counseling instead of lumping them together under the heading of pastoral care. It is also consistent with the approach and format of *The Pastor-Evangelist in Worship,* in which the pastor-evangelist's roles as preacher and as worship leader were discussed from an evangelistic perspective. The unifying theme of this study of pastoral roles, as has been stated, is evangelism.

Pastoral care and evangelism are, or ought to be, intimately related. Evangelism and pastoral care are both concerned for the whole person. Evangelism that is not pastoral is insensitive; pastoral care that is not concerned with the person's spiritual well-being is incomplete (see chapter 6).

2

Planning Home Visits

The most obvious place to begin a discussion of the pastor-evangelist as visitor is where most of our visiting takes place: in the home.
A number of questions come to mind immediately.

To Call or Not to Call?

Before we consider some of the evangelistic implications of the
ministry of pastoral calling, I need to make the case for what some
pastors seem to feel is simply not their cup of tea and, hence, not their
responsibility. The first definition of the transitive verb "to visit"
given in *Webster's New International Dictionary* is Going or coming
to see someone to provide help or comfort.[4] The intention expressed
in that definition is one I would certainly want to apply to the
pastor-evangelist as visitor.

In the Bible, as in the dictionary, a visit can be for the purpose of
affliction, judgment, or punishment (for example, Ex. 32:34; Isa.
26:14), as well as to comfort, reward, or benefit (for example, Gen.
50:24; Jer. 29:10). The Hebrew word for the verb "to visit" is *paqad,*
which means to look over or after, inspect, investigate, search, or (in
its passive forms) to be looked after, inspected, and so on. The fact
that in the Old Testament Prophets, a divine visitation *(pequddah)*
was usually an occasion of judgment and punishment may account
for the aversion of some pastors to the term "visitation evangelism."
They forget that God's visitation[5] in Jesus was one of blessing, not
of affliction (Luke 7:16).

The Greek word that the New Testament uses for the Hebrew verb
paqad is *episkeptomai,* meaning "to look upon," "have regard for
something or someone," or "to visit" (especially the sick). Jesus was
well aware of the high value that rabbinic tradition placed on visit-

ing. He said that people will be judged on the basis of whether or not they have visited the sick and the imprisoned.

> It is not a question of isolated acts but of a fundamental attitude. One has to realize that one does not exist of and for oneself, but of and for the other. This is to be expressed in one's actions. . . . Even when *episkeptomai* means "to seek out someone" in the NT, it never implies merely "to visit" that person in the usual sense, or for selfish ends, but always "to be concerned about them, with a sense of responsibility for others."[6]

This is the spirit in which Paul says to Barnabas, "Come, let us return and visit the brethren in every city where we proclaimed the word of the Lord, and see how they are" (Acts 15:36).[7]

The verb "to visit" has been used to translate other Greek verbs in the New Testament, each with its own shade of meaning.[8] It is interesting, for example, that in Galatians 1:18 ("Then after three years I went up to Jerusalem to visit Cephas") Paul chooses to use the verb *historeō,* the only time it appears in the New Testament. In this context it means "to visit in order to get to know."[9] As a new convert to Christianity, Paul wanted to get to know the man he had heard so much about. The two spent fifteen days getting acquainted.

"To visit in order to get to know" is one important purpose of visitation evangelism, as church members reach out to their neighbors. It is also a reason for the pastor-evangelist to visit people in their homes. It is too bad that while some ministers do not see visiting as their responsibility, others do very little calling because they do not view home visitation as one of their top priorities. Of course, they agree that pastoral care does necessarily involve some calling. They may argue, however—and with validity—that the responsibility for "routine" parish calling is not theirs alone but should be shared by the officers and members of the church.[10] Thus the pastor's time, they rationalize, is better spent equipping others to do it. That, to be sure, is time well spent, but it does not provide an excuse for pastors to shirk their own responsibility as visitors.

How different their attitude is from that of one pastor-evangelist who, writing of his ministry in New York City many years ago, expressed his commitment to evangelistic calling in these impassioned words:

> If the people would not come to church and if they would not heed my message from the pulpit, I meant to toil in the streets of the city until there was no more strength in me. I intended to meet people in their homes and offices and bring them if possible to the personal choice of Jesus Christ as their Saviour. I went into it with the determination to win or die, and before God, I would have kept my word.

Morning, noon and night I was at it. My prayers and my efforts went together, and I walked the streets of New York every hour in the afternoon until it seemed to me that if all the stairs I had climbed had been put on top of one another I would have been a long way towards the moon.[11]

I believe that the ministry of visitation is tremendously important to us as pastor-evangelists; it enhances and augments our total pastoral care ministry. The fact is, most people genuinely appreciate a visit by the pastor. It is a matter of calling not because they expect us to but because they like us to; not because we have to but because we want to.

From a pastoral standpoint, there are advantages to visiting people in their homes. First of all, we are on the other person's turf.[12] That in itself has helpful psychological implications for the person we visit, who has the security of his or her own surroundings and is often more open to honest dialogue and receptive to faith sharing. Second, our coming shows our concern and under normal circumstances creates a positive impression. Third, calling in our parishioners' homes gives us an opportunity to see them in their natural habitat, in a comfortable setting, and, perhaps, in a more relaxed attitude. Fourth, home calls foster a feeling of belonging in those we visit, who want to be able to identify with their pastor. Thus our ministry of visitation helps to build up the body of Christ, not to mention our own relationships with our parishioners. The old adage still pertains: "A home-calling pastor makes a church-going congregation."

There are times when the relationship with the person visited may be anything but friendly. At such times the home visit affords an opportunity for reconciliation. People can be reconciled without having to agree. Paul exhorted the Philippians to be of one mind (attitude, spirit) (Phil. 2:2), even if not of one opinion. I confess, however, that my pride often gets in the way. Instead of seeking to be reconciled, I find myself seeking to be right. Instead of trying to win the person, I try to win the argument, and I end up winning neither. As a pastor-evangelist I need to keep reminding myself why I am there.

At the same time, home visits are an important context for exercising pastoral leadership. When there is conflict in the church over a controversial issue, the pastor-evangelist can do much to resolve it by meeting with members in their homes. It has been my experience that people's biases and prejudices are changed more often through one-to-one encounters than from the pulpit. That is not to discount the power and importance of preaching but to recognize the value of interpersonal dialogue in effecting attitudinal change.

When my first congregation was experiencing what for some was the trauma of racial integration in the community and in the church, I spent many an hour, week after week, month after month, in people's homes, often dealing with bitterness and hostility born of prejudice and bigotry, ignorance and intolerance. In these encounters, many people's minds and hearts were changed by the power of the Holy Spirit. There was much faith sharing, as people struggled with what it means to be one in Christ. The next logical step of faith was clear but not easy for some: to acknowledge the Lordship of Jesus Christ and to affirm their commitment to an inclusive outreach and ministry.

The visits were not always successful. Often I had to eat humble pie. That was not a diet I enjoyed, and I live with the indigestion of my failures. But I also live with the knowledge that at least I made the effort. I was doing the work of an evangelist.[13]

To Prioritize or Not to Prioritize?

Most pastors admit they are unable to do as much calling as they'd like to do, simply because they are so busy. Certainly, priorities have to be established, and these should be communicated and interpreted to the congregation. The parishioners need to know our philosophy and what it is we are trying to accomplish in our calling ministry. It can be very difficult to keep up with all the demands on our time. Often, there are so many emergencies, problems, and needs that we don't have time to make so-called routine calls. Early in my ministry I concluded that I had to give priority to calls about serious accidents, illnesses, or death, and to calls about weddings, baptisms, joining the church, and specific problems or needs, including those of people who were homebound. My ever-growing calling list included both members and nonmembers.

Please note that the prioritizing of all pastoral visitation, including what has traditionally been thought of as evangelistic calling, should be based on need, not on receptivity. Partly because of a success-motivated mentality fostered by an undue emphasis on church growth, some pastors have bought the receptivity principle; that is, Concentrate on the people whom you consider to be most receptive to the gospel. It makes practical sense from a church-growth point of view. Why waste time on resistant people? Why beat your evangelistic head against the stone wall of a secular heart?

I have problems with such an attitude. In the first place, it discounts the work of the Holy Spirit, who may not agree at all with our human assessment of a person's readiness, and who can radically transform people's hearts in ways that confound our best predictions. Second, even if we are right about resistant people, they are the very ones who need most to hear the gospel. Who evangelizes them, if we who should—and could—do not? "How are they to believe in him of whom they have never heard?" (Rom. 10:14b). Third, even if our evangelistic efforts seem to bear no immediate fruit, who knows when the seeds we have planted or watered may sprout and grow? Again, it is God who gives the growth (1 Cor. 3:6).

Some pastors have unwittingly been practicing a kind of evangelistic triage: Ignore those who can save themselves, toss out those who can't be saved, and concentrate on the ones who (in their opinion) can be saved.

Since time is a limiting factor, the key word for me has been availability—my own availability. As a pastor I knew I had to prioritize to be available to call where my pastoral services were most needed. If I were to spend my time making routine social visits, as much as I enjoy that part of my ministry, I might not be available for the ever-increasing number of priority calls. Conversely, if I wanted to be available when and where I was most needed, I realized I had to limit the time spent on social calls. Availability requires prioritizing.

Although I love to visit socially, as a pastor-evangelist I came to view no call as strictly social. Whether it was a routine call or an emergency, I did my best to make it a faith-sharing visit—always. The key, as I have said, is availability. There is a burden to being available, but I find the burden is lighter if I prioritize.

To Plan or Not to Plan?

The answer to the question of planning is—both! As a pastor I did a lot of spur-of-the-moment calling. That is, I might be in a given area or neighborhood for some reason, and while there I would often pop in on parishioners or nonmembers on my calling list. It was simply a matter of stewardship of time. When one's parishioners are spread out over a large geographical area, be it urban, as my parishes have been, or rural, it is wise to take advantage of one's proximity to parishioners living or working in the vicinity. This, by the way, is one time when brief "routine" visits are definitely in order. Pastoral needs often surface unexpectedly during these unplanned visits. Indeed, some of my most meaningful faith-sharing conversations have occurred during such spontaneous visits, confirming my sense that it was the Holy Spirit who prompted them.

At the same time, I was always systematically mapping out calling schedules, including the names of persons or families I wanted to visit. These lists were the product of my general pastoral care of and concern for people, especially during my intercessory prayer times, when the Holy Spirit would present certain people to my heart. The list was always longer than I was able to keep up with, for it included not only parishioners but nonmembers as well, persons with whom I had established a relationship and who I felt needed a pastoral call.

I know pastors who are admirably organized but so locked into their schedules that they have no flexibility or freedom to be spontaneous in their pastoral visiting. They miss the serendipitous joy of seizing the opportunity. That raises the next logical question.

To Phone or Not to Phone?

In my seminars on visitation evangelism, probably the question most frequently asked by pastors and lay people alike is, Should you telephone first to make an appointment? My answer is deliberately provocative: Only if it is to your convenience. I wouldn't want to drive twenty-five miles to visit a couple, only to find them not at home. In that case it would be wise to telephone first.

But if we try to set up appointments in advance for all our calls, we find ourselves having to spread our visits over many days without any control over their geographical proximity. That, in my opinion, is no way to run a visitation railroad. It took me about two weeks in my first pastorate to discover that what I learned about this at seminary was simply not feasible. I dutifully phoned for appointments to call on the families in a particular neighborhood, only to be told that this one could see me on Tuesday night, and that one on Saturday morning, and some other one on Sunday afternoon, and so on.

That is not an efficient way to operate. It is better to identify a group of calls we want to make in a given area and take our chances on finding people at home. One category of people we can invariably expect to see are those who are homebound. If a call is not convenient for those whose doorbells we ring, we can say hello and good-bye and leave. They won't resent our coming unannounced if we don't force ourselves upon them, especially if we have let it be known in advance that we'll be calling in the area, and if our philosophy and style of visiting are communicated to the congregation. What I am saying applies to routine calling. If there is an emergency, or if there is a specific reason for wanting to see a particular person or persons, it is better to telephone first to set a time. This is for our benefit as much as theirs, so we won't spend time driving a distance to see someone who isn't home. Even so, if we do call and no one is home, we can leave a card and a note. Just the fact that we were there is important.

There's another dimension to this question: the use of the telephone as a medium for pastoral care. In that sense the answer to the question To phone or not to phone? is definitely yes. I learned much too late in my ministry the immeasurable value of a pastoral telephone call. So often I kept thinking I could get around to making certain visits that I never had time for, when I could have accomplished the same purpose with a telephone call. I now consider visiting on the telephone to be part of my role as visitor.

I have learned three lessons in regard to making pastoral telephone calls.[14] The first is the principle of vocal compensation. Back in the days when I was courting Margie, we used to talk as often via long-distance telephone as our meager finances would allow. She was a student at Wellesley and I was at Princeton. During one of our telephone conversations not long after I had been incurably bitten by the love bug, Margie interrupted me at one point to ask if I were unhappy. "Not at all," I replied. "Why do you think I'm unhappy?"

"Because you *sound* unhappy!" Actually I was moonstruck—madly in love—but I wasn't unhappy, and I had no idea that I sounded unhappy. "I can't see you," Margie explained. "All I have to go on is your voice." I've never forgotten that lesson. The person at the other end of the line cannot see your facial expression or body language. She or he does not know whether you are smiling or frowning. To come across as happy, you have to sound happy; to come across as friendly you have to sound friendly. Your voice has to compensate for what your face and body cannot communicate. That is what I mean by vocal compensation, an evangelistic principle for which I have my wife to thank, and one that is extremely important to remember when bearing witness on the telephone.

The flip side of vocal compensation is the principle of auditory accommodation. Because you cannot see the other person, you have to listen all the more carefully. That includes pausing more often to give the other person opportunities to speak and being extra careful not to interrupt. All the rules of interpersonal witnessing apply. The only difference is that since your eyes cannot help you, you have to rely on your sense of hearing. Your ears have to accommodate for what your eyes can't tell you. Have you ever had the experience of being cut off, without realizing it, from the party with whom you were conversing on the telephone? You feel silly when you discover you have been talking and there's no one on the other end of the line. That's all the more reason to pause for frequent feedback. It is a cardinal rule that to be an effective witness one must first be a good listener, especially when witnessing by telephone.

The third lesson, one that took me far too long to discover, is the value and effectiveness of the telephone as a medium for faith sharing and for prayer. I call it telephonic inspiration. I always believed that there was no substitute for being present in person, and because of that conviction I lived constantly with a frustrated, if not guilty, conscience for all the visits I hadn't been able to make. I'm not referring to visits with persons who had experienced a death in the family, a serious illness, or some other crisis or event that necessitated an immediate pastoral call. Like most pastors I tried hard to be available in cases of emergency or when I was really needed. I'm thinking of those persons whom, in the course of my pastoral "brooding" over and praying for the members of my flock and others on my intercessory prayer list, I felt I needed to visit, for whatever reason.

The result was that my list of calls to be made was always much longer than I could ever possibly accommodate. Out of a sense of desperation I started to make more use of the telephone. It took me a while to realize and appreciate how effective a medium the telephone can be for pastoral care and for faith sharing. Although a telephone call can be a good substitute for being with someone face-to-face, it should be viewed not as a way of avoiding actual visits but as an opportunity for a personal conversation that might not otherwise take place. It certainly is not an excuse to eliminate pastoral visitation, but it is the next best thing to visiting in person. I say that because I've experienced the reality of telephonic inspiration.

The pastor-evangelist has to be sensitive to the person on the other end of the line. I would never want to impose a prayer on someone under any circumstances, nor do I ever tack on a perfunctory prayer at the end of the conversation as a matter of routine. But if it seems appropriate, or if the conversation has been one of faith sharing, I believe in asking the other person if she or he would like me to pray. Never once has anyone refused the offer, and people have been not just appreciative but tremendously moved by the experience. People can feel amazingly close to each other and to God when they pray together on the telephone. The Holy Spirit and the electronic medium transcend the distance that separates you from the other person, as your prayer is carried directly to his or her heart. Many times I have found this to be an even more intimate experience than praying with someone in person. The spiritual impact is heightened by the very absence of visual or tactile contact. Anyone who has had this experience knows what I mean by telephonic inspiration.

So the conclusion I have reached regarding the question To phone or not to phone? is to phone when I can't visit in person and not to phone when I can visit in person, except when for convenience' sake I want to make an appointment to be sure someone is at home. That policy has worked very well for me and for others who follow it.

To Solo or Not to Solo?

Another question with which I often used to wrestle as a pastor-evangelist was, Should I take someone with me when I visit, or go alone? The open-ended conclusion I reached was, That depends.

There were certain kinds of pastoral calls that I preferred to make alone, especially those of a sensitive nature. I discovered that when someone was with me the dynamics were quite different. Sometimes I found it easier to focus and concentrate on spiritual things when I was visiting solo, but not always; it depended upon the agenda and the person or persons upon whom I was calling. There were times, for example, when having my wife, Margie, with me was immensely helpful and greatly facilitated the pastoral dialogue.

There is also the training factor to consider. It is good for a pastor to take a layperson or two along in order for the latter to learn by observation. That, of course, assumes the pastor's own interpersonal communication skills are worth observing. I was never confident that mine were; consequently, for far too long I neglected my responsibility and missed the wonderful opportunity a pastor has to train others by modeling. I was well aware of the importance of modeling in other evangelism training programs,[15] but these were highly structured, propositional approaches that lent themselves much more readily to modeling. I was doubtful that my own nonstructured, open-ended style, which calls for a total dependence on the guidance of the Holy Spirit, could be reduced to demonstrable rules.

As I became more and more involved in training people to do evangelism, I began to reflect on my interpersonal witnessing style to see whether I could identify any principles that might be helpful to others. At the same time, I became aware that there are certain interpersonal communication skills that probably can be taught best by modeling, such as listening, asking sensitive questions, and knowing how to terminate a call. That was when I started to take others with me on selected calls for training purposes. I have come to see the value of this kind of training—even, and maybe especially, for the style of interpersonal witnessing I advocate and try to represent.[16]

When you do take someone with you, it is important to make sure that the person knows beforehand what her or his role is in the calling situation, and that you talk together about the visit afterward. Reflecting on the dynamics of the call is an essential part of the learning experience.

3

Making Home Visits

It is important for the pastor-evangelist, when visiting, to be in charge of the conversation, not as a dominator and certainly not as a monopolizer, but as a facilitator and an enabler. That simply means that most of the time, although not always, it is up to the pastor-evangelist to initiate a faith-sharing conversation.

To Lead or Not to Lead?

In this sense the pastor-evangelist is the conversation leader. This is especially true when visiting unchurched persons with whom, if it is to be a faith-sharing experience, the pastor-evangelist is almost always the one who has to enable it to happen. The role of the leader, however, is to be a listener and to free the other person to share whatever is on his or her mind. Using what I call come-in questions, one can transform an ordinary conversation into a faith-sharing experience—instantly.[17] Come-in questions are low-structured questions that invite the other person to relate whatever he or she has been talking about to his or her faith. Low-structured questions begin with words like How . . . ? What . . . ?

For instance, after a person has related an unhappy experience (the "come-in point") I might say, sensitively and caringly, "My, you have certainly been through a lot, Linda. How has it affected your faith in God?" Or, "What a difficult choice, Bill! What part did your faith play in making that decision?" Or, "That's quite a story, Pat. Where do you think God is in all that?"

As the person responds from her or his own faith perspective, be it positive or negative, the conversation has been transformed at once into a faith-sharing experience. My role is still to be an active listener, affirming and relating to the other person's experience, but not before he or she is ready for me to respond. I call that moment the "plug-in point," when faith relates to faith. Facial expressions and body language are the important signals of that moment. Evangelistic sensitivity requires that we also listen with our eyes and speak with our ears. That is, what we see interprets what we hear, and what we hear determines what we speak. This is a rule I borrowed from a fund-raising consultant; it applies equally well to faith sharing.

A faith-sharing conversation is always a meaningful experience. With unchurched persons or prospective members, however, the visit ends too often without any commitment to a next step. That failure is almost always the fault of the conversation leader. An essential skill in effective witnessing is knowing how to help a person take the next logical step of faith. I call that climactic or terminal moment in the conversation the "decide-to point," when the witness asks a sensitively worded, high-structured question that gives the person an opportunity to make a faith decision. High-structured questions begin with words that call for a definite answer, usually yes or no, such as Will you . . . ? Are you . . . ? Do you . . . ? Is it . . . ? Have you . . . ? Extremely high-structured questions attempt, usually inappropriately, to force the answer: "You do want to join the church, don't you?"

If possible, the decide-to question should be related to the person's need, or whatever the faith-sharing conversation has revealed to be the next logical step toward God: "May I tell the nominating committee that you are ready to serve if asked?" "Would you be willing to come to the inquirers class next Wednesday night?" "May I have someone stop by for you and bring you to church next Sunday morning?" "Would you like to pray about that right now?" In other words, you are asking the person to make a commitment to do something, recognizing that to do so means she or he is opting for God. It is putting one's belief in or quest for God to the test. It is stating one's intention to take the next obvious step toward a deeper, fuller, more obedient relationship with God.

To identify what that next step is, the pastor-evangelist needs to know where the other person is spiritually.[18] Is the person a church member or unchurched? If unchurched, is the person a professing believer in God or a nonbeliever? If a nonbeliever, is the person a seeker after truth, or not a seeker? This last question is the key evangelistic question in determining how to witness to nonbelievers. A person who is a seeker is, humanly speaking, winnable. One who is indifferent to or apathetic about ultimate questions (justice, righteousness, truth, immortality) presents a totally different challenge. The pastor-evangelist needs to know more about this person before deciding how to approach him or her. Is the person reasonable or unreasonable? There are people who simply will not listen to reason. If the person is unreasonable, there is still one more question to be answered: Is the person friendly or unfriendly? I have known some friendly but unreasonable people. They squirt through the fingers of logic. They never arrive at the obvious conclusion. They can't see the inconsistencies in their statements. But they are pleasant, friendly people.

Unreasonable people, however, are more likely to be unfriendly. Trying to reason with unfriendly, unreasonable people is an exercise in futility. The best thing to do is "shake off the dust" (Matt. 10:14; see Mark 6:11; Luke 9:5; Acts 13:51). I think of that text, however, as a proof text for getting out, not for giving up. Before we get out, we offer our friendship and, if it seems appropriate, our continuing availability. Our evangelistic responsibility to the person does not end when the door shuts behind us. The person's name is referred to the church's intercessory prayer group, and someone from the church—the pastor or an evangelism calling team—pays another visit to the home in a few months. Who knows? The person may have had a change of heart. The Holy Spirit works miracles! I never discount the possibility of a delayed response. Pastor-evangelists should not give up on anyone until that person joins a church (any church), moves out of the community, or dies. Too many pastors and too many churches are not persistent enough in their evangelism to learn that persistence pays off.

I should mention briefly two other faith-sharing points. "Take-off points" are those moments in a conversation when the witness becomes a question answerer. This is a helpful and necessary part of interpersonal evangelism, but it can easily become a trap for unwary pastor-evangelists, who have answers to so many of the questions people ask. The temptation is for the witness to become the instructor. The unfortunate result is that the pastor-evangelist does most of the talking, and the resulting monologue precludes faith *sharing*.

Then there are "take-on points," when the Christian witness may have to challenge something the other person has said. Evangelistic sensitivity requires that this be done not arrogantly or abusively but in a positive and constructive way, by asking questions that help the person to see the reasonableness of a contrary point of view. This is an appeal to reason, not an attack on integrity. Two things I have learned in this regard are (1) that it is best to be up-front with my feelings, or whatever it is that is bothering me, and (2) that I can say the hard thing if my face and body language communicate an accepting, nonjudgmental attitude and a caring, sympathetic heart. This is "speaking the truth in love" (Eph. 4:15).

The essentials of this style of interpersonal evangelism are the ability to ask sensitive questions and the art of being a good listener. Some listening skills can be learned, but only God can make someone a good listener, for good listening is more than listening skills.[19] We can learn to ask questions, but only God can enable us to be the sensitive, caring, generous persons good listeners must be. Compassion and sensitivity are gifts of God. It behooves us, therefore, to pray that God will give us a heart for others.[20]

As the conversation leader, the pastor-evangelist also takes the initiative in dealing with whatever circumstances may be adversely affecting the communication process. One of these could be the seating arrangement. To avoid cross-firing, sidetracking or yoo-hoo-ing, I have often asked if I could move my chair or take another seat in order to see or hear better.[21] The request is always politely and sometimes humorously made. "Is that chair next to you an antique?" I might ask. The reply indicates that it obviously is not. "Then would you mind if I sit in it, so it's easier for us to talk?"

If the television is on, I make sure I'm not interrupting a favorite show. If there is any hesitancy at all to turn it off, I offer to come back another time, and if it still isn't turned off, I make my exit graciously. I don't want to compete with a television set for attention. Even if the person turns it way down, that's a clear signal that he or she wants to watch it, so I make my visit very short and get out as fast as I can. People don't resent an unexpected visit from someone who is sensitive to the possibility of intruding on their time and privacy.

The question is, When is an intrusion not an intrusion? The answer to the conundrum is, When the intruder is welcome. I don't ever want people to resent my coming, and they won't, if I apologize for the intrusion and don't overstay my welcome. Evangelistic sensitivity demands no less.

The pastor-evangelist is ready also to take the lead in dealing with interruptions. When the telephone or doorbell rings and a lengthy interruption ensues, it is sometimes very difficult, if not impossible, to resume the faith-sharing conversation you were having before the diversion. If another visitor arrives and joins the conversation, the intimacy of the previous conversation may be lost. You simply have to assess the new situation and decide whether or not to stay. If you do stay, remember that a change in the number of persons involved greatly affects the dynamics of interpersonal witnessing.[22]

There are many other distractions that can be a challenge to the pastor-evangelist as visitor. A too-friendly dog can be annoying, and a hostile dog can be dangerous. I'm not a cat lover, so why, if there's a cat in the house, does it inevitably insist on climbing into my lap? I have long suspected that cats sense my disdain and deliberately try to force themselves upon me. Cats have no evangelistic sensitivity whatsoever! I was calling on a couple one night, and before I had even sat down, a Siamese beast sprang from some lofty perch behind me and landed on the back of my neck, scaring me out of my wits.

In retrospect, I think I resented the owners' amused laughter as much as I did their cat's behavior. It is difficult to have a faith-sharing conversation under such circumstances, to say the least.

Young children can also be a distraction, when they are demanding attention, fussing, or simply by their presence and activity interfering with their parents' concentration. It is difficult for adults to have an in-depth conversation under those circumstances. One can still have a meaningful pastoral visit and, perhaps, even a faith-sharing experience. It's just more difficult. A skilled conversation leader can bring the child or children into the discussion. My strategy with little children is to use some gesture or word well calculated to gain their interest. Pulling a penny out of a child's ear always works, but if you haven't the gift of prestidigitation, a wink and a smile does equally well. I'm just as eager to establish a relationship with the children as with their parents. The fact remains, however, that they can be a hindrance to adult conversation.

Children and pets are not the only distractions, of course. A radio blaring in an adjacent room, someone incessantly practicing scales on the piano, loud traffic noise outside, someone scurrying around in the kitchen, or any number of other such things can be disconcerting. When such distractions occur, the visiting pastor must play it by ear. If further conversation is too difficult, it's time to leave.

You may also have to take the lead when there is a disinterested spouse or other adult in the home, who either walks out of the room when you arrive, never emerges from the kitchen, or, worse, remains in the same room with you but is totally aloof or demonstrably disinterested. You can't be sure what is going on in the mind of the person slouching in the easy chair on the other side of the room, whose face is hidden behind a newspaper.

I'm always wary about that situation. The question is, What do you do? One thing is sure: You can't just pretend he or she doesn't exist. Evangelistic sensitivity requires that we at least be circumspect in our conversation. The person behind the newspaper or in the other room may be listening. That possibility changes the way we relate as witness to the person we came to visit, whoever it is. The dynamics of faith sharing are radically changed by the presence of an observer.[23]

My own inclination has always been to attempt to engage or involve the nonparticipant. How to do that depends, of course, on my relationship with the individuals present. If I don't know the spouse who has remained in the kitchen, I might say, "Do you think Mr. Smith would like to join us?" Mrs. Smith may make excuses for her husband, in which case I might say, "I understand. Do you think he'd mind if I just said hello? I'd like to feel that I have at least met him."

More often than not, however, the person in Mrs. Smith's position will make the effort to get the spouse to appear, as a matter of common courtesy, if nothing else. The exchange between Mrs. Smith and her husband in the kitchen depends entirely on their relationship. Religion could be a sore point in their marriage, or it could be that Mr. Smith is working on something he can't interrupt. Whatever the reason he chose not to appear, once he emerges I want to be sure I neither impose on him nor hold him captive. I might ask a question to see if he is willing to engage in conversation, or if he is simply complying with his wife's request. Under no circumstances do I ever want him to feel that I have been enlisted by his wife to recruit him.

Early in my ministry, I made the mistake of allowing myself to be put in that position. A member of the church asked me to call on her unchurched husband, who turned out to be a very passive person, a veritable Mr. Milquetoast. My hard sell succeeded in coercing an agreement ("decision" would not be the right word) from him to join the church, but he never showed up for the new members class and he never attended church throughout my entire tenure. On my next visit he was sullen and totally noncommunicative, and his wife told me how angry at her he had been for "siccing your minister on me" (his words). Although he warmed up a bit as time passed and was cordial and polite when I visited, he never joined the church.

Back to Mr. Smith. Having learned my lesson, I intend to be friendly and affirming and, if possible, to establish my own relationship with him. I use a very low-key approach. If I detect any resistance or resentment at all, I don't push. I don't have to solve the problem then and there; rather, Mr. Smith becomes a subject of my intercessory prayers and continuing evangelistic concern; I need to know much more about him before I know how to proceed.

The case of the disinterested person in the same room is more difficult to deal with. Let's assume young Sally Jones is curled on the sofa with her face in a book. I can't talk *about* her to her mother. Any comment about her not being involved in the conversation would sound like a criticism to Sally. ("What's wrong with your daughter? Doesn't she like to talk?") Nor would it be appropriate to say, "Would you mind asking your daughter to join us?"

On the other hand, I would never feel comfortable simply ignoring Sally or pretending she isn't there. This is a situation where the pastor-evangelist can take the lead, and usually the best way to do that is to speak directly to Sally. I might walk over to where she is sitting and, in a friendly way, say something like, "Excuse me, Sally, I feel bad that we haven't included you in this conversation. I'd like to get to know you, too. Do you mind if we move our chairs a little closer so we can talk a bit?"

What I would say after that depends on Sally's response. The point is that I would take the lead in reaching out to Sally. I want to establish my own relationship with her, so that she thinks of me as *her* pastor, not just as her mother's pastor. That might never happen unless I take the initiative.

As conversation leaders, pastor-evangelists do not do most of the talking. On the contrary, our task is to free the other person to talk. We do that by asking sensitive questions and by listening. If possible, every pastoral visit should be a faith-sharing experience. We'll have our chance to share the gospel, but it may not be until the next visit.

To Stay or Not to Stay?

It is never wrong not to wear out your welcome (double negative intended). The length of a home visit depends on several factors:

My reason for calling. Have I a specific purpose, or is it a just-happen-to-be-in-the-neighborhood call? Am I dropping off a book or calling to discuss baptism?

Whether or not the person is expecting me. Have I made an appointment or announced that I would be calling in the area that day, or am I popping in unexpectedly? Drop-in calls are usually briefer than others. When people are expecting you to come, they usually expect you to stay a while.

The situation in the home. Is it a convenient time? Have I interrupted something? Is there a problem or a need?

My relationship to the person. Is this someone I need to check on periodically, or is it someone requiring more extensive pastoral care? Is this my first call, or have I been there before, so that it is just a matter of touching base?

Fifteen or twenty minutes is sufficient for most calls. It is possible, even easy, to turn an ordinary conversation into a faith-sharing experience and to be on the heart-to-heart level with another person much more quickly than I at first realized.[24] If the situation is not favorable for a visit, I offer to come back another time and then make a quick and gracious exit. I never want to stay a second longer than I'm wanted, especially if my visit was unexpected. But if my presence is really wanted, I'll stay as long as I'm needed. This rule applies to calls on members and nonmembers alike.

For example, early one evening I knocked on the door of the first floor apartment of a family I knew was having financial difficulties. The mother and her two older children had recently joined the church. The door was opened a crack by the nine-year-old daughter, who asked in a frightened voice, "Who's there?" When she saw who it was, she unlatched the chain, flung open the door, and threw her arms around my waist, sobbing almost hysterically. When she calmed down, I learned that she was home alone and terrified that her father, who was an escaped convict, had come home. The man was a vicious sadist who had brutalized his wife and children for years. When his wife finally divorced him, he threatened to kill her if he ever got out of prison.

The little girl had expected the rest of her family to be home before this, and when they didn't come, she was sure her father had done something to them and was coming after her. By no means was I about to leave that frightened little girl before her mother returned, which she did about a half hour later. The mother had been unavoidably delayed, and she was terribly distressed for having caused her daughter to become so upset. I should point out, parenthetically, that our church was a source of great comfort and support to that family in their time of need, and the young people and their mother have done admirably well since then.

That particular call is an extreme illustration of a situation in which the right thing to do was to stay as long as I was needed. Whenever there is an obvious need, that's the rule. We stay with a family experiencing the shock of losing a loved one, or with a wife who is waiting to hear if her husband has survived an operation, or with a homebound older person who is starved for company, or with a lonely man who needs someone to whom he can unburden his soul. If there is a reason to stay longer, then stay. Generally speaking, however, a pastoral visit can be relatively brief and still be meaningful.

One good way to initiate a faith-sharing conversation with homebound persons is to offer to read a passage of scripture. I always ask if they have a Bible I can use; I have yet to be in a parishioner's home without one, although I have been in many nonmember homes where there was no Bible. (That's when a pocket New Testament comes in handy.) If there is an opportunity to read scripture, the passage itself becomes the starting point for a faith-sharing conversation, leading naturally and acceptably into a closing prayer.

Serving Communion to homebound persons is a marvelous opportunity for faith sharing. In the context of the sacrament, the pastor-evangelist can ask a come-in question that frees the other person to share some experience of God. Here are some examples: "Can you remember the first time you took Communion, Doris?" (high-structured question to trigger her thinking). "Where were you in your faith journey then?" (low-structured question to facilitate her response). "What do you think about when you're having Communion, Bob?" "We speak of the sacraments as a means of grace, and we believe Christ is present with us in this Communion. When do you feel closest to God, Elizabeth?"

If Elizabeth has difficulty replying, we can ask another high-structured question to which she can respond with a yes or a nod. The purpose of our come-in questions is to make the experience not more difficult for her, but more meaningful.

To Wait or Not to Wait?

Pastor-evangelists can afford to take the long view. That is one of the advantages of the incarnational approach. Relationships are established. Conversations can be continued later. Mass evangelists, street-corner witnesses, and hit-and-run preachers have to get it all said each time, because they won't have another chance with the same audience.

To be sure, there are many times when the pastor-evangelist, having earned the right to be heard by first being a listener, will be an active witness and want to make the case for Christ as winsomely and persuasively as possible. Faith sharing is not a one-sided affair. Depending on the situation, the pastor-evangelist can sometimes prime the other person's faith-sharing pump by sharing something meaningful and appropriate from his or her own faith experience. The openness and sincerity of the witness frees the other person to share.

I define faith sharing as three-way communication in which two or more people relate to each other their personal experiences and perceptions of God and, in the process, reexperience the reality of God.[25] It is three-way communication because God is involved in the conversation too. God is always present when people are sharing their faith. It is God who inspires them to do so.

The question for the pastor-evangelist as visitor, therefore, is when to bear witness to Christ, whether to wait or not to wait. Our evangelistic sensitivity may cause us to think, This is not the time; I should wait till the next visit or the next meeting. Sensitivity is not timidity. One waits not because one is afraid but because the timing is not right. The purpose for waiting is a strategic one. One visit can pave the way for the next, when the situation may be more favorable and the reception much more positive. It is the Holy Spirit who prompts us to wait or not to wait to make the case.

It can be a meaningful experience, furthermore, whether or not we've made a case for Christ. Our very presence and caring attitude bear witness to the Christ in whose name we have come to call. There are times, too, when it may be better to say nothing, because there is nothing one can say. There is indeed value in a ministry of presence. What I mean by an incarnational approach, however, is more than a ministry of presence. It is being *with* as well as being *there.* When our son died, we were visited by a well-meaning pastor who, after greeting us, said practically nothing. We sat for twenty minutes staring at the floor, occasionally trying to break the awkward silence with some inane pleasantry but getting no response. Admittedly, the man did not know us or our son, and I suspect he thought we were too grief-stricken to want to talk. How helpful it would have been had he asked us about our son, or asked us how we were doing, or just agonized verbally with us! But he just sat there with his head down, without a word, perhaps thinking all the while that his "ministry of presence" was sufficient. It wasn't. We appreciated his coming, but it wasn't a meaningful visit.

To Pray or Not to Pray?

Prayer can make a visit meaningful, but the other person may not want us to pray. It is always appropriate, therefore, to ask rather than to assume one way or the other. If it seems appropriate, I might say something like this: "Would you like me to offer a prayer before I go?" Or, "Would you like to have a word of prayer with me?" If I think the other person might want or be willing to pray aloud, I might put it slightly differently: "Would you like to say a word of prayer with me?" The wording depends on the situation. I don't just "lay one on them" without consent. I read the person's face and body language, then listen carefully to what the person says and how he or she says it. It takes evangelistic sensitivity to know whether to pray or not to pray. Prayer should not be automatic, and it should never be perfunctory.

I can still remember how uncomfortable and even embarrassed I felt when a well-meaning visiting minister, as he stood up to leave, took my wife's hand and mine and started to pray. We had visited his church but were not members. I can't say exactly why I felt uncomfortable; the man obviously meant well, but I simply wasn't used to that sort of thing. Perhaps it would have helped if he had eased into it, or at least asked us if we wanted him to pray. I don't know what my response would have been, but I'm sure I would not have felt as embarrassed about holding hands if he had said, "Would you mind if I offer a little prayer?" and then, after obtaining our consent, added something like, "May we join hands as a symbol of our new friendship?"

Some people have not arrived at a point in their spiritual journey where they are comfortable praying aloud with another person. As a pastor-evangelist, I want to be sensitive to that reality, both in how I initiate a prayer and in what I say during it. That is true whenever and wherever I may be calling, whether in someone's home, office, or hospital room. Such occasions are always an evangelistic opportunity, as we sensitively try to help people to become aware of the God who is already at work in their lives, and to discover how easy and natural it is to talk with that God.

Every now and then someone will decline outright our offer to pray. Evangelistic sensitivity is knowing when to pray, as well as what and how. That, of course, is a gift of God, who alone deserves the credit if and when we happen to do things right. If we ourselves are in tune with the Holy Spirit, we sense when the circumstances are appropriate for prayer. If we do pray, it should be from the heart and not just routine. It need not—indeed, it should not—be too long. Martin Luther once commented to the effect that it is not the length of a prayer but how good it is and how it comes from the heart that counts with God.

There's a big difference between praying and preaching. A prayer is not a sermon. Some pastoral prayers sound more like sermons! Nor do I view prayer as a medium for witnessing. It is itself a witness. It is also a channel that the Holy Spirit can use to touch and to teach the hearts and minds of those who pray. The very act of praying can be a powerful source of inspiration. Indeed, often our most effective witness is the prayer itself. Previously unresponsive hearts can melt, attitudes can be changed, new thoughts expressed, new commitments made, as a result of prayer. As a pastor-evangelist and as a Christian witness, I am always grateful for opportunities to pray with those who are seeking to know and to do God's will. Prayer is a powerful dimension of interpersonal witnessing, but it should never be imposed or forced on others.

All of what I have been saying about prayer so far applies to our praying *with* others. As far as our private prayers *for* others are concerned, the answer to the question To pray or not to pray? is obviously and emphatically to pray! Every visit, whether planned or unplanned, is preceded, and, I hope, directed, by prayer. For me it has become a habit. I always pray before and after every visit; I consider the time I spend in the car, when I'm making calls, a wonderful opportunity for intercessory prayer, especially for the people I'm going to visit.

Then, too, I pray silently even (and especially) during the visit. The other person doesn't know I'm praying. These are open-eyed "mini-prayers," silent petitions relevant to the conversation, which I am continually sending Godward. "Lord, I'm not sure what Mary is trying to say. Help me to understand. . . . Lord, help me to know how to respond to Frank. . . . They're not communicating, God. Please open their hearts to each other and to you. . . . Forgive me, God, if I didn't say that right."

Far from distracting me, these instant mini-prayers make me a more sensitive listener, for I know that it is only God who enables me to listen empathetically and compassionately to others. As a pastor-evangelist I know I must depend entirely on the Holy Spirit, who alone can equip me to be a faithful witness.

4

Hospital Visits

There are only so many places where intentional visitation can take place. The home is the most obvious and the best place to see most people most of the time. That is why I am such a strong advocate of what, for want of a better term, is called visitation evangelism. The only way to reach everyone in a community is to go to where people live, their homes. Evangelism done in any other geographical location is limited to people who happen to be there or who pass by (for example, street corners and airports) or who are accessible and available (for example, offices and other workplaces) or who are there for a particular reason (for example, hospitals and nursing homes).

Other kinds of pastoral calls present their own challenges and opportunities to the pastor-evangelist as visitor. As I have already indicated, in addition to the general principles regarding what I call evangelistic sensitivity and style, there are unique considerations relating to other places where visiting occurs that are not necessarily pertinent to home visits, and to these we now turn. In this chapter I want to share some thoughts about hospital visits, concentrating on the differences rather than on the similarities.[26]

Biblical Precedents

Visiting the sick is a biblical priority, as demonstrated and commanded by Jesus himself. He commissioned the Twelve to "heal the sick, raise the dead, cleanse lepers, cast out demons" (Matt. 10:8; cf. Mark 6:7–13; Luke 9:1–6). He appointed seventy others and sent them out two by two with instructions to heal the sick and to announce the kingdom of God (Luke 10:1–12). He told his disciples a parable to the effect that as they visited or did not visit the sick, they did it or did it not to him (Matt. 25:36–45).

So much of Jesus' own ministry was healing people. Great multitudes of people came to him to be healed (Matt. 4:23–25),[27] and sometimes he went to them, as when he took Peter, James, and John with him to Jairus' house, where he healed a little girl everyone thought had died (Mark 5:22–24, 35–42; Matt. 9:18–26; Luke 8:40–56), and when he went to Bethany to raise Lazarus from the dead (John 11:1–44). Wherever he went, Jesus healed people.

The apostles continued their Lord's ministry of healing (Acts 3:1–10; 5:15–16; 8:5–7). If we need a proof text for visiting the sick, why not this passage? "It happened that the father of Publius lay sick with fever and dysentery; and Paul visited him and prayed, and putting his hands on him healed him" (Acts 28:8). We are reminded in James 5:14 that this is a shared ministry; it is not the responsibility of the pastor alone. James writes: "Is any among you sick? Let that person call for the elders of the church, and let them pray over the person, anointing him or her with oil in the name of the Lord."

Some Guidelines for Visiting Hospitals

The biblical mandate for visiting the sick is clear. The question I now want to consider is, How do we as pastor-evangelists fulfill that mandate today? What are some of the things we ought to think about with regard to hospital visits?

Style of Visit

Every pastor has his or her own visiting style. One point I need to make is that my own basic style as a visitor does not vary with the type of visit. By that I mean that I try, with God's help, to be consistent with the principles identified in the previous chapter, regardless of where I am visiting. I am committed to a style that is incarnational (being there and being with), relational (personal and ongoing), service-oriented (ministering to people's needs), God-centered (a faith-sharing approach), and Christ-informed (when I've earned the right to be heard). As a pastor-evangelist I never want to be manipulative, overly aggressive, or insensitive to the feelings and needs of others. Rather, I want to be a good listener who can help others discover and talk about their faith experiences, and I am ready to employ the five points of faith sharing wherever and whenever I am visiting with someone. I want to depend on the Holy Spirit for guidance in knowing when to speak and what to say, and for forgiveness if I feel I've blundered or failed, which I sometimes do—and always do when I run ahead of God.

Having declared my commitment to a particular style for all visiting, I must quickly add that hospital visits require some subtle adjustments in the application of the principles of style described in the preceding paragraph. Some differences are matters of degree, but they are worth mentioning nevertheless. Take the question of scripture reading. Few unchurched and not very many church members think about bringing a Bible with them to the hospital. Thanks to the Gideons, however, there is almost always a Bible in the room. If there's time, I like to get out the Gideon Bible, read a few verses, and suggest a passage for the patient to read later, if she or he is able.

Because hospital calls tend to be briefer than home visits, there is not always time to read a Bible passage, in which case I have often quoted a verse or two. My hope is that patients will see how relevantly and helpfully the Bible speaks to their needs.

Reading scripture had a powerful impact on one young man I had been visiting regularly over a period of several months. I'll call him Skip. A victim of acquired immune deficiency syndrome (AIDS), Skip was in pain most of the time and in much discomfort all of the time. He did not belong to any church, nor could he say he believed in the divinity of Jesus, but he had a genuine spirituality to which I related very positively, and an intellectual integrity I respected immensely. He had his own understanding of God, and he was definitely a seeker after truth. As I would read the Bible to him, he would listen intently and ask searching questions about every passage.

One day I chose to read part of 2 Corinthians 12, beginning at verse 7: "And to keep me from being too elated by the abundance of revelations, a thorn was given me in the flesh, a messenger of Satan, to harass me, to keep me from being too elated." My young friend was pensive. "What do you think Paul meant by that thorn in the flesh?" he asked me. I resisted the temptation to give an academic answer and waited for him to verbalize what he was thinking, for Skip had his own thorn in the flesh.

We talked about that for a while, and about what the inner voice said to Paul: "My grace is sufficient for you, for my power is made perfect in weakness" (12:9). Because of his faith, Paul could say, "For the sake of Christ, then, I am content with weaknesses, insults, hardships, persecutions, and calamities; for when I am weak, then I am strong" (12:10). Paul was strong because his strength was in Christ.

The message seemed to get through to Skip. He wanted to believe. Because of our talks and prayers, he felt free to talk with me about his disease, his life, his sexuality, his regrets. I asked him if he could, what would he want to say to the gay community? "That we're committing suicide. Gay people have to stop being so flagrantly promiscuous. It's not unusual for gays to have as many as a thousand different sex partners. Now I have a monogamous relationship, but it's too late for me. Homosexuals have got to stop killing themselves."

The Bible opens the door for that kind of honest talk. The Word convicts, and convinces, and converts those who dig into it with open minds and hearts; and hospital patients, if they are well enough, have time to read it.

Prayer is also an extremely important part of hospital calls. Nevertheless, the rule about asking applies even more in a hospital room. We are wise to make sure the patient wants us to pray. Most patients do, but we should not assume that. One night I was making a hospital call on an inactive member who was facing open-heart surgery the next morning. He was obviously anxious about the operation. As I was preparing to leave, I asked him if he would like me to offer a prayer. "I'd rather you didn't," he replied. So I didn't. I paused for a few moments, to give him a chance to express whatever feelings he may have wanted to express, but he made no further comment. It was not the time to press him for his reasons. I simply said, "I understand, Jake," and left.

Nor did I bring up the subject on my subsequent visits to the hospital. Following his recovery, however, he showed up at my study one morning and proceeded to explain what he had been going through spiritually and why he had declined my offer to pray with him that night in the hospital. His refusal had been on his conscience ever since, and now he wanted to recommit his life to Christ and the church and to be baptized again. The Holy Spirit had used that incident as a catalyst to lead Jake back into the church. Since, according to my Reformed theology, a person receives the sacrament of baptism only once, whether as an infant or as an adult, I suggested that Jake attend the next new members orientation series, at the conclusion of which he could publicly reaffirm his faith and his membership vows and receive a special anointing as a sign and seal of his newfound faith. That he did, and he has been an active church member and devoted servant of Christ ever since.

Hospital prayers should be brief but specific and relevant. The pastor-evangelist is always aware of and sensitive to the presence of others in the room. If I have already started my prayer and a doctor or nurse comes in, I end quickly, including him or her in my prayer as I close. I don't want to pray on and on while someone is waiting to see the patient. On the other hand, I make it a point in every case to include all hospital personnel in my prayers (such as orderlies, attendants, pink ladies, and candy stripers), as well as other patients and their families. If a doctor comes in just before I've started to pray, I usually introduce myself and say something like, "I was just about to offer a brief prayer; would you like me to step out while you see your patient?" As often as not the doctor will say, "No, no. You go right ahead. I can wait." In that case I usually invite him or her to join us. In any case, I include the doctor in my prayer.

That practice has led to some interesting conversations with doctors, nurses, and other hospital personnel. I think immediately of a fascinating conversation that began as I was waiting for an elevator after visiting with a patient one night. (There's nothing slower than a hospital elevator.) A doctor came by, recognized me, stopped, and came over to where I was standing. "You're out late, Pastor," he said, smiling. I explained that I had been sitting with a patient. He suddenly became very serious. "Would you have a moment to talk?" I said sure. So we went into an empty visitors' lounge, where for two hours he talked about the pressures and demands of his work and about his own faith struggles in the midst of human suffering. He needed to talk, and I was glad to listen. It was a beautiful faith-sharing experience, which led to other conversations and to his eventual involvement in the church.

The point of the illustration is that when as visiting pastors we are sensitive to the presence of others, they will be aware of our presence in their hospital. So, too, we need to be sensitive to the presence of other patients when we're visiting in wards or semiprivate rooms. If I am calling on Mr. Gomez and the next bed is also occupied, I introduce myself to the other patient before I pray (assuming he's awake) and ask him if he would like to join in the prayer. If he appears to be asleep or unconscious, I include him in the prayer nevertheless. I've learned not to assume that a patient whose eyes are closed is necessarily asleep, or that a comatose patient is unaware of a touch or a voice. It is appalling to hear some doctors and nurses discussing a patient's condition when the person is semiconscious. They forget that the patient is a person, not just a "case." They should know better.

Most medical professionals do know better now. They have learned from experiments showing that when positive things are said in the presence of patients who are unconscious, they recover faster. One doctor claims that patients recover more quickly from surgery when music is played in the operating room. It is good to have this kind of verification of what one has long believed to be true.

Semiconscious and comatose patients can respond to our touch as well as our voice. Touching is a very important part of our ministry to the sick, whether we are gently holding someone's limp hand, placing our hand on someone's shoulder, anointing someone with oil (James 5:14–15), or joining with an elder or two in a more formal laying on of hands (Mark 16:18b). I either hold the patient's hand or touch the patient's shoulder when I pray, depending on the circumstances.

In a semiprivate room, when the patients' beds are close enough,

I have often stood between the two and, if the patients are willing and able, have taken the hand of each as I pray. Otherwise, I stand by the person I'm visiting and include the other patient in the prayer. I also want to make sure the roommates know each other, so they can minister to each other afterward. If they are sensitive to each other's physical or emotional pain, they can comfort each other, cheer each other up, and even pray together, and in so doing ease their own suffering.

If there are other visitors present when I arrive, I have a decision to make: Do I visit with all of them, or do I come back later to see the patient alone? It depends on who the visitors are. This may be an opportunity to minister to the family as well as to the patient. If the room is crowded and the people are noisy, I'm inclined to want to come back later. If visitors are with the other patient, it may be difficult for me to have a private talk with the person I came to see.

On one such occasion the other visitors were so noisy I assumed they neither heard nor cared what my parishioner and I were saying on the other side of the thin curtain that separated the two beds. Despite the noise, we had a prayer together. As I was leaving, a loud voice shouted from behind the curtain, "Say one for me sometime, Rev!" I did an about-face, walked around the curtain, and said to the four visitors and the other patient, "What about right now?" They all smiled sheepishly, nodded their assent, and bowed their heads, as I offered a brief prayer for them and their sick friend. When I finished, the man with the loud voice shook my hand warmly and said, with tears in his eyes, "Thank you, Reverend. I really needed that." You never know who's listening!

Our bedside prayers do not necessarily end the visit. The pastor-evangelist is always prepared for the possibility that the prayer itself will evoke some kind of faith response from the patient. Some of my most meaningful faith-sharing conversations, in hospital rooms as well as in living rooms, have occurred *after* the prayer. Many times I will begin my visit with prayer, having exchanged greetings, and having said something like this: "While we have a moment alone, Michael, may I offer a prayer? Then we can visit." If I happen to be there when a meal is served, I often take the opportunity to say something like, "Would you like me to say grace?" This would not be a perfunctory prayer but would incorporate the specific needs of the patient in the context of giving thanks to God.

Length of Visit

One obvious difference between hospital visits and home visits has to do with the length of the visit. For several reasons, hospital calls are usually briefer than home visits. The pastor-evangelist does not want to risk tiring the patient—or the patient's roommate, if there is one. Nor does the visitor want to interfere with the medical staff members as they perform their various duties. Hospital rooms are often busy places. There may be other visitors in the room, or people waiting to visit; it would be inconsiderate for the pastor-evangelist to usurp or monopolize their private time with the patient. Hospitals have rules about visiting hours and the number of visitors allowed at one time. Depending on how long the patient will be in the hospital, the pastor-evangelist usually has an opportunity to come back again. Frequent visits, however brief, are greatly appreciated.

Hospital visits can be brief without being rushed. I try hard not to appear to be in a hurry. If I am wearing a topcoat or raincoat, I deliberately remove it and sit down as if I am going to stay awhile. If I stand there with my coat on, the patient gets the feeling I'm just passing through, rushing in and out. I want my actions to convey my sincere desire to give the patient my complete attention for the time I am there. It's a matter of making my body language conform to my pastoral intentions.

Time of Visit

Pastors are not restricted to the usual visiting hours in making hospital calls. The best time for the pastor-evangelist to call, therefore, depends on the status of the patient and the purpose of the pastor. If possible, I like to see patients before and after they undergo major surgery, and before and after they receive the report of tests regarding a serious problem. Unfortunately, we pastors don't always get the word in time, and some parishioners can be in and out of the hospital before we ever hear about it.

In addition to those special times, we see people at various stages of their recuperation or deterioration. If I want to visit alone with a patient, I prefer to call other than during visiting hours. Except in emergencies, I usually avoid the morning hours, as those are the times when the nurses and orderlies are busiest and the doctors are making their rounds. One of my favorite times is in the evening after visiting hours, when patients seem to be more open and receptive spiritually. Maybe it's because hospitals are quieter then and things are more relaxed. Or maybe it's because another long, lonely night is about to begin, and the patient is grateful for the peace and comfort your visit brings at that hour. It's like tucking someone in for the night. Whatever the reason, this is a great time for faith sharing.

If, on the other hand, I also want to see the spouse or other members of the family, I prefer to call during visiting hours, when I know they will be present. These are precious opportunities for a pastor-evangelist to engage the family and their hospitalized loved one in a faith-sharing conversation.

Purpose of Visit

As a pastor-evangelist, I hope that if the patient is feeling well enough to talk, every hospital call, however brief, will be a faith-sharing experience. It almost always is, as people are more receptive to the gospel when they are in the hospital than they may be at other times. If a patient wants to talk, it is easy to engage her or him in a faith-sharing conversation.

The reality of suffering, with its accompanying fears, anxieties, and insecurities, the reminders of their mortality and the questions evoked by such awareness, the threat of incapacitation or recurrent illness, the worry about unattended work not done or time lost, strained financial resources, dependent loved ones at home, difficult decisions to be faced, or any of a host of other problems can be come-in points for faith sharing. Most hospital patients are open and receptive to the gospel when they see how it speaks to their needs.

The pastor-evangelist can anticipate that the faith sharing of some patients will be expressions not of their gratitude for God's goodness and love but of their anger at God because of their suffering, their agonizing struggle to believe in the midst of their pain, their conviction that they are being punished by God, or their own guilt, shame, doubt, or sense of failure. Faith sharing includes the sharing of our experiences of the absence as well as of the presence of God, our spiritual lows as well as highs, our unbelief as well as our belief. If that is what Mrs. Park is feeling, it is helpful and good, even therapeutic, for her to have a chance to voice it. The pastor-evangelist need not be threatened by a patient's anguished outburst against God. Rather, it is a plug-in point, an opportunity to identify with the person in his or her struggle.

At such times I lean heavily on God and pray hard for the Holy Spirit to put the right words in my mouth, so that my response will be true to the gospel and helpful to the person. I am never confident in my own wisdom, but I am confident in the power of God to redeem my earnest efforts to be faithful, even if my words sometimes miss the mark. People can tell when we really care, and our witness will have integrity if our words are sincere expressions of our own faith, hope, and love.

After more than thirty years as a minister of the gospel and far more hospital calls than I could ever count, I can honestly say that very seldom has a faith-sharing conversation with a patient ever evoked anything other than a positive, appreciative response from the patient. It may have been a simple "Thanks for listening." Or, "I'm sorry for sounding so negative, Pastor. Thanks for letting me get it off my chest. Your prayer really helped." Or, "I still have trouble believing in a God who lets people suffer like this. I'll think about what you said." Or, "Thanks for helping me to see God's hand in all this. Could we talk about these things again sometime?"

After the Visit

Our relationship with hospital patients does not end with the final visit. It is sad but true that too often we forget about them after they leave the hospital. We ordinarily do a good job of following through with those who need our continuing pastoral care. As pastor-evangelists we also need to keep in touch with those persons who, during our hospital visits, we discovered were having faith problems. When next we visit them at home, we can rejoice in their recovery, if that is the case, and give thanks for God's healing grace. If they are still sick or incapacitated, we continue our pastoral care, of course. In either case, if they are still having faith problems, we can renew our previous faith conversation, responding as their situation demands, giving thanks for answered prayers and for God's patience and forbearance with us when the lamp of faith burns low.

Let me reiterate an important point: It is to be expected that other officers and members of the church are participating with us in this ministry of pastoral care. We need not—indeed, we should not—bear the burden alone. However, the topic here is the *pastor-evangelist* as visitor. The focus is on the pastor's role in this ministry, a role we are viewing along with other professional roles through evangelistic glasses.

5

Other Kinds of Visits

In this chapter we will consider the nature of visits in nursing homes, workplaces, and prisons.

Nursing-Home Visits

What has been said about hospital visits applies also to calling on people in nursing homes. However, there are one or two ways in which visiting a nursing home is different from visiting a hospital. The pastor-evangelist needs to be sensitive to these unique circumstances.

First, nursing-home patients are usually in for the duration. They need permanent health care; with rare exceptions, they will not be returning to their former homes. They are in varying states of health. Some are emotionally disturbed or mentally confused. Some are ambulatory, some permanently bedridden. Some are totally or partially paralyzed by stroke or another ailment. Some have families; others are completely alone in the world. Many entered the nursing home as a last resort, the decision having been made for them by a doctor, family members, or both. Some have come directly from their former residence, others by way of a hospital. Their circumstances vary in many respects, but they have one thing in common: They are all living on borrowed time. It is a reality of which they are aware but seldom speak.

What an opportunity for the pastor-evangelist to bear witness to the promises of the gospel to these beautiful older people, who need so much to hear a comforting word from someone who understands and cares about them! It means that they may be living on borrowed time, but time is all they have, and there are very few pleasant ways to spend it in a nursing home. Some of the residents are unable to read or even to watch television; they just lie there, waiting to be fed, waiting to be bathed, waiting to be turned over, waiting to die.

If they are lucid and alert, they are most receptive to the gospel. I have found them very willing to have me read a brief Bible passage to them and very appreciative of my prayers. What was said in regard to Communion for homebound persons applies also to people in nursing homes (see chapter 3). If they are able to converse coherently, the sacrament can be a beautiful context for a faith-sharing conversation.

Faith sharing usually comes easily to those who know their days are numbered. How important it is for the visitor to be a good listener to people who may have no one else to talk to. Even sensitive, caring nurses and attendants often don't have time really to listen to the hurting human beings in their charge.

For two years, with the assistance of members of the Oak Lane Presbyterian Church, I conducted worship services every other week for the patients in the main ward of a large nursing home not far from our church. Other patients were wheeled in for the half-hour services. It was an interesting congregation of persons of various religious backgrounds—"churched" and unchurched, believers and unbelievers. They were my second flock, many of whom I came to know as individuals, persons of dignity and worth. I soon realized that I could preach the same kinds of messages to them as I did to my church congregation. In some ways the people in those beds and wheelchairs were even more responsive than the people in the church pews. The worship services led to many faith-sharing conversations, as one-to-one relationships were established with individual patients.

These experiences helped me to see the residents of nursing homes not as an amorphous group of dependent, institutionalized creatures waiting for their demise but as unique individuals with their own identities, roots, personalities, characters, feelings, opinions, beliefs, and experiences of faith and life. Infirm they may be, confused and forgetful perhaps, but they have not ceased to be God's children simply because they have grown old. Who better than the pastor-evangelist can help them face their limited future with the hope that God inspires and the peace that passes understanding? If our visits are not directed to that end, we are not doing the work of an evangelist.

Another difference between nursing-home and hospital visits has to do with the families of the patients. It is safe to say that nursing-home residents, generally speaking, receive fewer visitors than do hospital patients. The latter may have daily visits from family members and friends, whereas nursing-home residents may not see their closest family members more than once a week, if that often. Chances of running into visiting relatives in a nursing home are rather slim, therefore, unless the pastor-evangelist makes a special effort to visit at a time they are expected.

Pastor-evangelists may want to do just that, as I have found that the family may need help as much as the patient. A son may be harboring guilt about having to put his elderly, infirm mother into a nursing home. That guilty feeling may be aggravated by the constant complaining of his mother, who wonders why she has to be where she is. The theme and variations are repeated in family after family. The problems relating to the care of aging relatives have to be at or near the top of the list of problems one encounters in pastoral ministry.[28] The pastor-evangelist who can bring some peace and comfort into the troubled lives of a family having to go through this experience, with all its related emotional turmoil, physical stress, and financial strain, is performing an invaluable service. Evangelistic sensitivity is needed to help family members deal with the situation in the context of their faith in and obedience to God. If they are not spiritually minded people, the challenge is greater, but the need is the same.

Pastors can be a source of much-needed support to those who face the traumatic experience of moving from a room or apartment in a retirement community into the related permanent-health-care facility. Even if the presence of this facility was one of the reasons they entered the retirement community in the first place, they dread the implications of having to move into it, knowing the change signifies their need of special care and, in most cases, the end of what little mobility and freedom they enjoyed in their former apartments. What a comfort and relief it is to the families of such people when they can make the change with an attitude like that of an elderly friend of ours, who expressed her feelings about it in writing. Here are some excerpts:

> As I think about it, it seems illogical and a little blind—that feeling of panic when for health reasons one must give up one's cozy room and move to the Care Center. *I don't want to go over there to live,* we think rebelliously. What we really mean, and it is a laudable reason, is our unwillingness to surrender our independence, our feeling of running our own lives. . . .
>
> I am learning to think of "the other building" as a refuge, a place where other eyes help me see, and a strong young shoulder is there to lean on when I totter. It is a place where they understand how pain and sleepless nights can wear down the spirit, and are tolerant when I become fretful and unreasonable. On the bright side, I can relax the strain of trying to keep up. And what a pleasure to find myself among some good old friends and to make new ones.
>
> When I move over, my job is to cooperate. Let me try to keep my

room a pleasant place that friends and hard-working nurses will not shrink from visiting. Let me be a comfortable neighbor.

O yes, the "other building" is a haven of security that takes the worry out of facing a helpless future.

Workplace Visits

Jesus was an itinerant rabbi with, as he said, "nowhere to lay his head" (Matt. 8:20; Luke 9:58). He preached, taught, and healed people wherever he encountered them, in the marketplace, in the temple, along the road, on the hillside, by the lake. We know Jesus made many house calls, and we could also say he visited with people at their places of work. The New Testament records at least three such encounters: with two fishermen, Simon and Andrew, as they were casting a net into the sea (Mark 1:16; Matt. 4:18; cf. Luke 5:1–11); with their two partners, James and John, as they were in a boat mending their nets (Mark 1:19; Matt. 4:21); and with "a man called Matthew sitting at the tax office" (Matt. 9:9; Mark 2:14; Luke 5:27). If we stretch a point, therefore, we could claim biblical precedent for workplace visits.

Most employees, blue-collar or white-collar, are not in a position nowadays to receive a visit from a pastor at their places of work. We're not Jesus, and we can't expect them to be called off the assembly line to talk religion with us. Our visits to people's workplaces are generally limited to calls on business executives, professional and self-employed people, and others who have some control over their own schedules. Even Jesus' workplace visits were with people who were their own bosses. Our office visits are also limited to people who know us or who know who we are. That is, a relationship of some kind has been established, so there is a plausible reason or justification for our being there.

In visiting the average working person, the pastor-evangelist may find that the best alternative to the workplace during the day might be a nearby lunch counter or restaurant. Appointments would have to be made for such meetings, obviously. If Harry's job brings him into contact with the public (for example, if he is a waiter or a salesclerk), we could also show up sometime at his restaurant or store and exchange a few words, but the circumstances might not be right for a faith-sharing conversation.

If a person has the kind of job that permits it, a visit at the office can make a powerful impression. Calling on people at their places of work offers some advantages to the pastor-evangelist. For one thing, people tend to be more honest and open about their beliefs and doubts on their own turf.[29] They seem more willing to share their faith. Our calling at their office is itself an impressive witness to them, and they are inclined to be more receptive, especially when we listen well to what they don't get a chance to say to us in church.

It is important, however, to be sensitive to the fact that we are interrupting their valuable work time. The rule for office visits is just the opposite from the rule for calling in nursing homes. Bed-bound patients have lots of time to visit; desk-bound employees have very little. It behooves us, therefore, to be brief, unless the person we are visiting has a good reason for insisting otherwise.

I always make sure it is all right for me to be there in the first place, either by telephoning in advance for an appointment or, if it's a drop-in visit, by inquiring of the receptionist or secretary whether it is convenient for the person to see me briefly. Although I may not be expected, the fact that I am a pastor is a tremendous door opener. Never has anyone refused to see me, but if someone appears the least bit pressed for time, I immediately offer to come back another day. The best indication of a working person's availability is whether or not I'm invited into his or her office. If not, that's a clear signal it's not a convenient time, for whatever reason, for me to be there. In that case I might say something like this: "I apologize for dropping in on you like this, Susan, but I was in the area and thought I'd take a chance on seeing you, just to say hello."

If this is a drop-in visit, Susan will be curious, and sometimes suspicious, as to why I am there. My rather disarming approach is intended to put her at ease. She may respond by inviting me into her office, or we may remain standing in the reception area. In either case, my next comment would normally be a sensitively worded expression of pastoral interest and concern, such as, "I'm really interested to see where you work, Susan, and to know something about your vocational life, so that when I pray for you I know what to pray for."

Susan's response would predictably be some expression of appreciation, such as, "Thanks, I need all the prayer I can get!" Or, less often, the reply may be more negative; for example, "It'll take a lot more than prayer to help me!" Either kind of response is a come-in point for faith sharing, when it is appropriate for the pastor-evangelist to ask a come-in question, if the setting is favorable. Assuming we are alone and can talk privately, I might lead into the question in this manner: "I can imagine the kind of pressures you must face every day in the business world, Susan. How does your faith help you handle your responsibilities and the difficult kinds of decisions you have to make?"

I never will forget the response of one man to my asking him about how his faith helped him in his work. He was a top executive with a major charitable foundation. "I couldn't make it without faith," he replied. "I have to make decisions that may be the difference between life and death for some worthy cause or program, some institution or organization seeking a grant. Every day on my way to work I pray, 'Lord, help me not to play God today.' "

The amount of this kind of calling a pastor can do is limited. For that reason office visits for me had to be more than strictly social, although social visits have their place and purpose. As a pastor-evangelist, I wanted every pastoral visit to be a faith-sharing and faith-building experience, if at all possible, and most office visits turned out to be just that. People welcomed the opportunity to talk about their problems and temptations, successes and failures, fears and frustrations, hopes and dreams, their struggle to be faithful in their everyday lives and what it means to be a Christian on the job.

In the privacy of a person's office, it is natural to offer to close such a faith-sharing conversation with a prayer, and I have never walked out of an office after that kind of visit without feeling that I had been doing the work of an evangelist.

Prison Visits

There is strong biblical precedent for visiting people in prison. In one of the Servant passages in Second Isaiah, the prophet uses the image of prisoners as a symbol for all who are in bondage of any kind: "Thus says God, the LORD . . . 'I have given you as a covenant to the people, a light to the nations, to open the eyes that are blind, to bring out the prisoners from the dungeon, from the prison those who sit in darkness' " (42:5, 6b–7). "The LORD sets the prisoners free," proclaims the psalmist (Ps. 146:7). "He leads out the prisoners to prosperity" (Ps. 68:6).

In the synagogue at Nazareth, Jesus read from the book of Isaiah these words: "The Spirit of the Lord is upon me, because he has anointed me to preach good news to the poor. He has sent me to proclaim release to the captives and recovering of sight to the blind, to set at liberty those who are oppressed." Then he shut the book and declared to those assembled, "Today this scripture has been fulfilled in your hearing" (Luke 4:17–21).

It is no wonder, therefore, that one of Jesus' criteria for separating "the sheep from the goats" (Matt. 25:32), the righteous from the unrighteous, will be on the basis of whether or not they visited those in prison; as they did it or did it not to others, they did it or did it not to him (Matt. 25:36–45).

"Remember those who are in prison, as though in prison with them," wrote the author of the letter to the Hebrews (13:3), and he commended them for having compassion on the prisoners (10:34). The apostle Paul was in and out of jail many times, claiming "far more imprisonments" (2 Cor. 11:23) than those he referred to as "false apostles, deceitful workmen" (2 Cor. 11:13). So were Peter and the other apostles. They and countless numbers of the early Christians knew what it was to be a prisoner. They followed a Lord who was himself taken prisoner and executed. Paul referred to himself as "a prisoner for Christ Jesus" (see Philemon 1:1).

It is true that few convicts today are in prison for the same reason as were the apostles, who were persecuted for following Jesus, not for committing crimes. The church, nevertheless, has accepted Jesus' parable in Matthew 25 as a mandate for a continuing mission to those in prison, who surely need to hear the gospel and to see it in action. The members of some churches have ministered in various ways to the inmates of nearby prisons, conducting services, teaching classes, visiting privately, corresponding, serving as sponsors, and providing support in various ways. Some of the men of the Oak Lane Presbyterian Church taught vocational and language skills to young detainees in the Youth Study Center in Philadelphia.

If there is a prison in the area, a pastor may want to equip some volunteers for this kind of ministry, which lay people find rewarding and for which they are ideally suited. There are occasions, however, when pastors themselves will need to visit a person who has been incarcerated. Sooner or later one of our church members, a friend, or the friend of a friend may get in trouble with the law and have to go to jail. When that happens, a visit to the prison becomes a top priority, part of the pastor's ministry to the prisoner and his or her family. All of them have their own emotional needs, which vary according to the circumstances of the imprisonment, the relationships of the individuals to the prisoner and to one another, their spiritual as well as material resources, and their own personalities, perceptions, and principles.

What good news do we have for those who are in prison? The most important message of all is that there is a God who loves them, no matter what they've done. Because God loves them, they have the possibility of a new life. This new life may not result in their release from prison, but it will result in their relief from the burden of their guilt and shame. The new life can begin for them whenever they are ready. While still in prison, they can identify and relate to other believers in faith and start living the new life. This will have a bearing on how they relate to the other prisoners, how they react to their guards, and how they view their own future.

The focus of this discussion is the pastor-evangelist's ministry to the person in prison. Since whatever I have to say about visiting people in prison is entirely the product of my own experience, perhaps the best way to address the topic is to describe some of my own attempts to do the work of an evangelist as a prison visitor.[30]

A few months after I was installed as pastor of the Oak Lane

Presbyterian Church, Grace made an appointment to see me in my study at the church. She wanted to talk about her son Tom, who had gotten into trouble with the law and had just been sentenced to serve five months in a prison in an adjacent county. A few days later I visited with Tom at the jail, where we talked across a wooden table in the presence of one of the prison guards. Tom seemed in good spirits and talked freely about his experiences in the Air Force (I later learned that he had received a dishonorable discharge), but not about his present difficulties. Nor did he express any remorse about what he had done. I was not able to engage him in a faith-sharing conversation. For the most part I just listened, but before leaving I assured him of my availability and support. I did offer a brief prayer at the end, but I felt awkward and self-conscious, as I was thinking at the time that neither the tone nor the setting of the conversation seemed conducive to prayer.

At Tom's request I called on his wife, Alicia, who appeared embarrassed by her husband's situation, concerned about their financial needs, and bitter at the world in general. She was totally unchurched and not the least bit responsive to my overtures in that regard.

I did not visit Tom again in prison before his release. My attempts to contact him at his apartment were in vain, but I spoke often with his mother, who reported that her son was having difficulty finding a job and that he was "acting up again." Later I learned that Tom and his wife had separated. He moved in with his mother for a while but eventually left home "because he couldn't stand my lecturing," as Grace put it. "If he wants to live at home, it'll have to be on my terms." When his grandmother died, Tom did not attend the funeral. For a long time Grace didn't know her son's whereabouts. After two years without any response to our efforts to contact him, we deleted his name from the church roll.

I could not help second-guessing myself about Tom. In retrospect I wondered if the outcome might have been different had I or someone else from the church, perhaps an elder, followed up on my initial visit. I had established a relationship with Tom, but I realized later that one visit was not enough. Subsequent visits are needed to show a person behind bars the kind of care and support the church can give. Making disciples calls for a continuing relationship, not just one pastoral visit. My experience with Tom taught me that doing the work of evangelism among convicts is of necessity a time-consuming ministry.

That conviction was confirmed by my experience with Bruce, who had been sent to prison for fraudulent conversion of clients' accounts (a felony). Like Tom, he was on the roll of the church but totally inactive. I had visited Bruce and his family in their home a few times; his wife, although not a member, attended our church regularly, and their two little children were in our Sunday church school. Bruce was always pleasant but totally unresponsive. On my first home visit he had expressed surprise that he was still on the roll and informed me that he considered himself an atheist. I did not know anything about his legal troubles until I read about them in the newspapers.

When I visited Bruce in prison, he seemed genuinely pleased to see me. I was permitted to visit with him in his cell, where we had a lengthy conversation. Bruce was depressed and convinced that his only hope for a new life after prison was to move to Germany, where he had spent time during and after World War II. He thought there he could begin again without the stigma of a prison record. In the meantime, we were focusing on the problems of his adjusting to prison life. Over a period of several weeks and after many hours of conversation, we progressed from head-to-head talks about religion to heart-to-heart talks about God. I kept bringing him books, which he eagerly devoured. His attitude changed completely, and one day, there in his prison cell, he professed his faith in a personal God and in the revelation of Jesus Christ. It took a while for Bruce to come to the point where he could honestly accept Christ as his Lord and Savior, but he said he wanted to with all his heart.

I was so impressed with Bruce that as I was leaving one day, I planted the thought of his becoming a minister and using his own experience to help other people. During our next visit he could speak of nothing else. The more we talked about it, the more excited we both became about the idea, and we prayed for God's will to be revealed. There followed many weeks of frustration and discouragement, as I met with prison officials, lawyers, psychiatrists, seminary administrators, college professors, business creditors and colleagues, family members, neighbors, friends, and the judge who had sentenced Bruce. At times I wondered whether God was telling me to cease my efforts or testing my perseverance. Was God really calling Bruce into a full-time Christian vocation, or was I trying to impose my own will on God? Time and again, just when I was ready to give up, another door would open, admitting a new ray of hope. When the hearing was finally held, the judge ordered Bruce released on probation under my sponsorship. The Jewish magistrate did not understand Bruce's conversion experience, but he was a compassionate man who was impressed by the church's support and Princeton Seminary's willingness to accept a convicted felon.

The congregation welcomed Bruce with open arms and gave him their generous financial support. Throughout his three years at seminary, Bruce served as my student assistant minister. Following graduation from Princeton Seminary, he was ordained as a Presbyterian minister and has been an effective servant of the church ever since.

The prison experience with Bruce was totally different from the one with Tom. No one is more aware than I that the credit for the changes in Bruce's life belongs solely to God. I was merely one of the human instruments whom God used to bring them about. That lesson I had learned long before. What I now had experienced in a new way was the powerful influence of the church in the evangelization of people in prison. By Bruce's own testimony, it was the acceptance and tangible support of the congregation that opened his heart to the reality of God's acceptance and the possibility of a new life, not in Germany but in Christ. I learned that a ministry of presence is important, but that it is perseverance that makes presence believable. I learned that availability is a commitment to spend and be spent, and that submissive prayer and dependence upon God's mercy and grace are the only ways to face the dilemma of whether to view as green lights or red lights the events that occur along the road of faith.

In the course of visiting Bruce I had opportunities to chat briefly with some of the other prisoners, who would call out to me, "Hey, Rev!" as I walked past their cells or through the recreation area. One of them was a sixty-one-year-old man who had been in and out of prison many times for vagrancy and alcohol-related petty crimes. Bruce had told me about Fred and was convinced that he could be successfully rehabilitated, to use a somewhat outmoded term. After visiting with Fred a few times, I agreed. The parole officer did not, however, and my intercession on behalf of Fred was treated as the well-meaning but naïve plea of one who had been duped by a clever con artist. "I tell you, Pastor, he'll be back in prison in less than two weeks. He's a boozer with a record as long as your arm. He can't make it out there."

Recidivism is a major problem in any penal system. The assistant warden may have been more realistic than cynical when he commented to me grimly that "there are probably not more than ten percent of these men worth trying to reclaim for society. The vast majority are criminal types who will return to their old ways until they're caught and locked up again. And every one of them will tell you he's in here on a bum rap."

Despite statistics that corroborate the warden's gloomy assessment, I believed Fred was one who, with help, could make a successful readjustment. When I reported that our church would be supporting Fred financially until he found a job, and that one of our elders would provide him a room free of charge until Fred could afford to rent a place on his own, the parole officer finally, though still somewhat reluctantly, agreed to release Fred under my sponsorship.

Fred had a Roman Catholic background but had not been in church for many, many years. He had a beautiful philosophy of life, however, and a simple faith in God, which he shared during our prison visits. The Session did not make church attendance a condition for helping Fred, but we did encourage him to seek out a nearby Catholic church. Instead, he expressed interest in attending our six-week orientation class for new members, at the conclusion of which he decided to join our church. His expertise as a chef was a welcome asset in our church kitchen, and he became a popular member and eventually president of the Men's Bible Class. After seventeen years without seeing his family, he was able to locate and reestablish contact with his son and daughter.

By then Fred was gainfully employed, had his own apartment, and was no longer on parole. Some months later he moved to Connecticut to be near his children. He was still "on the wagon," and happily employed as a chef, when he died suddenly of a heart attack. His son and daughter drove down from New England one weekend just to see the church that had helped their father regain his self-respect and become a useful member of society. With tears in their eyes, they said, "We can never put into words what it has meant to us to have Dad back in the family again after all these years. We just had to come and express our thanks to you in person."

Once again the crucial role of the church in the rehabilitation of former convicts is powerfully underscored by our experience with Fred. His case was another testimony to the effectiveness of a service-oriented evangelism, for what impressed Fred, as it did Bruce, was not anything I said but what the people of God did. They reached out to him in love and welcomed him into their hearts and homes. At the same time, the opportunity to do that might not have occurred if I had either ignored him or related to him on just a superficial level. I say that simply to emphasize the importance of our prison ministry. The pastor-evangelist can help unlock the physical as well as the spiritual cell doors for at least some prison inmates. One Fred or Bruce can make any amount of effort worthwhile. As pastor-evangelists we don't have to limit our efforts to helping prisoners face life in prison, as important as that is. We can also help some of them to set their sights on a better life outside.

There are bound to be disappointments, of course. Tom was one. Another was Roger, a young man whose release I helped to gain. Despite all my efforts and the gracious support of members of our congregation, Roger returned to a life of crime and became a fugitive. None of my "wise" counsel had any effect.

Still another of my failures was Elmer, who could never overcome his alcoholism. He was intelligent and capable when he was sober, but mean and sometimes violent when under the influence of alcohol. One time he terrified my two young sons by announcing his intention to kill me. Elmer would telephone at any time of the day or night, always collect, and always to demand money. Or he would show up unexpectedly on the doorstep of the manse, usually with a huge unpaid cab fare, which he expected me to pay. He lied repeatedly and broke every promise he made, until finally I told him I never wanted to see him again unless and until he was completely sober.

A few months later Elmer was back again, drunk as ever, with a $27 unpaid cab fare. I refused to pay and surreptitiously told the distraught driver to take him to the nearest police station. He did, and Elmer was locked up. A couple of days later I visited him in jail and later spent a day in court, where he was tried and sentenced. By then he was sober and remorseful, but I had seen him like that many times before. Never would he admit that he was an alcoholic or even that he had a drinking problem. On my last visit I told him that when he was ready to join Alcoholics Anonymous and try to straighten out his life, I would again offer my help, but until that point I was no longer available.

The last time I heard from Elmer was via a collect call from New Orleans. He was drunk and as nasty as ever. I hung up on him and have never seen or heard from him again.

Thus ends the sad tale of Elmer, who needed far more help than I was able to give. His response to my prison visits was always a manipulative effort to use me or to involve me in one of his nefarious schemes. Elmer was totally unreceptive to the gospel. When I think of the most difficult evangelistic challenges I have encountered over the years, his name always comes to mind.

Even so, I have him to thank for what he taught me about belligerent, antagonistic people, especially those who are alcoholic. There are many like him in prison, and they present a difficult problem for the pastor-evangelist, because they don't want the kind of help they need. Whereas the challenge with Bruce was discerning God's will for his life in the midst of all the confusing and conflicting signs, the challenge with Elmer was how far to go with an uncooperative, unresponsive, unrepentant sinner. To put it another way, the challenge for me with Bruce was seeing people's no as God's yes, whereas the challenge with Elmer was seeing his no as God's no. Bruce was responsive and hence redeemable; but was Elmer unredeemable because he was unresponsive to me? All I know is that I wasn't able to help him. Maybe someone else could have. Maybe someone has.

These are actual cases. There are others I could describe, but those I have chosen should suffice to make the point that visiting people in prison is a difficult and demanding challenge to the pastor-evangelist. It requires much more of us than a routine pastoral call, and it must of necessity be done in the context of the church's corporate ministry of evangelism, for a pastor cannot do all that is required for any rehabilitation program to be effective.

Evangelistic calls on prison inmates can lead to frustration and disappointment, or to the exciting renewal of broken lives. Whichever is the case, we are called to persevere in this ministry and to leave the results to God.

PART TWO

The Pastor-Evangelist
as Counselor

PART TWO

6

Biblical Precedents for Counseling

Counseling has always been an important aspect of pastoral care.[1] As a counselor the pastor-evangelist seeks through the medium of interpersonal dialogue to help persons to live as spiritually and emotionally healthy individuals. The task involves the pastor-evangelist in every aspect of people's lives, always with the hope of being an instrument through whom God can help people to face and handle the demands and difficulties, successes and failures, opportunities and challenges, decisions and commitments, joys and sorrows, pain and bereavement, and whatever other exigencies and pleasures life presents.

That is not intended to be a definitive description of the role. Professional counselors may prefer a more technical definition, although some define the process quite simply. For Carroll Wise, for example, "Counseling is fundamentally a process of communication between two persons for the purpose of helping one of them solve life problems."[2] My colleague in the Department of Practical Theology at Princeton Theological Seminary, the late Seward Hiltner, also viewed counseling as a process of helping people help themselves.[3] Another friend and colleague, Donald Capps, Professor of Pastoral Theology, in a recent conversation commented, "I don't think I've ever tried to define it. I suppose I would use Howard Clinebell's definition. He is sort of the unofficial spokesperson for the profession."

Clinebell, whose writings I have found most useful and whose "growth counseling" approach I subscribe to, distinguishes the related terms as follows:

> *Pastoral care* is the broad, inclusive ministry of mutual healing and growth within a congregation and its community, through the life cycle. *Pastoral counseling,* one dimension of pastoral care, is the utili-

zation of a variety of healing (therapeutic) methods to help people handle their problems and crises more growthfully and thus experience healing of their brokenness. Pastoral counseling is a reparative function needed when the growth of persons is seriously jeopardized or blocked by crises. They may need pastoral counseling at times of severe crises, usually on a short-term basis. *Pastoral psychotherapy* is the utilization of long-term, reconstructive therapeutic methods when growth is deeply and/or chronically diminished by need-depriving early life experiences or by multiple crises in adult life.[4]

The somewhat restrictive use of the term "counselor" has led to the adoption and use in Protestant circles of the designation "spiritual director," so long a part of the Roman Catholic tradition. The relationship between pastoral counseling and spiritual direction is a matter of much discussion and debate, although all would agree that holistic pastoral care includes both. The role of the spiritual director and that of the pastoral counselor, as they have evolved historically, can be distinguished in terms of their focus and purpose. The counselee's motivation to seek help is different, and for that reason so is his or her relationship to the counselor. The two roles need to be understood, however, as mutually dependent functions. As a pastor-evangelist I prefer to think of spiritual direction not as a form of pastoral counseling but as a dimension of it, just as counseling can be part of spiritual direction.[5]

Is Jesus a Role Model for Counseling?

Counseling is, to be sure, an incredibly demanding role and one that can be unhealthfully time-consuming for a conscientious pastor. Unfortunately, there are no role models in the New Testament for the pastor-evangelist as counselor. That is to say, there are no illustrations to which we can point for a description of what a pastor-evangelist must do to fulfill the professional role of counselor, as we understand that role today. It is *not* to say that the Bible cannot be a powerful aid and an extremely useful tool in counseling, as in all interpersonal witnessing, to illustrate, illuminate, punctuate, and authenticate.[6]

The Synoptic Gospels

What about Jesus as a role model for counseling? The Synoptic Gospels record a number of verbatims of varying lengths between Jesus and different individuals, but these incidents bear little resemblance to a typical modern counseling situation. In most cases we find Jesus responding to people's physical and/or spiritual needs, often with a comment regarding their faith. The stories are told to demonstrate Jesus' authority to heal people's infirmities and to forgive their sins, not to display his counseling skills. Almost always there are other people around when the verbal exchange is taking place.

The following incidents, in which Jesus is engaged in conversation with various individuals, could hardly be classified as pastoral counseling sessions:

- The exchange between Jesus and the leper, whom Jesus heals and charges not to say anything about it but to show himself to the priest (Matt. 8:1–4; Mark 1:40–45; Luke 5:12–16)
- The exchange between Jesus and the centurion, whom Jesus commends for his great faith and whose servant he heals (Matt. 8:5–13; cf. Luke 7:2–10)
- Jesus' response to Jairus' appeal for the ruler's dying daughter (Matt. 9:18–19, 23–26; Mark 5:22–24, 35–43; Luke 8:40–42, 49–56)
- Jesus' reaction to the woman with the hemorrhage, who touches the fringe of his garment in order to be healed (Matt. 9:20–22; Mark 5:25–34; Luke 8:43–48)
- The table conversation between Jesus and Simon the Pharisee, and the woman who anoints Jesus' feet (Luke 7:36–50)
- Jesus' encounter with the Gerasene demoniac, from whom he exorcises the unclean spirit (Mark 5:1–20; Luke 8:26–39; cf. Matt. 8:28–34)
- The exchange between Jesus and the Syrophoenician woman whose daughter is demon possessed (Mark 7:24–30; cf. Matt. 15:21–28)
- Jesus and the blind man of Bethsaida, whose sight he restores (Mark 8:22–26)
- Jesus' exchange with the father of the epileptic boy, whom the disciples were unable to cure (Matt. 17:14–21; Mark 9:14–29; Luke 9:37–43a)
- Jesus' response to a lawyer who asks, "What shall I do to inherit eternal life?" and "Who is my neighbor?" (Luke 10:25–37; cf. Matt. 22:34–40 and Mark 12:28–31)
- Jesus' gentle rebuke to Martha when she complains about her sister's not helping her (Luke 10:38–42)
- The exchange between Jesus and the one leper who turns back to thank him after Jesus heals ten (Luke 17:11–19)
- Jesus' dialogue with the rich young ruler and discourse on the perils of wealth (Matt. 19:16–30; Mark 10:17–31; Luke 18:18–30)
- Jesus' call, healing, and commendation of Bartimaeus, the blind beggar (Mark 10:46–52; Luke 18:35–43; cf. Matt. 20:29–34)

- The exchange between Jesus and Zacchaeus the tax collector (Luke 19:1–10)
- The exchange between Jesus and a scribe regarding the greatest commandment (Mark 12:28–34; cf. Matt. 22:34–40 and Luke 10:25–28)
- The interchange between Jesus and Peter about Peter's denial (Matt. 26:33–35; Mark 14:29–31; Luke 22:31–34)
- The exchange between Jesus and Pontius Pilate the next day (Matt. 27:2, 11–14; Mark 15:1–5; Luke 23:1, 3–4)
- The resurrected Christ's instruction to Cleopas and his companion on the road to Emmaus (Luke 24:13–35)

It would take some clever eisegesis to interpret any of these texts, and others that could be cited, as models for pastoral counseling. Shall we say, for example, that Jesus was doing family counseling with the sons of Zebedee and their mother when they came to him with their improper request? Jesus' encounters do, however, provide us with a composite word picture of the way he related to persons in different situations. Jesus responded to their needs, yet he did not hesitate to confront them when necessary. He could hardly be used as a model for nondirective counseling, yet he often asked questions to make people think. He treated people with respect, but he could be quite confrontational in his approach, especially when dealing with hypocrisy ("Woe to you, scribes and Pharisees, hypocrites!").

The Gospel of John

Turning to the Gospel of John, we can add a few more incidents to those we have identified in the Synoptic Gospels. Two pericopes from the Fourth Gospel come closest to resembling pastoral counseling situations, in that both involve private and lengthier conversations. The first is Jesus' session with Nicodemus (John 3:1–15), who comes to Jesus by night—with or without an appointment, we don't know which. We do know that Jesus receives him; he does not say, "Sorry, Nick, it's past my office hours; perhaps I can work you in sometime next week."

In a paper describing what he wanted his future congregation to know about his pastoral counseling ministry, one of my students wrote, "I will not tolerate anyone's calling me at home after nine o'clock at night." He made the same comment in a class discussion, prompting another student to remark, "Don't worry, nobody will want to!" We can learn much about what it means to be available to people by observing how Jesus handled the tremendous demands on his time and energy and how he dealt with interruptions.

In John's verbatim of the conversation, Jesus is both direct and directive in relating to Nicodemus: "Are you a teacher of Israel, and yet you do not understand this?" (v. 10). He does not merely listen; he challenges the Pharisee to be born anew (vs. 3–7), and apparently his evangelistic effort is successful, as we are told that Nicodemus later helps Joseph of Arimathea to prepare Jesus' body for burial (John 19:39–40).

The other pericope is the story of Jesus' encounter with the woman of Samaria at Jacob's well (John 4:7–26). In this fascinating dialogue, Jesus does not talk down to the woman or over her head but, in his typical fashion, makes her think. First he arouses her curiosity by asking her for a drink, in effect putting himself in her debt, "for Jews have no dealings with Samaritans" (v. 9b). Then he challenges her intellectually by replying to her question with a cryptic play on words: "If you knew the gift of God, and who it is that is saying to you, 'Give me a drink,' you would have asked him, and he would have given you living water" (v. 10). The woman does not know who he is, what the gift of God is, or what he means by living water. "You have nothing to draw with, and the well is deep; where do you get that living water?" (v. 11). Jesus has definitely hooked her interest, but she doesn't know what he means.

Nor does she understand when he tells her that whoever drinks of this living water will never thirst: "Sir, give me this water, that I may not thirst, nor come here to draw" (v. 15). Whereupon Jesus abruptly shifts the conversation and challenges her morally: "Go, call your husband, and come here" (v. 16). "I have no husband," she replies (v. 17a). "You are right," says Jesus; "you have had five husbands, and he whom you now have is not your husband" (vs. 17b–18). With that the woman realizes that Jesus can look into her very soul: "Sir, I perceive that you are a prophet" (v. 19). Jesus has pricked her conscience, so she changes the subject: "Our fathers worshiped on this mountain, and you [Jews] say that in Jerusalem is the place where people ought to worship"; namely, the temple (v. 20). This was one of the main issues between Jews and Samaritans. The woman undoubtedly is thinking, Maybe this prophet has the answer, and besides, it will get him off my case.

This time Jesus' response challenges her spiritually as well as morally: "Woman, believe me, the hour is coming when neither on this mountain nor in Jerusalem will you worship the Father" (v. 21), for "God is spirit, and those who worship him must worship in spirit and truth" (v. 24). In other words, it's not the place that matters but the spirit of the worshiper. It's not ceremony but truth that counts with God.

Jesus' words have the ring of authority. As if thinking aloud, the woman says to him, "I know that Messiah is coming . . . when he comes, he will show us all things" (v. 25). In a fitting climax to this engrossing exchange, Jesus replies, "I who speak to you am he"—an outright pronouncement by Jesus that he is the Messiah (v. 26).

Just then the disciples come, and the woman rushes off to tell everyone back in her town of Sychar, "Come, see a man who told me all that I ever did. Can this be the Christ?" (v. 29). Many of the Samaritans believe in Jesus because of her testimony, and they persuade him to stay there for a couple of days (vs. 39–40). Many more believe, and they say to the woman, "It is no longer because of your words that we believe, for we have heard for ourselves, and we know that this is indeed the Savior of the world" (v. 42).

Was Jesus functioning as a pastoral counselor in this story? Some might argue that he was, but it seems to me that his role was more that of a teacher. True, the two roles often overlap, but Jesus was first and foremost a rabbi (teacher). He was pastoral in that he cared for "the whole person," but he had his own agenda and he spoke with authority. As with Nicodemus, so with the woman; his words were instructive, directive, and prescriptive. He always called for a response, and in the case of the woman of Samaria the response was positive.

So even in this story we cannot correctly point to Jesus as a role model for the professional counselor. Once again, that is not to say there are no valuable lessons to be learned. Jesus' encounter with the Samaritan woman beautifully illustrates the personal nature of Christian faith, because it is *about* a person (Jesus), is transmitted *through* persons (the woman told the townspeople about Jesus), is intended *for* persons (even those with whom Jews had no dealings), and, most important, because it is a relationship *with* a person (the living Christ). The question I want to address in this and the following chapter is, How does the pastor-evangelist as counselor bear witness to these truths? We are not Jesus, and we cannot relate to people the way he did.

Before tackling the question head on, let's see if there are any other incidents in the Fourth Gospel in which Jesus could possibly serve as a role model for pastoral counseling:

- An official begs Jesus to heal his dying son (4:46–54)
- Jesus heals a sick man by the Sheep Gate pool (5:2–9)
- Jesus converses with the man blind from birth, whom he heals and later seeks out (9:1–7, 35–39)
- Jesus visits with Martha and Mary after their brother Lazarus dies (11:17–40)
- Jesus responds to questioning by Annas (18:19–24)
- Jesus responds to Pilate's questions (18:33–38)
- Mary Magdalene speaks with the resurrected Christ (20:11–18)

The only one of the above incidents in which Jesus' role remotely resembles that of a pastoral counselor is the visit with Mary and Martha when, out of his compassion for and empathy with the grief-stricken sisters and their friends, Jesus himself weeps (John 11:35). His tears are a reminder that, in counseling with grieving persons, that kind of identification with the pain of others is sometimes entirely appropriate for the pastor-evangelist.

I learned the hard way the value of genuine tears. In the incident I am about to relate I was functioning as a preacher and worship leader, not as a counselor, but the principle is the same.

As I was delivering my message at the memorial service for the eleven-year-old daughter of some very dear friends, I looked down at the drawn faces of the distraught parents. Their little girl had died of a staphylococcus infection a few days following surgery to correct a congenital heart defect. Having lost a child of our own, who would have been the same age as their daughter, I could identify with their terrible pain and sorrow. Suddenly I felt myself overcome by grief, and I started to weep. My voice choked, and for half a minute or so I was unable to speak. I was terribly embarrassed by my lack of control and prayed hard for God to help me regain my composure. At last I was able to continue through the rest of the service. Afterward, the parents hugged me for a moment without a word, and then, with tears in her own eyes, the mother said, "Your tears meant more to us than anything else you said." Others made similar comments.

That would not have been the case if my tears had been contrived. They were the spontaneous and genuine expression of what I was feeling for my friends at that moment. I still feel some embarrassment when I think about it. I had shared many tears with hurting people in their homes and in my study, but that was the first time I had ever broken down in the pulpit. It was an unsettling experience for me to lose control like that, but I know that God used my human emotion that day to help comfort a grief-stricken family.

Are There Role Models Among the Apostles?

Verbatims in the Book of Acts

Turning to the Acts of the Apostles, we again find no role models for our pastoral counseling ministry. A perusal of the verbatims of the following conversations between the apostles and various individuals reveals the apostles primarily as either teachers or healers, but always as witnesses:

- Peter speaks with the lame beggar, whom he heals by the temple gate (3:1–10)
- Philip teaches and baptizes an Ethiopian eunuch (8:26–39)
- Ananias calls on, heals, and baptizes "Brother Saul" (9:10–19; 22:12–16)
- Peter bears witness to and baptizes a Roman centurion named Cornelius (10:1–48)
- Paul confronts Elymas the magician (13:6–12)
- Paul casts out a spirit of divination from a slave girl (16:16–18)
- Paul and Silas witness to a frightened Philippian jailer (16:25–37)
- Paul gives his personal testimony before Felix, the governor (24:10–27)
- Paul speaks with Porcius Festus (25:1, 6–12)
- Paul bears witness to King Agrippa (26:1–32)

Guiding Principles Underscored

We don't learn much about counseling techniques from these incidents, but some important guiding principles for the pastor-evangelist as counselor are underscored.[7] The first is the obvious point that opportunities for counseling can occur any time, any place, as they did for the apostles—by the temple gate, in a chariot traveling along the road, in someone's home, in jail, in a palace, wherever they happened to be. The counseling we do is not restricted to the pastor's study. In fact, some of our most effective pastoral care occurs in our unplanned, unscheduled, informal encounters with people.

Second, we are often directed by the Holy Spirit to counsel and bear witness to people we would rather not see at all. Philip, Ananias, and Peter were prompted by the Holy Spirit to go to persons they would not otherwise have sought out. The Spirit told Philip to approach a man of much higher station than himself, a minister of the queen of Ethiopia (Acts 8:29). It is not likely that Philip would otherwise have initiated a conversation with that high-ranking official sitting in his impressive chariot. The Lord told Ananias in a vision to go and heal Saul, the man whom Ananias knew as the dreaded persecutor of the saints (9:10–14). Peter was told by the Spirit to go to Caesarea and bear witness to a Roman centurion named Cornelius (10:19–22), despite the Jewish prohibition against associating with a Gentile (10:28). When we are open to the leading of the Holy Spirit, we will be directed to people who need our help and will be guided in our counseling task.

Third, we must remember that the Holy Spirit has preceded us and prepared the way for us with the people God wants us to see. Philip found the Ethiopian reading the prophet Isaiah (8:30). The way was well paved before Philip ever arrived on the scene. God had already been at work in that man's life. Unbeknown to Ananias, Saul's life had been changed by a heavenly vision on the way to Damascus (9:1–9; cf. 22:6–16; 26:12–20). He was ready for what Ananias would do for him. So, too, Cornelius had been told in a vision to send for Simon Peter and hear what he had to say. As counselors, we need to be sensitive to the ways in which God has been at work in people's lives before they ever come to see us. The pastor-evangelist knows how to help people identify and talk about their faith experiences and how to plug into those experiences without violating the counselor-counselee relationship. There will be more about that in the next chapter.

Fourth, pastoral counseling and evangelism are not separate and distinct functions but are intimately related and mutually dependent aspects of holistic pastoral care. The apostles, following the example of their Lord, ministered to the whole person, to people's spiritual needs as well as their physical and emotional needs. They remind us that our pastoral care is inadequate and incomplete if it does not include persistent attention to people's spiritual needs. The issue for the pastor-evangelist, therefore, is not when to be a counselor and when to be an evangelist, but how to counsel with evangelistic sensitivity and how to evangelize with pastoral sensitivity.

Fifth, and following on the previous point, the incidents from scripture serve as a reminder that the basic medium for counseling as well as for evangelism is, after all, conversation. It behooves the pastor-evangelist, therefore, to be a good conversationalist. Conversation involves both speaking and listening. For conversation to be communication, there must be understanding as well as hearing. As I stated in chapter 3, we listen with our eyes, as well as with our ears. Our eyes help us to know the feelings behind the words. The conversations reported in the New Testament do not always convey the feelings and emotions behind the words. That is why biblical scholars and commentators often differ in their interpretations. They were not present when the conversations took place; they couldn't see the facial expressions or the body language of the participants. Biblical interpretation is often a matter of conjecture, if not speculation. We cannot always know for certain where the biblical character is "coming from"; that is, what else was going on in his or her life before the reported encounter with Jesus or one of the apostles. The point is, again, that pastor-evangelists, in order to be good conversationalists, must be good listeners.

The sixth and final observation, one to which I have already made brief reference, is that the interpersonal style of Jesus and the apostles was often confrontational. Jesus often rebuked people, sometimes gently (for example, Martha, when she complained about Mary[8]), sometimes sternly (for example, his mother at the wedding feast in Cana[9]), sometimes bluntly (for example, Peter, for trying to deter him from his purpose[10]), and sometimes very harshly (for example, the scribes and the Pharisees, for their hypocrisy[11]). He confronted the woman at the well about her marital status,[12] and Peter about his brash claim.[13] So, too, we find Paul blasting Elymas[14] and challenging King Agrippa to believe the prophets.[15] In his letter to the Galatians, Paul writes about confronting Peter for being intimidated by the circumcision party (Gal. 2:11–14).

These illustrations from the New Testament underscore the importance of knowing when and how to be confrontive.[16] The pastor-evangelist as counselor must be able to recognize the difference between appropriate and inappropriate guilt and understand the relationship and distinction between guilt and shame. Those who are really guilty, and have not acknowledged it, need to be confronted. Those who have something to confess should be helped to see that. The sensitive counselor, however, does not add to the burden of someone already overladen with inordinate feelings of guilt or repressive shame. Howard Clinebell describes a five-stage process for resolving healthy guilt feelings: confrontation, confession, forgiveness, restitution, and reconciliation.[17] When one helps a counselee to understand these stages from a theological perspective and to move through them in a faith-sharing context, one is doing the work of an evangelist.

Some Guidelines for Interpersonal Witnessing

Although the verbatim material is limited, the incidents taken as a whole do suggest, in addition to listening, some other guidelines for effective interpersonal witnessing, such as discovering and ministering to the other person's need, identifying where the other person is spiritually and responding appropriately, and, most important, relating the gospel to the situation. The subject of the apostles' witness was Jesus Christ. It was "in the name of Jesus of Nazareth" that Peter healed the lame beggar (Acts 3:6). Philip baptized the Ethiopian eunuch after telling him "the good news of Jesus" (8:35). "Brother Saul," said Ananias, "the Lord Jesus who appeared to you on the road by which you came, has sent me that you may regain your sight and be filled with the Holy Spirit" (9:17).

Peter told Cornelius about "the one ordained by God to be the judge of the living and the dead. To him all the prophets bear witness that every one who believes in him receives forgiveness of sins through his name" (10:42–43). Paul, filled with the Holy Spirit, denounced Elymas in the name of the Lord (13:10–11), and to the unclean spirit in an exploited slave girl he said, "I charge you in the name of Jesus Christ to come out of her" (16:18). To the Philippian jailer's question, "What must I do to be saved?" Paul and Silas replied, "Believe in the Lord Jesus" (16:30–31). To Felix, the governor, Paul bore witness to his faith in God and in the resurrection of the dead (24:10–21), and to King Agrippa he related the story of his conversion on the road to Damascus (26:1–23).

"Counseling" in the Bible

One reason there are no role models in the New Testament for the modern-day counselor is betrayed by the very use of the word in the Bible. In the Jewish scriptures as well as in the New Testament a counselor is primarily an adviser, a giver of advice. I suspect that connotation would not be acceptable to Carl Rogers, whose name is so closely associated with nondirective counseling!

The English word "counselor" occurs in its singular or plural form thirty times in the Revised Standard Version of the Old Testament and only five times in the New Testament. It is used four times in the Gospel of John to translate the word *paraklētos,* [18] which in the Authorized (King James) Version is translated "Comforter," referring to the Holy Spirit. The word literally means "called to one's side," but it has presented linguistic problems for biblical scholars.[19] In secular Greek *paraklētos* came to mean an advocate or legal adviser, a person called in to help someone in court. The KJV's use of the term "Comforter" for *paraklētos* in John's Gospel is not consistent either with the secular use of the word or with the equivalent Old Testament concept of "advocate." The translators of the RSV rejected the word "comforter" in favor of "counselor," which embraces more clearly the two concepts of helper and advocate. While pastors may function in either of these roles in their ministry of pastoral care, neither word is an adequate synonym for a certified pastoral counselor today, whose professional expertise includes far more technical knowledge and psychoanalytic skills than any translation of *paraklētos* implies.

All things considered, the Bible provides neither a role model for nor a definition of what it means to be a pastoral counselor. There are, however, as I have already indicated, biblical principles to guide us in our counseling ministry, as in all our professional roles, even though the unique function we call pastoral counseling has no identifiable parallels in the Bible. That fact has a large bearing on what I have to say about the pastor-evangelist as counselor, to which task I now turn.

7

Theology, Psychology, and Counseling

The boldness of the apostles in bearing witness to their Lord serves as an indictment of our failure as well as a reminder of our responsibility to do the work of an evangelist in our counseling ministry. If there are no role models for the way pastoral counseling is understood and practiced nowadays, perhaps we practitioners should rethink what we are doing and why we are doing it the way we do.

Identifying Our Presuppositions

To do pastoral counseling with integrity, we have to come to grips with and resolve some fundamental questions. What presuppositions inform our understanding of the role of a counselor? What assumptions shape our approach to the people who come to us for counseling? What is our doctrine of God? Of humanity? Sin? Redemption? Atonement? The Holy Spirit? The authority of the scriptures? Is our understanding of human nature basically psychological or theological? Are the categories we use to explain human behavior primarily psychological or theological?[20]

I long ago concluded that as a Christian and as a pastor I would view my counseling role from a theological perspective. I start with the unprovable assumption that there is a God, a personal God, who is responsive to our prayers and to whom we are responsible. That is a statement of faith, the faith that is a gift of the God I believe in. I am dependent upon the God I believe in to go on believing, but because I believe, my understanding of humanity is fundamentally biblical and theological. It is biblical in that I view human beings holistically, as psychosomatic unities. We are not bodies with souls; we are body and spirit together. It is theological in that we are created in God's image—not that God looks like us, but that we are dependent upon God, the way an image is dependent upon that which it reflects.

I believe, furthermore, that God's purpose, will, and nature are revealed through the testimony of the Holy Spirit, speaking to the hearts of believers through the scriptures, and made visible, understandable, and accessible through the life, words, and works of the historical Jesus, to whom the Spirit and the scriptures bear witness.

I believe in the reality of sin, which is our prideful and willful disobedience of God's will. It is to put oneself in the place of God, to give one's allegiance to or put one's trust in anything or anyone other than God. It is to transgress or fail to conform to the law of God.[21] I reject all dichotomies that attempt to view humanity as basically good or basically evil. I act on the biblical premise that God's creation was good, but that human beings from the start have misused their God-given freedom, so that all humanity is tainted by sin. Thus all human beings who are capable of making moral choices and spiritual decisions, and of ordering their priorities and commitments, have sinned or will sin and fall short of the glory of God.

I also believe that human beings are affected by, but not totally determined by, their environment, for God can intervene in human affairs in totally unpredictable ways and redeem the most unlikely situations. I believe that in everything God can work for good with those who love God and are called according to God's purpose, that God never tests us beyond our endurance, that God's grace is sufficient, and that nothing can separate us from God's love, which is offered and available to all through the living Christ, who reigns eternally as Lord and Savior of the world.

I believe God has been revealed to humankind sufficiently for our salvation in Jesus Christ, whom to know is life, whom to trust is wisdom, whom to love is joy, whom to serve is freedom. Christ came to reconcile human beings to God and to each other. I believe that our unique function as pastoral counselors is to help people get in touch and in tune with the God who can change their lives.

These are affirmations of faith, the basic assumptions that shape my self-understanding and my view of humanity. They are the givens in my counseling ministry, and I state them here without apology or argument.

The Peril of Psychology Without Theology

The insights of the psychological disciplines should inform but not displace our theological presuppositions. Most secular psychological theories of human behavior are fundamentally or ultimately deterministic. Their practitioners act on the assumption that human beings are the products of their environment, and if one probes deeply enough, one can discover the causes of human behavior. That is to say, if the past is known, the present is understood and the future can therefore be predicted, or so it would seem. In other words, we are conditioned by our life's experience, and our behavior is the result of sociological, physiological, and psychological forces that explain why we act as we do. If, however, human behavior is explainable, it is easy to assume one's actions are also inevitable, the necessary result of a cause-and-effect relationship. Aye, there's the rub!

Most psychological theorists have no place for sin in their understanding of human nature; the word is missing from their vocabularies.[22] There are notable exceptions, such as the late Karl Menninger, whose book *Whatever Became of Sin?* dramatically called attention to that lack.[23] But so many of the psychological fads, such as transactional analysis, leave no room for the reality of human sin. There is no understanding of the Christian doctrine of redemption or the power of the Holy Spirit, whose radical transformation of human personality cannot be explained or explained away. In demeaning the reality of guilt, secular psychology has undercut a basic tenet of biblical theology, which testifies that "all have sinned and fall short of the glory of God" (Rom. 3:23); "None is righteous, no, not one" (Rom. 3:10; see Ps. 14:1–3).

It is difficult for me to reconcile the whole human potential movement, with its glorification of self, its overemphasis on personal fulfillment, its doctrine of justification by self-assertion, and all the other whims of a me-first, success-oriented generation, with Jesus' call to deny oneself and take up a cross, to turn the other cheek, to love our enemies, to pray for those who persecute us, and to seek first the kingdom of God and God's righteousness. Jesus came that we "may have life, and have it abundantly" (John 10:10). He showed us what it is to be truly human. In this sense, the human potential movement really began with Jesus Christ. As a Christian I believe it is in Christ and only in Christ that our true humanity is realized and our human potential is achieved. "I can do all things in him who strengthens me," declared the apostle Paul (Phil. 4:13). "For the sake of Christ, then, I am content with weaknesses, insults, hardships, persecutions, and calamities; for when I am weak, then I am strong" (2 Cor. 12:10).

The peril of psychology without theology in counseling is the presupposition that a person can be "explained" solely in psychological terms. It can lead a counselor into the trap of assuming that the counselee is either sick or incapable of handling his or her "problem" (and if you don't think you have a problem, wait till I get through with you!). That assumption may or may not prove to be correct, but it is a risky place to begin the counseling relationship. If a person is mentally or emotionally ill, she or he needs a doctor, a medically qualified person who can prescribe drugs, give or authorize shock treatments, or have a person institutionalized. However, in far more cases than some psychiatrists, clinical psychologists, psychotherapists, and other secular counselors will recognize or admit, the trouble is spiritual, not psychological. Too many spiritually bankrupt people are treated as if they are emotionally disturbed. They are not encouraged or helped to see how God can redeem and transform their lives. I agree completely with the clinical psychologist who commented, "There are very few professional psychiatrists or psychologists to whom I would want to entrust my *spiritual* life."[24]

The Peril of Theology Without Psychology

Conversely, it is also true that some pastors treat people who *are* emotionally disturbed as if their serious problems are religious questions. Such pastors do not recognize their own limitations. Knowing when to refer someone to a more highly qualified professional counselor is part of the wisdom and skill required of a counseling pastor. Neurotic or psychotic persons need professional help.

It is important for pastors to learn as much as they can from the various psychological disciplines, so that they can discern more accurately the needs of the persons who seek their help and can minister to them more effectively. It is good for pastors to be familiar with the latest counseling theories and techniques and to know what resources are available. It is as reprehensible for a pastor to ignore or violate the valid insights of psychology as it is to abandon the convictional truths of theology.

For the counseling pastor, psychology without theology is incomplete, and theology without psychology is irresponsible. Both perspectives are needed, but theology must take precedence over psychology in shaping the pastor-evangelist's understanding of human nature and his or her approach to the counseling task.

Reclaiming the Counseling Pastor's Rightful Place

In the trend toward professionalism and specialization that has characterized much of pastoral counseling, too many ministers have either sold out or copped out. Some have sold out by exchanging their theological vocabulary for the language of psychology. To augment one's theological vocabulary is one thing; to abandon it altogether is something else. The problem has been around for many years. Halford Luccock called attention to the danger in his Lyman

Beecher Lectures on Preaching in 1953, when he exhorted his hearers at Yale to "take the aid which psychology gives without allowing it to become a dilution of, or substitute for, the gospel."[25]

Those who have "sold out" have allowed the assumptions and categories of secular psychology to displace their biblical and theological understanding of human nature.[26] They have unwittingly bought into a deterministic view of human behavior, with no place for sin, redemption, or the radical and totally unpredictable intervention of the Holy Spirit. It is one thing to be informed by the invaluable insights of psychoanalysis, psychotherapy, and other secular disciplines; to abandon one's theological principles in the process is something else. It is one thing to be up on the trends in psychological theory; to embrace uncritically every fad that comes down the psychology pike is something else.

Others have copped out because they have been intimidated by the so-called professionals, with their certification requirements and esoteric jargon.[27] They feel they are no longer qualified to do what pastors have been doing well for centuries. They assume they don't know enough to help people cope with stress, or death and dying, or marriage relationships, or any kind of crisis. Some have acquired an inferiority complex as the result of put-downs by professionals, such as the remark I heard during a discussion involving a group of pastors and pastoral counselors. One of the pastors happened to mention something that had occurred in the course of a marriage counseling session with a couple he had been seeing. Ignoring the point of his remark, one of the "professionals" present looked at the pastor accusingly and asked, "What qualifies you to do marriage counseling?"

That kind of remark and the attitude it displays are neither helpful nor fair. They deserve the kind of retort made by one annoyed pastor, who, refusing to be intimidated by that put-down, commented, "The only difference between you professionals and us amateurs is that you charge people fees."

Pastors need to remember that the most important way they can help people is to be a caring listener and a faithful representative of and witness to the God who can change people's lives. Of course it is important to know when and where and how to refer people whom we are, in fact, not qualified to help. When people are sick they need a doctor. But most people with problems need to talk to a wise, sensitive man or woman of God, who can help get them back on track spiritually. They need to be in touch with a Savior whose grace is always sufficient and whose transforming power is available to those who love, trust, and obey him.

I am not appealing for pastors to keep doing things the same old way. I am calling for pastors to reclaim their rightful place as counselors, and I am cautioning all of us not to lose our theological perspective, which is the one thing we counseling pastors have to offer people that is unique. Why else should anyone seek counseling from a pastor, when there are professionals and specialists available, far better trained (albeit more expensive) to psychoanalyze them? Let me reiterate, however, that when people need expertise we cannot provide, they should be referred.

8

The Pastor-Evangelist as Counselor

Of all the persons who come to pastors for counseling, the number of those needing to be referred is usually comparatively small. For most people, we ourselves can fulfill the role of counselor. The question I now want to address specifically is, How does one do the work of an evangelist when counseling? In other words, How does one do counseling with evangelistic sensitivity?

There is no need to repeat what has already been said about faith sharing and interpersonal witnessing (see chapter 3). Counseling affords many opportunities for faith sharing. As these occur, the pastor-evangelist needs to keep in mind the unique relationship between the counselor and the counselee, lest in the interest of evangelism the professional relationship be violated. There are always the twin dangers of the counselee's overdependence on or emotional attachment to the counselor, who must know how to help the counselee transfer those feelings in a healthy way to God. To manipulate a counselee into making a faith decision by taking advantage of a counselee's dependency would be ineffective in the long run, as well as totally unethical.

Some Guidelines for Counseling

Here are some guidelines to keep in mind when doing the work of an evangelist as a counselor.

Be a Listener

The first rule of interpersonal witnessing applies as much to counselors as to anyone else: The witness must first be a listener.[28] I've heard professional therapists say things like, "I listen, and listen, and listen, and I don't know what happens, but somehow people are healed." Pastor-evangelists need not be intimidated, therefore; just our being there, listening, caring, and sharing are extremely helpful to the counselee. One professional counselor said to a group of pastors, "Don't worry about it. People will probably get better no matter what else you do, if you just listen!"

Maybe. But I'm sure it helps to listen wisely. I must not be hood-winked. I can take things at face value if I remember that there may be and there usually is more involved than meets the ear. That's why I have said, We listen with our eyes and we speak with our ears. What we see helps us to interpret what we hear, and what we hear deter-mines how we respond. As a pastor-evangelist I don't want to react too quickly, or too approvingly or disapprovingly, to what the coun-selee says. I don't want to reach premature conclusions or make snap judgments. It's better to follow Jesus' advice and be as wise as a serpent and innocent as a dove (Matt. 10:16). That's good advice for a listener.

Be a Friend!

Be a friend to the counselee, and listen as a friend. That means to listen caringly rather than judgmentally, sympathetically rather than censoriously. Some people listen in a way that makes the other person feel he or she is being evaluated. Their facial expressions communicate an unsympathetic reaction to what is being said. As a pastor-evangelist I want to establish a friend-to-friend relationship with the counselee and put him or her at ease. I try to communicate by my face and body language, as well as by my words, my accept-ance of the other person and my desire to be of help. Acceptance of the person does not mean condoning what the person has done or agreeing with what he or she says. It means neither condoning nor condemning. It means being friendly.

Be a Clarifier

The counselor wants to help the other person to identify his or her real need. What is it she or he wants? Why are you talking together? Is there a problem? What the counselee vocalizes may not be the real need or problem. Is there a hidden agenda? If so, is it conscious or subliminal? What does the counselee want to accomplish in regard to the identified need? Is the desire appropriate? Is the goal realistic? Is another session needed? As a pastor-evangelist I want to be sensi-tive to any come-in points in order to find out where the other person is spiritually. I also want to be sure the other person understands where I am coming from. I come not with my own agenda but with my own perspective, which I want the other person to know is that of a Christian minister who believes in a God who can change people's lives. It is crucial that I clarify my own role as a counseling pastor.

Be a Pastor

Even though I am not now serving as a parish minister, I still consider myself a pastor. I think and feel as a pastor. Because of the tendencies described in the first part of this chapter, however, I know that it is sometimes possible to forget that one is a counseling pastor, not a secular counselor. The *counseling* pastor needs to remember to be what he or she has been called to be—a pastor. The counselees are not "cases" but persons. As a pastor I cannot have a detached attitude about the people who come to me for help. They become part of my life, and I of theirs. My concern for them and my ministry to them is not confined to the counseling sessions in my study. I am not just their counselor; I am their pastor. That means they have a claim on me in the future, if they need my pastoral services, whether or not they are members of my church. I want them to know I am someone who cares about them and who will be available to them as long as I am in that role. I am first and foremost a pastor.

Be a Counselor

But I am also a counselor, who brings some special gifts and perhaps acquired skills to that task. I have never viewed myself as a problem solver. Indeed, I have very little confidence in my ability to solve people's problems. Rather I see myself as a caring listener, who in the process of active listening may help people to discover their own answers. As a counselor I try to help people sort things out, to define and focus the questions, and to suggest possible alternatives. Occasionally, I will do what the word suggests: give counsel. Advice giving is risky, but it is a legitimate part of pastoral care. It should not be done dogmatically or superciliously, but tentatively and gently, more by way of suggestion than by direction. The nature of the office of pastor permits us to be more prescriptive in our counseling than we might otherwise dare to be, but when we do give advice we should do so judiciously.

Be a Faith Sharer

Any advice given should be expressive of the pastor's own faith. Many sensitive pastors have long been doing what some contemporary psychologists have only recently been advocating: that is, revealing something of themselves to the counselee. The counselor's self-disclosure facilitates identification, builds trust and confidence, and frees the counselee to be more open and self-revealing. It makes sense. How much better for the counselee to talk to a real person rather than to a sphinx. As pastor-evangelists should we not be willing to share our own faith when it is appropriate and helpful? We do so, of course, as those who are themselves struggling to be faithful, wanting to grow, to learn, to be more Christlike. Counselor and counselee together are seeking to discern and do the will of God. As a counselor I want to be a faith sharer.

Be an Evangelist

Faith sharing is part of being an evangelist. We share our faith in the hope that our experience of God will confirm or strengthen or illumine the other person's experience of God, or awaken the other person's interest in God, or stimulate the other person's curiosity about God, or encourage the other person's decision for God, or attract the other person's loyalty to God. As an evangelist I want to help people discover how God can help them. But my interest in them is not limited to their immediate problems. I care about their ongoing relationship with the God whose help they need, and with a community of faith where they can find encouragement and support in their daily walk with God. My desire is always to help people to know and to come to grips with the reality of God. What place has God in their lives? What is their relationship to Jesus Christ and the church? If they call themselves Christians, have they taken seriously what it means to be Christ's woman or Christ's man in the world today? As an evangelist my desire is to help seekers to find their answers in Christ and to challenge nonseekers to become seekers. Without violating my role as counselor, I'll do my best to help each counselee to take the next logical step of faith. That includes leading the uncommitted to a point of decision and, whenever possible, bringing the unchurched into the body of Christ. Can I do all that? Not by my own wisdom or piety or power.

Be a Pray-er

By God's grace, I can, if I undergird my counseling ministry with prayer. I realized long ago that I must be above all else a pray-er. From the beginning of my ministry I have made it a practice to pray before, during, and after each counseling session. I'm not talking about having a prayer with the counselee, but about my own private prayers before the session, when I commit myself and the counselee, and our time together, into God's hands and seek the wisdom and guidance of the Holy Spirit. During the session I am continually sending up mini-prayers to God—silent, spontaneous, "instant" petitions—asking God to help me to be a better listener, a more caring pastor, a more convincing witness, a wiser counselor; to be with the other person in his or her struggle; and to help us both to be open and receptive to what God wants to teach us. After the session I pray that God will help the counselee to discern and do God's will, that God will forgive my inadequacies, redeem my mistakes, and in everything work for good. What an immense burden is lifted from our shoulders when we put our trust not in our own wisdom but in the grace of God, who hears and answers our prayers, when we are doing the work of an evangelist.

Some Guidelines for Referring

Why Refer?

We refer because our expertise is limited and we may not be sufficiently trained to deal with people who are having difficulty coping with certain kinds of stress or who are suffering from various kinds of mental illness or emotional disorder. We refer because there are professional counselors who are better equipped than we are to help people with certain types of problems or to deal with certain kinds of situations. Pastor-evangelists need never feel guilty about referring people to other professionals.

Whom to Refer

As a pastor, the persons I was inclined to refer included the following types:

1. Those whose problem or need would claim too much of my time in relation to my other pastoral responsibilities. This is always a judgment call. Every pastor has to determine her own or his own pastoral priorities. If it appears that a person will need intensive counseling over a prolonged period of time, you may want to refer, unless you feel you have the time to give to that individual. It is better to refer than to resent the person for demanding too much of your time.

2. Those whom I could no longer help (except in terms of maintenance). You know the type: You have done all you can do for them, but they want to keep coming simply because they like to talk to you. They're in a dependent relationship, and you have to help them make the transfer to an appropriate person—a spouse, a parent, or someone else.

3. Those who were totally unresponsive to or uncooperative with

me. It is impossible to help those who refuse to be helped or whose attitude is such that there is absolutely no communication between us. They are usually quite receptive to the suggestion that they be referred, if they have already reached that conclusion themselves. Ironically, however, I have found that the suggestion to refer may in itself break the communication log jam. I might say something like this: "We don't seem to be communicating very well. Perhaps you should be seeing a different kind of counselor. Would you like me to suggest someone?" To which the counselee might reply, "Not at all. I'm sorry; I guess I haven't been very cooperative. I'm perfectly satisfied to continue with you. Let's see how it goes from now on."

4. Those who had a medical problem, or who needed special professional help, or who required closer attention than I could provide, such as alcoholics, drug addicts, suicidal persons, criminal types, transients, neurotics, psychotics, and those with severe psychological problems. If someone came with a concern about a problem of weight gain or weight loss, for instance, or with an obsession for dieting, I would be quick to refer that person. Eating disorders can be symptomatic of such serious health problems as anorexia or bulimia. Some people use food as a means of escape, a way to avoid facing other problems in their lives.

When to Refer

The proper time to refer is as soon as you discover that any of the above conditions pertains. Often you will know this after the very first visit. Other cases may take two or more counseling sessions. If no progress is being made after you feel you have had an adequate opportunity to make that judgment, then refer. If you are making progress, you may want to continue in your counseling role until you and the counselee agree that his or her need has been met. The pastor-evangelist will want to continue to pray for those who are referred and to keep in touch with the professional persons to whom the counselees are referred.

How to Refer

It is to be expected that the pastor-evangelist will know how to refer people tactfully and sensitively, but honestly. For example, one might say, "I feel you may have some things you need to work on with a professional analyst, Shirley. Would you be willing to talk with someone I have in mind? I'll be glad to call her for you." I feel it is very important either to call or to go with the person to pave the way. I can't just push people out the door and forget about them. The pastor-evangelist can help the counselee make the transfer of trust. I have on occasion prevailed upon my colleagues in pastoral theology at Princeton Seminary for help with difficult cases, and I have been on the receiving end of referrals from colleagues as well. Over the years I have found that people do not resent or object to being referred when the reason for referral is properly explained. They can understand and appreciate a pastor's confessed limitations of time, training, or expertise.

I keep in touch with the professional person to whom I have referred someone to see if and when my further help is needed. The anorectic young woman may need my pastoral support, once her medical problem is under control. The spiritual dimension of her life should not be neglected simply because she needs medical or psychiatric help. That is why it is so important for pastor-evangelists to give serious consideration to the kind of professional persons to whom they will refer their counselees.

To Whom to Refer

Wherever I have been throughout my ministry I have made it a point to identify a number of professional persons to whom I can refer people when necessary. Having served in communities where plenty of professional help was available, I would customarily establish a close working relationship with at least one good psychiatrist, as well as a clinical psychologist or psychotherapist, to whom I could refer people who needed such help. I found these professionals were always happy to have that kind of association, which was as useful to them as to me, as well as helpful to our mutual counselees. My backup list would also include the names of Alcoholics Anonymous controls, certified pastoral counselors, social workers, marriage counselors, guidance counselors, attorneys, and other individuals and groups ministering to persons with particular kinds of problems (such as, Compassionate Friends, Parents Anonymous, Parents Without Partners). These persons came well recommended. I always made it a point to know them personally and to establish a relationship of mutual trust and good rapport. In addition, I kept on my desk a list of social, welfare, and public assistance agencies to whom I could refer transients. Most metropolitan areas have published directories of such agencies.[29]

As I have already emphasized, pastor-evangelists are concerned for the whole person. They are not restricted to matters of faith alone. That is why it is essential for them to have access to a range of professional expertise in their counseling ministry. On the other hand, pastor-evangelists do not want to lose touch with the individuals they counsel, whom they view not as clients but as persons for whom they may serve as God's witnesses and helpers.

9

The Counselor's
Evangelistic Opportunities

Pastors are called on to do many different kinds of counseling. Each type presents its own special challenge to the pastor-evangelist, who needs to be able to recognize and distinguish the different agendas each situation calls for. Here are a few thoughts about the evangelistic opportunities presented by some of the more frequently encountered counseling situations.[30]

Premarital Counseling

Premarital counseling affords some of the best opportunities for pastors to do the work of an evangelist.[31] Most conscientious pastors nowadays will not marry a couple without meeting with them an agreed-upon number of times, not just to plan a wedding but to discuss the implications of marriage and the relationship into which they are about to enter. At the same time, the pastor-evangelist knows that the purpose of premarital counseling is not to guarantee a successful marriage but to give integrity to the marriage service.

Ordinarily the couples who come to us to talk about a wedding are not seeking our advice about getting married. They have already made that decision! Their anticipated agenda and the pastor's agenda are quite different, and this clash of expectations needs to be dealt with at the very outset.

It is usually not at all difficult to do so. Most couples will welcome our desire to meet with them if the suggested counseling is seen as an opportunity rather than as a legal requirement and the whole matter is discussed in a positive context. They can easily see the value of premarital counseling, especially if there are matters they have not yet dealt with, and they can understand and appreciate our insistence that a Christian wedding be given its full integrity. Premarital counseling provides a structured opportunity for a couple to clarify their values, order their priorities, set goals, express their convictions, recognize their differences, and come to grips with their relationship to Christ and to the church.

My initial response to the couples who come to me is warm and friendly, mirroring their own excitement and joy. "So you want to be married—wonderful! Have you announced your engagement, or is it still a secret? . . . When did you decide? . . . How did you two meet?" These kinds of questions are simply to put them at ease, free them to talk, and show my genuine interest. Early on in the very first meeting, after the usual niceties, there are three questions I usually ask as a way of leading into a statement of my own expectations regarding the counseling relationship: (1) "Why do you want to be *married?*" (There are other options!); (2) "Why do you want to be married in a *church?*" (There are other options!); (3) "Why do you want *me* to marry you?" (There are other options!).

Their responses to each of these questions reveal much about where they are spiritually. If they have indicated they want to be married by a minister in a church, and specifically by me, I am free to state the conditions under which I am willing to marry them. It is not an automatic decision on my part. My agreement to marry them is contingent on their wanting to talk about the nature and meaning of Christian marriage and to discuss in depth their relationship with each other and with God. I put this to them gently but firmly, as a matter of my personal integrity as a pastor. I want them to think seriously about every aspect of the wedding service, so that when they take their vows they will do so with full awareness and conviction.

For some, this expectation comes as a surprise if not a shock. They may have had nothing spiritual in mind whatsoever when they walked into my study. ("We've driven past your church many times and have always thought, If we ever decide to get married, that would be the place. We want a church that looks like a church.") Perhaps they were simply following the conventional procedures suggested by a parent or a friend. ("My mother thinks it doesn't count if it doesn't happen in a church.") One or both of them may not be a member of a church or even a believer. Maybe they could not care less about the spiritual integrity of their wedding. That being the case, they have an immediate decision to make. Do they still want me to marry them, or should they go somewhere else?

Note that the decision is theirs, not mine. It is not a matter of my deciding whether or not to marry them, but of their deciding whether or not they want me to marry them on the terms I have stated. That puts the matter in an entirely different light, and it relieves me of the unpleasant task of having to tell the couple that I won't marry them. The ball is in their court.

Realizing that their answer will reveal the seriousness of their intentions regarding their marriage, most couples readily agree to premarital counseling, which can be arranged on a mutually convenient basis for an agreed-upon number of sessions. Over the period of time that the counseling takes place, we will be discussing in an intimate, faith-sharing context the various aspects of marriage, including the spiritual dimension. For most unchurched couples, premarital counseling sessions are a doorway to a new relationship with Christ through which the pastor-evangelist can lead them. When they have talked in depth about the vows they will be taking, they realize how much more meaningful the wedding will be for them if they speak their vows to each other and to God as believers who have joined or decided to join a church. The church they join does not have to be the counselor's church. Perhaps they will not be locating in the counselor's area, in which case it would be better for them to unite with a congregation in the community where they will be living.

If they are going to be living nearby, it is a good idea for the pastor-evangelist to arrange to meet with the couple a few months after the wedding to see how things are going. This postwedding session can be offered as a wedding present from the pastor in words to this effect: "I'd like to give you a gift of another counseling session six months from now, to see how you folks are getting along. Would you be interested in getting together to talk about your marriage?"

What if during the course of the counseling the pastor-evangelist has serious qualms about marrying the couple? These should be voiced, and if they cannot be dealt with to everyone's satisfaction, a referral is definitely in order. Again, this is a judgment call, and we pastors are not infallible. We do the best we can to prepare the couple for their life together, but our wisdom is limited, and so is our influence. That is why prayer is so important when we're doing the work of an evangelist.

Marriage Counseling

Professional counselors make a sharp distinction between premarital counseling, which they acknowledge to be a proper activity for pastors, and marriage counseling, which some feel is beyond the competency of most pastors and should be left to certified pastoral counselors and other professional marriage counselors. Marriage counseling does require greater counseling skills and it certainly demands far more time.[32]

As pastor-evangelists it is important for us to examine our theological assumptions concerning marriage. What theology informs our understanding of our role as marriage counselors? Do we believe it is our Christian duty to save a marriage at all cost? What is our view of divorce? Pastors' answers to these questions will differ according to their respective theologies. The woman whose frightened daughter I found alone one night lived in terror and torment for twenty years, married to a brutal wife beater and child abuser, because according to her Roman Catholic background divorce was a sin. In my view divorce was a lesser evil by far than her continued enslavement to such a man, whom she had married as a teenager.

Because of my high view of marriage, I do my best to be a reconciler and mediator. I believe a marriage should be saved *if possible*, but not at all cost, and I recognize my limitations in that regard. If both partners want their marriage to be saved, there's every hope it can and will be. If only one does, the possibility of saving the marriage is much less. As a pastor-evangelist I see my role as helping both partners to face the issues as Christians. This is easier said than done, when there is bitterness and rancor between the two. They may be so angry that they are unable or unwilling to approach their problems from a faith perspective. That's the challenge for the pastor-evangelist as marriage counselor. There is little any counselor can do to rekindle the flame of affection once the fire has gone out, especially if there is a third party involved. Our ministry may be primarily to the rejected partner, who needs to experience the redeeming and transforming power of Christ's love.

Doing the work of an evangelist in marriage counseling means being sensitive to the come-in points for faith sharing and encouraging both parties to be open to God's will rather than to impose their own on each other. They may *think* it is God's will that they separate, but they can be *sure* it is God's will that they try to be reasonable, fair, and honest with each other in the process. They may lack the spiritual discernment or the moral strength to do what God wants regarding their marriage, but that is something to be confessed as a failing, not offered as an excuse. They can't pump love from a dry well, but they can pray to the God whose love never fails. They may have a hard time forgiving each other, but they can think about the Christ who died that they might be forgiven.

These are the kinds of things the pastor-evangelist can bring into focus as a marriage counselor. There are many opportunities for faith sharing, which can transform the character and tone of the conversation. When the whole process is undergirded with prayer, miracles can happen.

Divorce Counseling

Divorce counseling has become a specialized field of expertise. When a couple is anticipating divorce, they can benefit greatly from counseling, which can encourage an amicable separation and a fair and equitable agreement regarding properties, possessions, custody of children, visiting rights, and so on. A divorce is like a death, especially for the spouse who may not have wanted or expected it. The adjustment can be extremely difficult and the emotional impact devastating.

The pastor-evangelist can be a source of comfort and support during the transition period for the spouse who is having to cope with loneliness, insecurity, anger, bitterness, guilt, fear, and perhaps the new demands of being a single parent. It is a time when the church can and should help fill the gap. Ministry to singles is an increasingly important service that churches need to provide for an ever-growing number of persons in our society, many of whom are divorced.[33] Church members can become a surrogate family for lonely people who have hitherto been ignored or neglected by too many congregations. They may feel locked out by family-oriented programs and worship services. Even the language we use has tended to be exclusive of single persons.

As churches become more aware of and sensitive to the needs of these people, pastors who counsel divorced persons (and other singles) have greater responsibility as well as opportunity to do the work of an evangelist. Hurting people are usually more receptive to the gospel. The pastor-evangelist will have little difficulty turning a conversation into a faith-sharing experience when counseling persons undergoing the stress of separation or divorce. Come-in points are easily discerned as people pour out their troubles. "What effect has all this had on your faith in God?" Such a question instantly moves the discussion to a deeper level, as the counselee's experience is viewed from a faith perspective. That's when real therapy begins. The counselee may begin to ask, "What is God saying to me in all this?" "Can God work for good even in this situation?" "How can God help me?" In time, the counselee may even be led to ask, "How can I help God?"

Prebaptism Counseling

Adults who decide to make a public profession of faith and to be baptized into the church have already been evangelized. I am not referring here to the evangelism that took place (if there was any) in order to bring them to the point of decision. Rather, I am referring to any counseling that takes place specifically to prepare for baptism those who have decided to join the church. Such counseling is, for the most part, instructional in its nature and intent, but that purpose does not preclude the possibility of faith sharing. The pastor-evangelist can discuss with the counselee the meaning of baptism and the implications of the baptismal vows, the duties of church membership, the spiritual disciplines, and other aspects of the Christian faith and life. What faith decisions does the counselee face and what is the next logical step of faith she or he needs to take? It is all part of the ongoing evangelization and discipling process.

Churches that practice infant baptism have a responsibility to help the parents or spiritual guardians to accept and fulfill their responsibility to bring up their children as Christians. In our Presbyterian tradition we will baptize a child if there is one believing parent. I have always made it a practice to spend two or three hours with the parent or parents before the baptism. These were usually group counseling sessions, since the sacrament of baptism was scheduled for certain Sundays and more often than not there were several couples and single parents involved. Godparents are not part of our tradition, but if parents have already asked someone to fill that role, I invite that person to the prebaptism session and include him or her in the baptism service.

These prebaptism counseling sessions have been a most meaningful part of my ministry. They provide some of the very best opportunities for doing the work of an evangelist, since many parents who inquire about having their children baptized are themselves unchurched or are only nominal Christians. In the meeting or series of meetings the pastor has with the parents, there is time to delve deeply into the meaning of the covenant, to present the doctrine of the church in a positive and compelling manner, and to explore with those present their own faith. Since it is the parents who will be declaring their faith in Christ during the sacrament and making solemn promises concerning their children, it is crucial that they understand what they will be doing and saying, so they can take their vows with integrity.[34]

After the welcome and introductions, a good opener for the discussion is to ask the parents why they want to have their children baptized. This leads naturally into a discussion of the meaning of the sacrament and of their role in the spiritual development of their children. Then I might say, "Since you are the ones who will be taking the vows during the sacrament, perhaps we should talk about the questions you'll be asked." That usually triggers a wonderful faith-sharing conversation, as the parents share their own beliefs and doubts. If there are some present who are unchurched or even unbelievers, it is a marvelous opportunity for the pastor-evangelist to introduce them to the person and work of Jesus Christ through the symbolism and theology of the sacrament.

For the parents, the prebaptism session is almost always interesting, usually inspiring, often fascinating, and sometimes even a life-changing experience, as they probe their faith more deeply and explore their priorities and values more thoroughly than they probably have ever done before. Many parents have joined or renewed their relationship with the church as a result of being in a prebaptism class. I think of one young father who was so challenged by the experience that he started to think about entering the ministry. A few months later he enrolled in seminary, and now he is pastor of a church. It is people like that who make doing the work of an evangelist so satisfying.

Family Counseling

As in other types of counseling, there are unique considerations relating to family counseling that require a high degree of sensitivity and professional skill. The interpersonal dynamics are complex and not always readily apparent or easily understood by an untrained person. Professional counselors have discovered, for example, that the impact on the family "system" by the removal or addition of one or more persons is immense. The needs of each individual are never exactly the same and are often divergent or contradictory. Each one has her or his own agenda.

The dynamics of faith sharing in family counseling are also unique. The number of persons involved is one of the key factors shaping the context for evangelism.[35] Readiness for, resistance to, or touchiness about any suggestion or effort on the part of the pastor-evangelist to bring God into the conversation may vary widely among family members or other persons involved. Depending on the level of anger and hostility among the family members toward one another, there may be no acceptance of any faith statements. References to God by one person may be greeted with sneers or sullen silence by the others. Come-in questions by the counselor may evoke a diatribe against the Almighty—which, by the way, *is* a form of faith sharing, albeit a negative one.

Nevertheless, the gospel is just as relevant for families as it is for individuals. The Holy Spirit can work with families as well as with individuals, especially if they are open and receptive to the gospel. As pastor-evangelists, how can we deny the families we counsel the opportunity to relate the good news of Jesus Christ to their situation? They deserve to be given the opportunity to respond in faith to the redemptive love of God and to experience the transforming and renewing power of the Holy Spirit.

The hope of the pastor-evangelist is that the members of the family can put their professions of faith in God into action in their relationships with one another, that their obedience to the Lord they say they believe in will be translated in terms of their mutual obligations. The pastor-evangelist can help families see that loyalty to Jesus Christ is expressed in our unity with one another. If the members of a family really want to learn to love one another, they can start by *acting as if they do.* Love is a verb; it is expressed in loving deeds. To paraphrase the words of Jesus, Whatever you do or don't do to the members of your own family, you do or don't do to Christ! (Matt. 25:31–46).

Crisis Counseling

Our primary concern for people in times of crisis is to be of help in whatever ways we can.[36] The sensitive pastor-evangelist would never want to force the faith issue when a person is too upset or desperate or consumed by pain or sorrow to respond. Evangelistic sensitivity is knowing the appropriate time and way to bear witness.

However, those who seek counseling in times of personal crisis may be especially receptive to the gospel. If they are functioning rationally—that is, if they are not too emotionally upset to listen to reason—they may respond readily to a come-in question ("How is your faith holding up, Dave?"). Sometimes I have begun with a high-structured question: "I've been wondering, as I listen to you, Dave—do you believe in God?" If the answer is yes, then I might follow with another high-structured question: "Do you think the God you believe in can help you with (whatever the need or problem is)?" Or I might ask a low-structured question: "How might God help you?" or, "How has your faith in God helped you?"

Often, the pastor-evangelist will think of biblical illustrations with which the counselee can identify. The prodigal son, the lost sheep, the man who fell among thieves, the grief of Mary and Martha when their brother died, Moses' crime, David's adultery, Saul's mental illness, Judas' betrayal, Peter's denial, and all the other object lessons that serve as reminders of the frailties of humanity are grappling hooks for our self-understanding and take-off points for the pastor-evangelist to witness to the God whose steadfast love endures forever (Psalm 136).

If we really believe in God, we can trust the God we believe in to honor our sincere attempts to be faithful witnesses to people in their times of greatest need. We don't stop doing the work of an evangelist when people are most desperate for good news. That good news may have to be understood in an ultimate sense, however. It may be that we have to help people live through the crucifixion before they can experience the resurrection. The good news does not eliminate the reality of the cross.

Counseling the Dying or Bereaved

Much of our pastoral care and counseling is with people who are terminally or seriously ill. Our theology of healing will determine how we view our role as counselor with such persons.[37] Some people make a work out of faith by thinking that God will heal them physically if they believe hard enough. I believe God can heal people even when medical science has pronounced them terminally ill. I do not believe in what is usually meant by faith healing, which in my view is an attempt to impose our will on God. It is not *our* faith that heals, but our faith in God's ability to heal those whom God wills to heal. The miracle is not that God grants the healing we request but that God works for good in *everything* with those who love God and are in tune with God's will. Healing, furthermore, involves more than a physical cure. When God makes a person whole spiritually, that person is healed in the fullest sense. Wholeness has to do with more than just one's physical condition. God may not cure the sickness, but God can always make the sin-sick whole.

The role of the pastor-evangelist as counselor is to help people to discover God's miracles in the midst of their pain, to recognize the healings God has already brought about in their lives, and to open them to the healings yet to be experienced. The pastor-evangelist wants the counselee to know that although God may not relieve the pain, God will provide the strength to bear it. For those whose suffering has blinded them to God's love, the pastor-evangelist hopes that in their suffering they may find their way back to God through the Christ who suffered and died for us all.

These same considerations apply to our counseling with the bereaved, whose sorrow over their loss may deepen or destroy their faith in the goodness of God. Some become bitter and blame God for their misery; others are stirred to a new awareness of their dependence on God for the strength to bear the terrible burden of their grief. In either case, the pastor-evangelist will find that people are more open to faith sharing in the wake of bereavement than at almost any other time. The bitter ones need to vent their anger; the others welcome the chance to share their experience of God's mercy and love.[38]

Career and Financial Counseling

People often seek counseling regarding career matters or financial problems. They may be facing a major decision about a job offer or a career change. Perhaps they have been laid off, forced to take early retirement, or fired and are facing unemployment for the first time in their lives.[39] Maybe they have recognized the narrowing possibilities for their future, or have realized their own limitations, and are depressed or discouraged about where they are, what they are, and who they are. Because in our Western society we tend to define who a person is in terms of what a person does, one's identity is inseparably related to one's employment.

No wonder pastors find themselves counseling so many people about work-related problems. To lose one's job after many years can be an emotionally shattering experience. After listening to many persons who have undergone it, I would say that being fired must be like an earthquake, when one's base of security, one's ground of reality, is rudely shaken by forces beyond one's control. Often there is the terrible feeling of helplessness, followed by fear, followed by depression.

This is the time when the pastor-evangelist can plug into the person's faith, helping him or her to look at all the options through the eyes of faith and to ask, What is God trying to teach me? What does God want me to do? Now is the time to seek God's will and to trust that God can indeed work for good in such a situation *with those who love God and are called according to God's purpose* (Rom. 8:28). The pastor-evangelist can pray with and for the counselee and teach him or her to pray boldly but humbly, honestly but submissively, earnestly but receptively.

There are, of course, practical ways to help such people, including referring them to a support group for unemployed persons, sorting out options, suggesting possibilities, opening doors, serving as a reference, making recommendations, perhaps even providing temporary work. The counselee may be financially hard pressed, in which case the pastor may be able to help. There may be some discretionary funds at his or her disposal, or perhaps the church has a fund set aside for helping in such situations. So as not to offend a person's pride, the offer must be made discreetly and tactfully, perhaps as an interest-free or low-interest loan, to be paid back when the person is able. Affirmation and support are extremely important to those who have suffered the humiliation of being fired, or whose self-confidence has been torpedoed by too many unsuccessful job interviews, or whose self-esteem has been demolished by an impatient and unsympathetic spouse. The pastor-evangelist can help to restore a sense of self-worth by reminding the person of a Savior who values people by other than worldly standards and in whose eyes every life is precious.

Career counseling does not always involve problems of this sort. The situation may be a positive one, in which the counselee is facing a choice between two or more acceptable offers and wants the pastor's help in weighing the alternatives. On more than a few occasions people have come to me asking for help in discerning God's will for their lives as they face a major career choice. One man said to me,

"You talked in your sermon about our being Christians on the job, and about our Christian vocation. How do I know whether God wants me to stay where I am or look for a different kind of job?" (Some people really do listen to our sermons!) Such a request presents a tremendous opportunity for the pastor-evangelist, who has experienced the reality of a God who guides and who provides, to bear witness to that reality.

Sometimes people seek our financial advice, not as investment counselors or professional estate planners but as persons who can help them be better stewards of their possessions.[40] They have taken seriously what they have heard us say from the pulpit about Christian stewardship. These are enjoyable occasions for me; I love to help people sort out their financial priorities and wrestle with what it means to be a steward of all that God provides. Doing the work of an evangelist includes challenging people to take seriously the truth that "the earth is the LORD's and the fulness thereof" (Ps. 24:1); we are the caretakers of God's creation and of all life. Our financial stewardship is part of the way we express that truth.

Counseling Homosexuals

A distinction needs to be made between counseling homosexual persons about the kinds of problems and needs everybody else has and counseling persons about their homosexuality. Counseling the former is no different from counseling anyone else. Counseling the latter merits some special consideration by the pastor-evangelist.

Most pastors, whether or not they realized it at the time, have counseled homosexuals. In the average-size church there are bound to be persons of homosexual orientation. Until recently many of these persons had never publicly revealed their sexual identity. Times have changed radically in that respect.

There are, nevertheless, persons who are still wrestling with their sexual identity. They may be heterosexuals harboring the fear that they are homosexual, or homosexuals nursing the hope that they might become heterosexual. I have counseled both. Some homosexuals may be burdened by a guilt complex imposed upon them by unaccepting parents. Some may be confused by the conflict in values represented between the teachings of the Bible and the sexual practices of the gay community, between the traditional teachings of their church and the liberated demands of the gay rights advocates, between the scruples of tradition and the permissiveness of the sexual revolution. Some may be bitterly resentful of their ambiguous sexuality or deeply committed to a person of their own sex and wanting a pastor's blessing on that relationship.

Added to these deeply personal and often agonizing concerns is the terrifying reality of AIDS, which is spreading throughout the world and, in our country, has reached epidemic proportions. Every homosexual is haunted by the grim specter of that dreaded disease, as the number of its victims multiplies daily. Safe sex is now the golden rule for gays, and monogamous relationships are becoming the norm, as the pleas of AIDS victims like my young friend Skip (in chapter 4) are heeded.[41]

I cannot treat the complex subject of homosexuality in any depth here. My desire, once again, is to focus briefly on the pastor-evangelist's role as counselor to people with the kinds of concerns I have mentioned. What is called for in every case is compassion and understanding. We can listen without being judgmental and without compromising our own theological integrity. We can represent a God who loves us and accepts us the way we are, a Savior who can help us achieve our true humanity, and a church that understands itself to be a community of forgiven sinners. The saints are a fellowship of the redeemed, not a society of the sinless.

My pastoral response to the homosexuals I have counseled has been determined by their own attitudes, which can range from the arrogant flaunting of their right to be different to their total despair of their right to be accepted, from defiant self-righteousness to pathological guilt. As a counselor I want to respond to each person in a way that is consistent with my theological presuppositions, including my understanding of and commitment to the authority of the scriptures.

I can understand the sincere love that two persons of the same sex can have for each other, but I must admit that I am personally repulsed by the sexual activity which that relationship often entails. In no way can I view sodomy, for example, as anything but an unnatural and repugnant act. That, by the way, is a physiological, not a homophobic, reaction. I deplore the cruel, belligerent, and excessively judgmental attitudes that characterize the hysterical homophobia in some churches. One ought to be able to detest the sin without hating the sinner.

When a young man (let's call him Ron), who in a previous counseling session had described himself to me as a passive homosexual, indicated his interest in going to seminary and asked my feelings on the subject, I told him that I share my denomination's stand against the ordination of self-avowed, *practicing* homosexuals, just as I would oppose the ordination of any heterosexual who demands the right to be ordained on his or her own terms. Ordination is not a right to be demanded by an individual but a call of God to be confirmed by the church. I could not support the ordination of anyone who insists on maintaining a life-style contrary to the teachings of the church. That includes heterosexual persons who insist on the right to carry on adulterous relationships with anyone they wish. They may believe in exoneration by mutual consent, but adultery is still adultery and fornication is still fornication, and both are condemned by the Bible and by the traditional teachings of the church. I would certainly support the ordination of any homosexual who has taken a vow of celibacy, assuming the other requirements for ordination have been met.

Ron, who was not a member of a church at the time, said he appreciated my frank response and that he would think and pray about his decision. We had a few more counseling sessions before he returned to his army post in another state. A few months later I received a letter from Ron informing me that he had abandoned his homosexual activity entirely and that he would be entering a Baptist seminary as soon as he completed his tour of duty with the army. He completed seminary and is now an ordained minister. He is also married and the father of two children (at last count).

Henry's case was quite different. He had been accused of sexually fondling a young boy at the school where he taught. He was terribly depressed and remorseful, and despite the deep trust relationship that I thought had been established between the two of us, apparently there was more to the story than he was willing to admit. After several sessions I suggested to Henry that he talk with a professional counselor and went with him to meet the other person, whom I knew personally. His main task was to assess whether Henry was a habitual child molester, and hence a menace, or whether what had occurred was an isolated and relatively harmless and misunderstood incident, as Henry insisted it was. My friend's professional assessment of Henry proved helpful in the school's decision to dismiss Henry and to provide for extended psychotherapy.

My role was to continue to provide spiritual support for Henry throughout his long ordeal. In no way did I condone what he had done (apparently to more than one boy, as it turned out), but I tried to help him to confess his mistakes, which he eventually did, to seek God's forgiveness and help in dealing healthily and constructively with his shame. Many months later he wrote to tell me that he was at peace with himself and with God.

In chapter 4 I spoke about my visits with Skip, a young man who was dying of AIDS. Some of those visits were counseling sessions, as he shared his feelings about his life as a homosexual. My task with Skip was to help him to face his inevitable death with confidence and hope, to trust in God's forgiveness, and to believe in Jesus' promise of eternal life. Skip was a seeker after truth, and eventually he was able to affirm the truth he saw embodied in the words and works of Jesus. Maybe one of the reasons he came to believe that he was accepted by God was his experience of being accepted by someone he viewed as God's representative. My acceptance of him meant God's acceptance. That's a reality we pastor-evangelists should recognize, and a role we need to take very seriously. Skip knew that I cared and that I accepted him for what he was, although I couldn't affirm his former life-style.

Counseling the Seekers

Seekers constitute a broad category, in which I include those persons who are sincerely seeking help in discerning God's will for their lives regarding any matter of conscience, faith, the Christian life, or the spiritual disciplines. Those who come earnestly wanting to grow in their faith and understanding are the most open, receptive, and teachable counselees. They are willing to hear the gospel demands as well as the gospel promises.[42] They know you haven't become their enemy by telling them the truth (Gal. 4:16). Because they come to be fed spiritually and theologically, the counselor's role is to provide spiritual direction. Doing the work of an evangelist with such people is helping them to apply the gospel to their situation and to take the next logical step of faith.

A word of caution is in order here. Some people who come ostensibly seeking help with a religious question have a hidden agenda. Before answering their intellectual question about a certain doctrinal point, the pastor-evangelist needs to find out if there is anything else on the person's mind or heart. Even if I suspect there is, I don't want to ignore the spoken question; I simply don't want to be sidetracked by it. I might say something like, "That's an interesting question. What is it that is troubling you about that?" Or, "I like that question, Carol. What is it that interests you about (whatever it is)?" Almost invariably, Carol, who has something else on her mind, will elaborate on her own question. She doesn't really want an answer from me; she wants to get something off her chest.

Whether or not there is a hidden agenda, the pastor-evangelist's task is to help people to share their faith, to talk about the God in whom they believe. Using the Socratic method of sensitive questioning, the pastor-evangelist helps them to articulate experiences of God that confirm their faith and to apply their awareness of God to their present question. "What makes you feel God cares about how we live our daily lives, Bob?" Bob's response will determine the direction of the next question. For example, "God really has been at work in your life, Bob. How do you think God wants you to answer your own question about stewardship?"

These kinds of faith-sharing conversations come easily when the counselee is a seeker. The seeker may be a young man wrestling with his conscience about serving in the armed forces and wanting to know what he should do as a Christian; or a high school student struggling to be loyal to Christ against all kinds of peer pressure; or a new member wondering what to give to the church; or a Sunday school teacher wanting the answer to a theological question; or a church officer saying, "Teach me to pray." A seeker could be a person wanting to be a more active member, a more faithful steward, or a more effective witness.

Those who come to us with these kinds of desires are the frosting on our counseling cake. They make doing the work of an evangelist enjoyable, and they compensate for the times we feel discouraged by people's apathy and frustrated by our own inability to make a difference.

We have been looking at the counselor's role through evangelistic glasses. As in our treatment of the pastor-evangelist's other professional roles, the focus of this chapter has been deliberately narrow. My purpose here and throughout this book is to see what it means for a pastor to do the work of an evangelist. Whether as a counselor or as a visitor, the pastor-evangelist sees every pastoral encounter as a faith-sharing opportunity. Evangelism is not a separate function that pastors perform from time to time. It's not a professional hat worn only when pastors are looking for new members. Doing the work of an evangelist means doing *whatever* we do with evangelistic sensitivity.

PART THREE

**The Pastor-Evangelist
as Teacher**

10

The Evangelistic Challenge

All pastors are teachers. Some may function primarily as preachers, or counselors, or youth ministers, or administrators—but whatever their role, teaching will always be a preeminent part of their ministry. Preachers teach in the pulpit. Pastoral counselors teach when they conduct a marriage enrichment seminar. Youth ministers teach when they lead a Bible study. Ministers of administration teach when they are advising a committee or leading a church officers training class. The teaching may be formal or informal, structured or unstructured, planned or spur-of-the-moment, but most pastors have opportunities galore to teach.

A survey of 400 pastors representing four different denominations indicated that their two most important congregational ministries by far are worship leadership and Christian education, in that order.[1] In the ministry of education,[2] teaching ranks first in importance among their various leadership roles. Yet 64.7 percent of 252 respondents reported that they devote less than 30 percent of their time to Christian education.

Even though most of the pastors had taken at least one course in Christian education at seminary, fewer than half—45.2 percent—indicated that they felt adequately prepared for their educational responsibilities in the parish. They were asked to list the courses they found most helpful and what more they thought could be done. The respondents, 66.3 percent of whom were solo pastors, were also queried about their strengths and weaknesses in Christian education.

Nowhere in the report was there any reference whatsoever, by even one pastor, to any need for training in evangelism. There was nothing mentioned in the list of courses taken, nothing in the list of courses needed, nothing in the list of strengths, nothing in the list of weaknesses. The survey is dramatic proof of my contention that few pastors have given any thought to the topic addressed by this section of the book—the pastor-evangelist as teacher. If the survey is any indication, doing the work of an evangelist as a teacher is the furthest thing from most pastors' minds. For them evangelism is not even on the stove, let alone on the front burner.

What a sad state of affairs! If pastors are not doing the work of an evangelist as teachers, who is? If pastors are not interested in learning, whom can they train? No wonder the mainline churches are not holding on to their young people! It is a pertinent question that we are addressing here: What does being a pastor-evangelist imply about one's role as teacher?

Accepting One's Responsibility

One implication is that there must be an evangelistic intentionality about our teaching. It is quite possible to teach religion without being evangelistic. That is why some ministers have abandoned the pulpit for the classroom. I know a former Episcopal priest who left the parish to teach in the school of religion of a major university, because, he said, "I could no longer preach with integrity." He had become uncomfortable with religious language and could no longer talk about a personal God. Prayer had lost its meaning, and the notion of a personal relationship with a living Savior had become for him an unintelligible concept. He had too much integrity to go on preaching what he himself could not believe. So he became a teacher of religion.

Others have done the same. As teachers they can talk *about* religion without having to declare themselves. They can discuss theology without having to commit themselves to the God who is the subject of all theology. They can speculate about the nature of faith without having to share their own faith. They can teach religious subjects without worrying about their students' religious convictions.

But some pastors apparently feel they don't have to leave the parish to teach like that. They teach that way in or out of the pulpit. They can teach the Bible without ever calling for a response to its message. They can conduct a communicants class without challenging the participants to make a decision for Jesus Christ. Those who engage in that kind of teaching are hardly doing the work of an evangelist! From the comments I often hear, it would not be too harsh to say that much of the teaching that goes on in many mainline Protestant congregations is not at all evangelistic, or even evangelical (gospel related).

As a teacher I know it is possible to theorize about faith without ever challenging people to be faithful. It is possible to study all about Jesus without ever inviting people to become his disciples. It is possible to discuss Christian doctrines theoretically without applying them existentially. It is possible to talk about God without encouraging people to talk *with* God. It is possible to conjecture about what it means to be a Christian without giving people a means of becoming Christians.

It is not just a matter of one's attitude or even of one's spirituality. The truth is that many pastors, as well as many seminary professors, have never had any training in communicating the gospel from any other podium than the pulpit. Nor have they ever been taught how to prepare a person to make a profession of faith and to take seriously what it means to accept Jesus Christ as his or her personal Lord and Savior. Consequently, some feel either uncomfortable with or unequal to the challenge of leading another person of any age to make a decision for Christ. Accompanying their feeling of inadequacy is a sense of uneasiness, if not guilt, for they know this is something they should be ready, willing, and able to do.

Not many, however, will admit their uneasiness. Instead, they defend what they are *not* doing by denigrating what others *are* doing. They exonerate themselves by ridiculing others' language, rejecting their theology, maligning their methods, or impugning their motives. They rely on disparagement by label to cover up their own shortcomings.

Pastors who resort to this kind of tactic (and I've known too many!) can hardly be expected to do the work of an evangelist in their role as teachers. The situation will not change until they take seriously their responsibility to lead others to Christ and to nurture them in their pilgrimage of faith. They are afforded no greater opportunity to do this than in their role as teachers, for that is when they can deal in depth with the kinds of soul-searching questions with which people are constantly struggling. Becoming a faithful disciple is a lifetime enterprise, and the pastor-evangelist as teacher has a crucial part to play in it.

Rethinking One's Own Faith

The unwillingness of some pastors to accept this critical responsibility may stem from their own theological confusion about the nature of faith and the validity of their own truth claims. In the Introduction I have briefly described my own struggle to understand and to articulate the paradoxical nature of faith and to make a rational case for an experiential faith. I knew I had to confess and come to grips with my own faith assumptions before I could help anyone else to do the same.

I wrestled with what I call the "gift-grasp paradox," my dependence on God for the faith to believe juxtaposed with my freedom to decide for or against God. If faith is a gift of God, how can I be held responsible? If faith is a responsibility, how can it be called a gift of God? I came to realize that ultimately faith has to be a gift of God. One knows that, however, only after the fact. Once I could say, "I believe," I understood that my faith was a response to God's initiative. God was there before I ever believed, but one doesn't know that when one is struggling to believe. The leap of faith appears to be totally an act of one's own free will until one asks oneself, Whence came the urge to leap? Having made the leap, one realizes and acknowledges God's prompting.

When I really understood and took seriously the *givenness* of faith, and when I recognized that my "reasons" for believing in Jesus Christ are not self-evident facts but faith statements, my approach to preaching, teaching, and interpersonal witnessing was radically transformed. That is when I discovered the value of and the possibilities for faith sharing.

As a teacher, therefore, the pastor-evangelist endeavors to make every class, every teaching situation, a faith-sharing experience. The pastor-evangelist knows the difference between "head talk" and "heart talk" and the proper place of each in evangelistic dialogue. The pastor-evangelist also knows the difference between *what* questions and *why* questions and how to respond to each. She or he is aware of the fact that *what* answers to *why* questions are not satisfying to the asker.

For example, if in response to Sue's asking me, "Why do you believe in Jesus?" I reply, "Because he is the way and the truth and the life" or "Because the New Testament declares him to be the Christ," I have answered a *why* question with a *what* answer. A *why* answer would be something like, "Because after learning about him, I found myself wanting to believe in him" or "Because the God I believe in has given me the faith to believe in him."

It can be seen from these examples that *what* statements are content-oriented, more dogmatic in tone, having to do with one's beliefs about God. They tend to leave unanswered *why* questions ("But *why* do you believe he is the way, the truth, and the life?"). *Why* statements are more confessional in tone, bottom line, having to do with one's experience of God. Their experiential quality is one clue to identifying *why* statements. *What* statements, on the other hand, usually have to do with the content of one's belief. Sometimes a statement has to be dissected in order for its *what*ness to be exposed. The pastor-evangelist knows that putting a "because" in front of a *what* does not make it a *why*.

More often than not, people who ask *why* questions are not merely curious about your reasons for believing what you believe. What they really want to know is, Can you give them reasons that would count for *them* to believe? The objective in answering a *why* question is to be believable; the objective in answering a *what* question is to be understood. The pastor-evangelist is aware of that subtle but important distinction.

Both kinds of statements are necessary. Our *what* statements give clarity to our *why* statements. Our *why* statements give integrity to our *what* statements. The pastor-evangelist understands that one's answers to the *why* of faith are not "proofs" to another person but rather the confirming evidence of one's own faith assumption. That is what I mean by taking seriously the givenness of faith. It is to recognize that ultimately faith is not something I can make myself have, but something I find myself with. It is to recognize and confess that although I am free to say yes or no to God, I am totally dependent on the God I believe in to go on believing! That's the paradox of faith.

A pastor can do the work of an evangelist in his or her role as a teacher if he or she has probed the meaning of faith and taken seriously the givenness of faith. There must be an intentional effort to do so, however. As with every other professional role, doing the work of an evangelist has to become second nature to the pastor-evangelist as teacher. One can begin by taking advantage of the various teaching opportunities that are customarily part of pastoral ministry.

11

The Evangelistic Opportunity

In addition to the classroom, there are a number of other contexts for evangelism, such as the study, the boardroom, and particularly the pulpit.

In the Pulpit

Much of our teaching is done from the pulpit. I have dealt with the pastor-evangelist as preacher in *The Pastor-Evangelist in Worship*. The focus here is the relationship between teaching and preaching and the implications of that relationship for the pastor who is serious about doing the work of an evangelist.

There is preaching and there is teaching. A pastor does both. As a pastor I sometimes found it difficult to draw the line between the two; it was no easier when I became a seminary professor. I can therefore understand why some scholars caution against making too sharp a distinction between preaching *(kēryssein)* and teaching *(didaskein)*. [3] They argue that all Christian preaching involves teaching and all Christian teaching includes preaching. Their argument is supported by the fact that the two words are often used together in the New Testament. [4]

Yet the very fact that the words have different definitions means that a distinction can and must be made between the two. Each suggests a different style, sometimes a different purpose, and often a different context. Although the stylistic difference may be largely a matter of emphasis, preaching is proclamation; teaching is explanation. A sermon, of course, may and usually does involve both, to varying degrees.

Each has its own special purpose, although this too may be a matter of emphasis. The basic purpose of preaching is to announce the good news; the primary purpose of teaching is to nurture the faithful.[5] Again, a sermon may combine both purposes.

Likewise, to our modern minds preaching and teaching suggest different contexts. The place for preaching, some would say, is the pulpit; the place for teaching is the classroom. That is an impression, not a rule. When people refer to preaching in a pejorative sense, it is usually because they feel the preaching is out of place. Preaching is never out of place in the pulpit, but it almost always is in the living room, and it can be out of place in the classroom. Teaching, on the other hand, is not out of place in the pulpit, but unless there is also preaching (proclamation), a sermon is incomplete.

It would seem that we have reversed the practice of Jesus' day, when the context for teaching was usually the synagogue, whereas preaching could take place "anywhere in the open."[6] The purpose was different then, because the hearers were different. In the synagogue the scriptures were expounded for the purpose of increasing the knowledge of the righteous believers. This was *didaskalia* (the teaching), whereas "*kērygma* [the proclamation] is the herald's cry ringing out in the streets and villages and in houses. The herald [*kēryx*] goes to all, to publicans and sinners; [the herald] attracts the attention of those who are without and who do not attend the gatherings of the righteous."[7]

A brief word study might be helpful here. Whereas the New Testament uses many different verbs that are translated by our one English verb "to preach," it is interesting to note that the noun "preacher" occurs only four or five times in the New Testament, depending on the English translation. The Greek word *kēryx* is used three times. It means a crier, or herald, or proclaimer; hence, preacher. The writer of the pastoral epistles twice refers to himself as a *kēryx* (1 Tim. 2:7 and 2 Tim. 1:11), and Peter refers to Noah as "a *kēryx* of righteousness" (2 Peter 2:5). The Greek word *kērys-sō* occurs only once, when Paul asks in Romans 10:14, "And how are they to hear without a preacher *(kēryssō)?*" Another Greek word meaning "preacher" is *kataggeleus,* which also occurs only once in the New Testament. In Athens some said of Paul, "He seems to be a *kataggeleus*"—preacher, RSV; setter forth, KJV—"of foreign divinities" (Acts 17:18).

Never is Jesus referred to as a preacher. Yet the New Testament has much to say about Jesus' preaching. He came into Galilee "preaching the gospel of God" (Mark 1:14). By his own testimony it was his mission in the world: "Let us go on to the next towns, that I may preach there also; for that is why I came out" (Mark 1:38). He was anointed "to preach good news to the poor . . . to proclaim release to the captives" (Luke 4:18). He was both the herald and the message, for the New Age began when he announced it: "Today this scripture has been fulfilled in your hearing" (Luke 4:21). "The time is fulfilled," he declared, "and the kingdom of God is at hand" (Mark 1:15). In that sense Jesus' preaching was on a different plane from that of anyone else.

So was his teaching, "for he taught them as one who had authority, and not as their scribes" (Matt. 7:29; Mark 1:22; cf. Luke 4:32). Thus, when Jesus taught in the synagogue at Nazareth, he was not expounding the scriptures as the rabbis did. He was preaching *(kēryssein)!* As Gerhard Friedrich put it:

> His teaching was proclamation. He declared what God was doing among them today: This day is this scripture fulfilled (Luke 4:21). His exposition was a herald's cry. His teaching concerning the coming of the kingdom of God was an address demanding decision either for it or against it. Hence his preaching was very different from that of the scribes at synagogue worship.[8]

Although Jesus is never referred to in the New Testament as a preacher, he is often called "Teacher." The principal Greek word for "teacher" is *didaskalos.* It is used forty-one times in reference to Jesus. He is also called *Rhabbi,* which is the transliteration of a Hebrew word meaning "a great man," or "teacher." In the King James Version it is translated as "master" eight times and transliterated as "rabbi" five times. In the Revised Standard Version the figures for the two words are reversed ("master" five times, "rabbi" eight times). The word *rhabbouni,* meaning "my rabbi," occurs only twice: in Mark 10:51 it is translated "Lord" in the KJV, and "Master" in the RSV; in John 20:16 it is transliterated in both English versions ("Rabboni"), and then translated in the biblical text itself ("She turned and said to him in Hebrew, 'Rabboni!' (which means Teacher)").

Whereas Jesus was called "Teacher" rather than "Preacher," pastors today are often addressed as "preacher," but hardly ever as "teacher." Although pastors are teachers, the word "teacher" is not used as a functional title. "Preacher" is an appropriate title for pastors, who are heralds of Christ and proclaimers of the good news. It would be equally proper to address a pastor as "teacher," as our Jewish neighbors do their pastors, who are called "rabbi" (teacher).

This titular omission, as it could be called, probably accounts for the tendency of some pastors to overlook or to discount the teaching opportunity that their time in the pulpit affords. We need to appeal to people's minds as well as to their hearts. How else can they fulfill the great commandment to love God with all their heart, soul, *mind,* and strength? Preachers and worship leaders need to be aware of the strangers in the pews and the agnostics in every congregation. There are in the minds even of many regular churchgoers great gaps of ignorance and doubt. The words we preach may be heard but not understood, as people's comments on our sermons often reveal. This is why we have to be teachers as well as preachers in the pulpit. The proclamation of the gospel calls for more interpretation and explanation than some preachers and worship leaders seem to realize. Assuming that everyone understands their theological language, they don't define their terms, identify their presuppositions, or explain their dogmatic assertions.

I have always taken for granted that in the pulpit I am a teacher as well as a preacher. Some sermons will contain much more teaching than others, but every sermon has some teaching in it. Even if we try to limit ourselves to "pure" proclamation, we cannot avoid the element of teaching. If all we say, for example, is "Jesus is Lord," even that statement contains an element of teaching as well as proclamation. There is *didachē* in the *kērygma!* But to teach with evangelistic sensitivity demands that we explain what we mean when we say, "Jesus is Lord," and that we show how this truth applies to our hearers as well as to ourselves. Insofar as we expound, explain, interpret, and apply the truths of the gospel and the facts of faith, we are teaching as we preach. Our awareness of the need to do this is the proof of our evangelistic sensitivity in the pulpit.

With regard to the pastor's responsibilities as a teacher, I do not intend to make any distinction here between preaching and worship leadership.[9] Everything I have said about teaching in the pulpit applies to teaching at the lectern, before the altar, behind the Communion table, or on the steps of the chancel. Whether preaching or leading worship, the pastor-evangelist is always seeking to help people understand what is happening, explaining why we do what we do, defining unfamiliar terms, clarifying difficult concepts, illustrating new ideas, and interpreting the elements of worship.

In the Classroom

The classroom is used generically here to symbolize the formal teaching that every pastor has ample opportunity to do. Whether it is an adult Bible class, a communicants class, an orientation class for new members, a prebaptism class, or a church officers training class, the pastor-evangelist as teacher is always sensitive to people's doubts, questions, struggles, and needs. He or she is constantly trying to help people to think theologically, to view life through the eyes of faith, to see God's hand at work in every dimension of their lives. All that is part of Christian education, "leading people out" to the kingdom of God.

To do the work of an evangelist in the classroom is not to be content with mere content. It is to be something more than just an imparter of knowledge. It is to challenge people to apply the content to their own lives and to take the next logical step of faith. It is to increase their desire and their ability to face honestly and coura- geously what it means to be Christ's man or Christ's woman in the world today. The pastor-evangelist knows when and how to call for a decision of faith in the classroom as well as in the pulpit.

Why should we hesitate to invite those we teach to make decisions for Christ? Are we teaching just to fill their heads with more facts, or do we hope also to inspire their hearts to greater faith? Is our task simply to be a good discussion leader, or should we not also be striving to help people to be more faithful disciples? There is no greater opportunity for the pastor-evangelist to do this than in the classroom, where a particularly close relationship between the teacher and those in the class can be developed.

Participants in new members classes can be challenged to think deeply about what it means to accept Christ as Lord and Savior, so that when they take their membership vows they can do so with integrity. Participants in an issue-oriented adult forum can be chal- lenged to expose their biased views to the truth of the gospel. Young people in a senior high Sunday school class can be challenged to approach their personal and social problems from a Christian per- spective. Church officers in a training workshop can be challenged to examine their role as leaders of and examples to the congregation.

If our task as pastor-evangelists includes inviting people to take the next logical step toward God, then it can truly be said that every teaching occasion is an evangelistic opportunity. The pastor- evangelist is as sensitive to the possibilities for faith sharing in the classroom as in the living room or anywhere else. Ways to initiate a faith-sharing conversation have been discussed earlier. Suffice it to say here that as a teacher the pastor-evangelist is always sensi- tive to opportunities to ask a come-in question that can transform an ordinary classroom discussion into an inspiring faith-sharing conversation.

When I became a seminary professor, I discovered that seminary students have faith questions too, just as I did when I was a student, and as I still do. No one ever challenged me about my beliefs as a Christian. Everyone assumed that my faith was intact, but I can say in retrospect that I could not talk about Jesus Christ as my personal Lord and Savior when I went to seminary. In fact, I felt uncomfort- able around people who used that kind of language, and if the presby- tery who took me under care had insisted on my using it, I probably would not be a minister today.

So I can identify with my students in their faith struggles. To those who complain about losing their faith in seminary, I want to say that it was in seminary that I found my faith in Christ. My seminary education opened up a whole new world to me, as I studied church history, and theology, and biblical introduction and exegesis. It was while reading the book of Acts one evening that the Bible came alive for me for the first time. I realized that I was reading holy history and that the scriptures were indeed inspired. I also realized that I had to come to grips with the person of Jesus Christ. Who was this man Jesus? Could I believe that he was indeed the Son of God, the Savior of the world and Lord of all life, and my personal Lord and Savior? For me that was a huge intellectual challenge.

I had felt a strong call from God to go to seminary. Yet I knew that I could not be a minister if I could not honestly profess my faith in Christ. How could I preach in his name if I could not believe in his name? I prayed constantly for God to help my unbelief and to give me the gift of faith. I cannot say when it happened, but sometime between then and the time I graduated from seminary it did happen, so that now I can understand and identify with Paul when he said, "For to me to live is Christ" (Phil. 1:21). It was a gradual process, not a sudden awakening (like my vocational call), but my prayers were unmistakably and convincingly answered. Years later I related that experience in a little poem, which I called "Looking Back, or Christology Delayed":

> My call to be a minister
>   I never will forget.
> In retrospect I know my faith
>   was not Christ-centered yet.
> I spoke not of a "call of Christ"
>   nor thought about it much;
> I should have been quite mystified,
>   were it described as such.
> A personal relationship
>   with Christ I couldn't claim,
> and it was even hard for me
>   to pray in Jesus' name.
> It truly was a call of God;
>   there's no doubt in my mind,
> but putting it in terms of Christ—
>   those words I could not find.
> I came to know the living Lord
>   on seminary sod,
> and now my faith in Jesus Christ
>   informs my faith in God.
> From God to Christ, from Christ to God,
>   thus with the Spirit's aid

by providential grace was my
Christology delayed.

In the Study

The pastor's teaching is by no means limited to the classroom and pulpit. Some of the most important teaching takes place in the pastor's study, where we are often meeting with individuals, couples, or perhaps a few persons at a time. Everything we have said about teaching is as applicable to the study as it is to the classroom. There are two reasons for distinguishing between the two contexts. The first is simply to impress upon the reader's consciousness the need to be thinking evangelistically when teaching in the study as well as in the classroom. The second reason has to do with the difference in the nature of the teaching that the two contexts suggest. Overlooking the fact that some studies are large enough to be used as classrooms for small groups, I am using the study as the contextual symbol for the more intimate kind of human interaction that usually takes place there. The study represents the teaching we do on a one-to-one basis, as individuals come to us for counseling, for example. Because we are not bound by a totally nondirective straitjacket, we can do much more than listen passively. We may need to confront a problem drinker, counsel a puzzled teenager, instruct a prospective church member, or advise a distraught parent.

Into our study also come couples for premarital or marriage counseling, parents for prebaptism instruction, church committees for help with their various responsibilities, and all kinds of persons with all kinds of needs. In each of these situations we are consciously seeking to teach with evangelistic sensitivity. For the pastor-evangelist that means knowing when and how to bring God into the conversation, and how to challenge and motivate people to want to discern and do God's will.

Like teaching and preaching, teaching and counseling are closely related and at times indistinguishable, since either function can include giving advice and guidance. Much of what has already been said in Part Two about counseling applies equally to teaching, especially the teaching that takes place in the study. Teaching and counseling, like preaching, may be evangelical without being evangelistic. They become evangelistic when they challenge people to *respond* to the gospel. The pastor-evangelist need be no less urgent in appealing for a decision in the study or in the classroom than he or she is in the pulpit. The study may call for a different delivery; the pitch, tone, volume, intensity, and even the language may be different, but the message will be the same, and the decision called for will be unmistakably clear. Once again, the decision called for will be the next logical step of faith.

In the Boardroom

The boardroom is the contextual symbol for the place where church boards and committees meet. If, as is so often lamented, pastors have to spend such an inordinate amount of time tending to their administrative responsibilities, why not resolve to make those hours as spiritually productive as any other hours in the day? We need to look upon church administration as ministry.[10] But just calling it a ministry does not make it a ministry. The pastor has to make it happen.

One place to make it happen is the boardroom. Perhaps the most time-consuming aspect of church administration is working with the official boards, committees, and organizations of the church. Every board meeting, committee meeting, or congregational meeting, every gathering of church memebers that the pastor attends, presents its own teaching opportunities for the pastor-evangelist, who is constantly seeking to help those present to relate the business at hand to the gospel and to be faithful stewards of all that God has entrusted to them as a committee and as a church. In every controversy there is the challenge of reconciliation. In every failure there is the possibility of redemption. In every sacrifice there is a test of faith. In every ethical issue there is the opportunity to decide for or against God.

Thus the pastor-evangelist as teacher can make every meeting a learning experience for everyone involved, where he or she can help the other participants to link temporal necessities to spiritual values and to ask, What would Christ have us do in this situation? What does it mean to be faithful to the one who is the Lord of the church? Even though those involved are church members, their faith and their discipleship are constantly being put to the test. It is that reality which enables the pastor-evangelist to view this kind of teaching as part of the work of an evangelist.

The pastor's teaching style in the boardroom is more informal than formal, more implicit than explicit, more collegial than authoritarian, more dialogic than didactic, more suggesting than demanding, more spontaneous than structured. I am not thinking here about a planned teaching segment that is built into the agenda at the start of a board meeting. During such times the boardroom literally becomes a classroom, in which the pastor assumes the role of teacher. The kind of teaching I have in mind is that which the pastor does as an ex officio member of a committee, without changing roles.

The pastor, of course, teaches as much by example as by words. One's priorities and values are highly visible when hard decisions about the church budget are being heatedly debated, for instance. It is axiomatic that the teacher is also a learner. The relationship between the pastor-evangelist as teacher and those to be taught is one of mutuality. Intelligent lay people have much to teach pastors, as well as one another. Acknowledging that learning is a two-way process, I need to remind the reader once more that the focus of our study is the pastor: here, specifically the pastor as teacher. The question we have been considering throughout the book is, How does the pastor do the work of an evangelist in his or her various professional roles?

Other Teaching Contexts

A pastor's teaching ministry is not confined to the church building. There are evangelistic opportunities everywhere, for the pastor-evangelist is always a teacher, always ready to help those who, upon discovering he or she is an ordained minister, have questions to be answered, needs to be met, problems to be solved. In a living room or an office, on a train or a golf course, in a hospital or a supermarket, the pastor-evangelist is always ready to help people who are seeking the truth. The pastor-evangelist knows the difference between a come-in point and a take-off point, between a plug-in point and a decide-to point, and responds appropriately.

Throughout my years in the ministry much of my teaching has taken place in people's homes, with church members and unchurched persons alike. Almost always the teaching has taken place in a very relaxed and natural way, during the give-and-take of the conversation, and usually it has been either a prelude or a postlude to a meaningful faith-sharing experience. It may have been with a young man asking about baptism, a prospective member wanting to know about the beliefs of our church, or a widow wondering what to do about a memorial service for her husband.

In every situation the teaching is aimed at building people's faith and commitment, as well as increasing their understanding. That is what makes it evangelistic, and that is why for the pastor as teacher the opportunities to do the work of an evangelist are unlimited.

12

The Evangelistic Style

Trying to define evangelistic teaching is something like trying to define evangelistic preaching.[11] Should not all Christian teaching be evangelistic? Or, to put it negatively, can any teaching that is truly Christian not be evangelistic? A distinction can be made, however.

The Nature of Evangelistic Teaching

Perhaps, as in preaching, the difference is largely a matter of degree, for much that can be said about Christian teaching in general applies to evangelistic teaching in particular, and vice versa. With that statement as a precautionary preamble, what follows is an attempt to describe what I mean by evangelistic teaching.

It Is Incarnational

The teacher is "there with" the students, "fleshing out" the message. The teacher is a role model, identifying with them in their faith struggles and sharing their experiences while setting them an example "in speech and conduct, in love, in faith, in purity" (1 Tim. 4:12). We teach more by example than by exhortation. Life-style is so important. The gospel is best understood and most believed when it is taught by a caring, loving, open, available, reconciling, mediating, humble, faith-full teacher.

It Is Relational

The principle of mutuality applies especially to evangelistic teaching, since teacher and student are both seekers after truth, learning from each other and from God. Evangelistic teaching assumes a relationship between the teacher and the student, a relationship that is not limited to the classroom or wherever the teaching takes place. It implies a commitment on the part of the teacher to follow through with people in whatever ways are necessary and appropriate. It is a friend-to-friend relationship that extends beyond the classroom and is based on mutual trust and respect. It is, in Parker Palmer's words, "to know as we are known."[12] Such a relationship takes time to build, for trust is something that is not demanded but earned.

It Is Informational

Although it is relational, evangelistic teaching is also instructional, for the teacher does have knowledge to impart. Classroom discussions call for more than a pooling of ignorance or a glorified religious bull session. One need not speak as an oracle, as the source of all wisdom, or as the final authority after which there is nothing else to be said. Rather, one can help people discover truth for themselves by asking creative questions (the Socratic method), by underscoring the validity and pointing out the truth of what is said by others, and by being enthusiastic when the point one wants to make is made by someone else. Good teachers know how to trigger a relevant response by a subtle use of suggestion. Evangelistic teaching is informational because people are learning new ideas in the process. It is evangelistic, because what they are learning is related to the gospel and its application to their own lives.[13]

It Is Motivational

The previous chapter made the point that evangelistic teaching involves more than merely imparting information. The instructor is also a motivator, a persuader, an apologist, an appealer. There is a difference between discussing our understandings of a biblical text and sharing our deepest convictions about God. In my teaching I wanted people to be convicted and convinced and converted by the Holy Spirit as they were confronted by the gospel. The goal of evangelistic teaching is not information, or conformation, but transformation—changed lives. The hope is that people will not only hear the gospel but also respond to it in faith. That is to say, evangelistic teaching is *intentionally* evangelistic. It has a motivational thrust.

It Is Transformational

Precisely because evangelistic teaching is intentionally *evangelistic,* lives *are* changed. This is one characteristic that distinguishes it from much ordinary teaching. The Holy Spirit is powerfully at work where the gospel is being faithfully presented and studied. It is the

Holy Spirit, not the teacher, who is the converter of human hearts. But the pastor-evangelist as teacher can be the instrument God uses to make it happen. God alone can change a person's life, but the teacher can try to cultivate an atmosphere in which that change is more likely to happen. As a teacher, therefore, the pastor-evangelist is always looking for and aware of opportunities to turn a class discussion into a faith-sharing conversation, where "head talk" becomes "heart talk." When that happens, people experience firsthand the transforming power of the Holy Spirit.

It Is Inspirational

Because it is transformational for some, evangelistic teaching is also inspirational for all. The shared experiences of growing Christians are mutually upbuilding. In his letter to the Romans, Paul spoke of his desire that they might be "mutually encouraged by each other's faith" (Rom. 1:12). A life that is obviously changed by the power of the Holy Spirit is an inspiring example as well as an encouragement to others. Evangelistic teaching is always within the context of prayer, offered in the confidence that where two or three are gathered in Christ's name, the Holy Spirit is present (Matt. 18:20).

It Is Facilitational

"Facilitational" (to coin a helpful word) means "facilitative," used here to remind us that evangelistic teaching frees other people to be evangelistic. Part of the teacher's evangelistic task is to equip others for the church's ministry of evangelism (see chapter 13). That, too, must be an intentional emphasis. By being evangelistic, the teacher models what it means to be evangelistically sensitive. Members of the class develop a sensitivity to and for one another. It might show, for example, in what they say when they pray aloud, knowing that some in their group are not professing Christians or perhaps are angry at God. They learn not to impose their faith on others and to respect one another's doubts, as well as their beliefs. They learn they can disagree in love, because they have watched the teacher do the same. They also become more aware of and concerned about those outside the church, about human suffering, about the world and all its problems, because evangelistic teaching facilitates that kind of compassionate concern for others. A service-oriented evangelism liberates people from the bounds of their own little worlds and expands their vision to embrace all of God's universe and all of life.

It Is Affirmational

Evangelistic teaching has a positive impact on people because it honors their uniqueness as persons and never "puts them down." The pastor-evangelist as teacher values the insights, questions, and experiences of others and is genuinely interested in and excited about their faith development. What a joyful change for so many folks, who are used to being kicked around and stomped on where they work and where they live, to be affirmed by a teacher and a group of Christians who really care for and respect them as individuals. People learn the meaning of Christ's love when they experience the love of Christ's people. They learn to love and accept themselves when they understand that Christ loves and accepts them as they are. And they are more ready to believe Christ accepts them when they are affirmed by those who bear Christ's name.

The Pastor-Evangelist as Teacher

Having described the nature of evangelistic teaching, what are the implications of doing the work of an evangelist, in terms of the pastor's evangelistic teaching style? It is a given that each person must develop his or her own style, one with which he or she is comfortable. It is a mistake to try to imitate someone else. The first and most important rule is the advice my wife, Margie, has always given me: Be yourself! In other words, respect your own individuality.

But I want to be my *best* self. If one is naturally dull and boring, it is no advantage to be oneself! One should not copy another's style, but one can learn from it. One can work to improve one's own style by correcting distracting or annoying mannerisms and bad habits of speech. One can also improve one's interpersonal communication skills, including one's faith-sharing and listening skills.

Having acknowledged the principle of individuality, here are some suggestions that can apply to anyone who sincerely desires to do the work of an evangelist as a teacher.

Be Enthusiastic

Faith is catchable. I used to say contagious; then I wondered, If faith is contagious, why don't more people have the disease? It is not automatically caught on contact. But it is catchable, and it is more likely to be caught if the transmitter is enthusiastic, filled with the Spirit of God.

Many years ago I heard a man speaking on the subject of enthusiasm. His message was so clear I'll never forget it. He said, "If you want to *be* enthusiastic, you have to *act* enthusiastic!" He made the rather staid, conservative members of the exclusively male audience stand and repeat that statement in the first person over and over again, pounding a fist in the palm of the other hand each time they said the word "act." After a couple of halfhearted, self-conscious tries, inhibited elderly gentlemen were pounding their fists and shouting at the top of their lungs, "If I want to *be* enthusiastic, I have to *act* enthusiastic!" We all got the point.

As a teacher in the classroom or boardroom as well as in the pulpit, the pastor-evangelist whose enthusiasm for Jesus Christ shows in a way that is winsome, appealing, genuine, and worth embracing will find that people do respond and that faith is catchable.

Be Forthright

Faith is challenging. As one of my high school coaches used to say, "Don't pussyfoot around!" I want the people I teach to know that faith is a challenge to the mind, to the heart, and to the will. A decision of faith calls for intellectual readiness, emotional involvement, and a volitional act.

For the pastor-evangelist as teacher, therefore, leading people to the point of commitment means helping them to understand the content of the Christian faith and to face their doubts honestly. It means teaching people that experiencing the grace, mercy, and love of God is not just an intellectual exercise; with genuine faith there is always an emotional reaction. It means helping people to sort out their priorities and to profess their faith in Jesus Christ as a volitional act of commitment.

How can we pussyfoot around with something as important as a person's faith in God? It is vital to give people the opportunity to declare themselves. Do they know what it means to accept Jesus Christ as their personal Lord and Savior? Do they *want* to believe in him? If not, do they *want* to want to? If so, they are seekers and eventually they will believe. "When you seek me with all your heart, I will be found by you, says the LORD" (Jer. 29:13–14). "And I tell you," echoed Jesus, "ask, and it will be given you; seek, and you will find; knock, and it will be opened to you" (Luke 11:9; Matt. 7:7). The pastor-evangelist needs to be forthright, therefore, about people's awareness, desire, and commitment.

Be Flexible

Faith is dynamic. It is experienced in countless and usually unpredictable ways. What excites one person may not impress someone else. Hence, the rule when one is doing the work of an evangelist as a teacher is, Flexibility is the key.

Not many days after I was installed in my first church, I found myself enmeshed in a juvenile jungle called the Daily Vacation Bible School, a phenomenon with which I had had absolutely no experience. But there I was on the first day, conducting the opening exercises. Knowing nothing better to do, I followed the customary format, which included some group singing. I remember thinking, as I stood in front of ninety squirming children, waving my arms in a vain effort to get them to sing louder, What am I doing here? I found myself laughing inwardly at the remembrance of my days as the public relations director for the Baltimore Orioles and wondering, What if the boys in the press box could see me now! (The press box was strictly men's territory in those days. No longer, I'm happy to say.)

We had a seminary intern working at the church that summer, who, I discovered, had played the drums in an orchestra. I pressed him into service the next morning, and the two of us had a jam session. What we did to those Bible school songs you would not believe! Jim's drumming covered up my mistakes at the piano, and the kids went wild. The next day the auditorium was packed for the opening exercises, as many of the kids brought along their parents and friends. They clapped and clapped to keep us from stopping, until we had to shoo them into their classes. Everything was upbeat from then on. The teachers were delighted, because their pupils were excited. At the closing exercises many parents came up to me to express their thanks for the school: "Our children loved it," they said, "and those opening exercises were great."

The point of this illustration is not that it's a great idea to have a daily jam session in vacation Bible school. The point is to be flexible and creative, and not to settle for worn-out ways that are not working. In those two weeks many people discovered, some undoubtedly for the first time, that religion can be fun and that expressing the joy of our faith can be exciting. Why not? If you have a drummer, a trumpet player, a magician, a juggler, a comedian, or anyone else with a special talent, make use of that person. Put people's talents to work and be ready to depart from the same old routine. Variety is the spice of faith, as well as of life.

Be Helpful

Faith is a struggle. Everyone needs help discerning and doing the will of God. What a privilege for us pastors as teachers to be with people in that struggle, as together we try to understand what it means to make Christ the center of our lives. Since one of the basic teaching responsibilities of a pastor is to help people to think theologically, that necessitates teaching people the facts of faith, introducing people to the subject of faith, and reminding people of the purpose of faith.

The facts of faith are the *what* of faith, the content of the gospel. That means the whole gospel, not just one element of it. The Bible is the textbook of our faith, written by inspired but fallible human beings and preserved by the church across the centuries for the edification of the faithful. As the apostle Paul reminded Timothy, "All scripture is inspired by God and profitable for teaching, for reproof, for correction, and for training in righteousness, that the person of God may be complete, equipped for every good work" (2 Tim. 3:16–17). People have to understand that studying the scriptures is a lifetime enterprise. If they want to do God's will, they have to know God's Word. That is one essential element of our teaching responsibility in the classroom and in the pulpit, and it is a never-ending task.

Equally essential and continuous is the task of introducing people to the subject of our faith, Jesus Christ. The good news in one word is Jesus, who is the object as well as the subject of our faith. In our teaching as well as in our preaching we bear witness to him, whom Christians affirm as God's Messiah, who "reflects the glory of God and bears the very stamp of God's nature" (Heb. 1:3). If you want to know what God is like, look at Jesus. If you want to know what God has done and can do for you, study Jesus. If you want to know what God demands of you, listen to Jesus. He is the perfect revelation of God.

It is also the teacher's task to remind people of the purpose of faith, which, in a word, is discipleship. The focal question of my ministry as a pastor and as a teacher has always been, What does it mean to be Christ's woman or Christ's man in the world today? The question focuses the purpose, guides the direction, and determines the content of my teaching as well as my preaching. Helping people to understand what it means to become, and motivating them to become, new persons in Christ should be the emphasis of every Christian education program. For the pastor-evangelist every sermon, every class, every Bible study, every prayer group, every board meeting, every pastoral visit, every counseling session—in short, every teaching opportunity—will be appropriately related to that purpose.

It may seem that doing the work of an evangelist is an incredibly demanding responsibility. Indeed it is. It takes every bit of energy, every ounce of commitment, every speck of ability a person has, and more. Who is sufficient for such a role? Except by the grace of Christ, none of us is. "I am the vine, you are the branches," Jesus told the disciples, " . . . apart from me you can do nothing" (John 15:5).

As pastor-evangelists we identify with the apostle Paul when he writes to the church at Corinth, "But by the grace of God I am what I am, and his grace toward me was not in vain. On the contrary, I worked harder than any of them, though it was not I, but the grace of God which is with me" (1 Cor. 15:10). So he could claim, "I can do all things in him who strengthens me" (Phil. 4:13). Prayer is our only lifeline to that power.

Even so, to be a conscientious pastor-evangelist is a tremendous burden. Being concerned for those outside as well as inside the church, for the evangelization of the world about us as well as the nurture of those in the household of God, can be emotionally as well as physically exhausting. One thing that can help us survive is a sense of humor. In fact, I think it is indispensable.

13

Evangelism in the Church School

The pastor-evangelist as teacher has the additional task of training church school teachers to recognize and accept their unique opportunities to share in the church's ministry of evangelism. Within the church itself, the most important group of people needing to be evangelized are the children of the congregation. Parents have to be helped to fulfill their key role in the faith development of their children. Many if not most parents feel they are doing their job if they see that their children attend Sunday school. The practical reality is that church school teachers, whose privilege it is to instruct the children Sunday by Sunday, are the church's main hope for the evangelization of its children. Yet how many Sunday school teachers have ever been trained to lead a teenager or anyone else to Christ?

I once put that question to a gathering of 150 Sunday school superintendents, and not one person present had ever had any such training. Take a look at the church school curriculum materials of your denomination. Do they equip a teacher to do the work of an evangelist in the Sunday school classroom? Church school teachers should be among the very first people to be trained to do the work of an evangelist. The pastor does not need to be an expert in current faith development theory in order to fulfill this training responsibility, but some familiarity with the writings of James Fowler and others in the field might be helpful.[14] As has been already stated (see chapter 7), the pastor-evangelist can learn from the psychological insights of these and other theorists without selling out to them.

Enlisting Teachers

Before teachers can be equipped, they must be enlisted. Depending on the size of the church and its educational program, the responsibility for recruiting people to teach may belong to the Sunday school superintendent, the chair of the Christian education committee, or some other person assigned the task. Regardless of who that person is, the pastor-evangelist will want to help define the qualifications by which people will be selected. That may sound too idealistic for a church that has trouble finding *anyone* willing to teach! To the extent that some selectivity is possible, however, here are some of the qualities to be considered.

Their Christian Virtues

A teacher's Christian virtues include such things as a vital faith, a sincere commitment to Jesus Christ, a strong devotion to the church, a disciplined life-style (including stewardship, worship and personal prayer, and study), a social conscience, and a genuine concern for the needs of others. How can anyone know these things about anyone else? Jesus gave us the answer: "You will know them by their fruits" (Matt. 7:16). Even so, it is not easy to evaluate someone's spiritual qualifications. For this reason recruiters for the teaching ministry of the church must always pray that the Holy Spirit will guide them in their selections.

Their Personal Qualities

People who are friendly, caring, affirming, positive, enthusiastic—in short, people who like people—make the best evangelists. Other things being equal, they also make the best teachers. "People persons" are good company wherever they are, including the classroom. Their students know that such teachers genuinely love and care for them.

Their Teaching Ability

Some persons are born teachers. Others learn to become teachers. It is to be hoped that the teaching in the church school will be of no lesser quality than that in secular schools. Certainly it should be no less dedicated. The ability to conceptualize, articulate, and communicate ideas is extremely important. So is the ability to listen and to encourage participation.

Their Work Habits

A thorough knowledge of the lesson materials is essential. This requires conscientious preparation, which in turn depends on the teacher's personal dedication to the task. The Christian education of children and adults alike is an awesome responsibility, which should never be discharged in a perfunctory or slipshod manner. To emphasize and express liturgically the importance of the ministry of teaching, lay volunteers should be consecrated to their ministry in a service of worship in which the entire congregation participates.

Their Learning Capacity

Closely allied to teachers' work habits is their capacity to grow in effectiveness as teachers. This requires both willingness and the ability to learn. Some people are not teachable. They are too set in their ways, too resistant to new ideas, too tied to their own limited experience. Even an experienced teacher should welcome more training. Experience is helpful; training is necessary! The agreement to teach includes a commitment to attend meetings and training sessions, to study the curriculum materials and other resources, and to take advantage of whatever help is offered.

Equipping Church School Teachers

Within the church school as a context for evangelism, what is it that teachers should be equipped to do in order to teach with evangelistic sensitivity? To put it simply, they need to be taught to do six things.

1. Identify

Who are the unchurched persons in the class? Who are the unreached? Identifying such persons requires two-way communication between the teachers and the evangelism committee of the church (including the pastor), who need to inform each other about unchurched family members, visitors, newcomers, neighbors, and other persons who do not belong or may never have belonged to a church.

2. Invite

In addition to such persons of whom the teachers or the church office may already be aware, there are unchurched persons in the community to be evangelized. Teachers and students alike need to be reminded continually, until it becomes habitual with them, to invite their friends, neighbors, and others with whom they live, work, and play to attend a Sunday school class, a worship service, or some other church activity. Slogans like "Each one bring one" and "Bring a friend to church" are helpful. It is especially important that teachers be trained to visit prospective members at home, as well as to make pastoral calls in the homes of their students. Their mission is not to present the gospel but to *represent* the gospel by their coming and caring; the hope is that people will want to come to a class where they can study the Bible with others and learn what it means to be a disciple of Jesus Christ.

3. Instruct

Learning is a mutual process. Teachers and students learn from each other and together learn from God. In that sense the teacher is also a student. But the teacher is still the *teacher*. In terms of the teacher's evangelistic task, that means more than covering the content of a prescribed lesson plan. It means teaching not just about Christ but what it means to accept Christ as Lord and Savior, not just what the church is but what is required of a church member, not just who the disciples were and what they did but what it means to *be* a disciple and how to become one today.

4. Involve

The best way to teach people the meaning of Christian fellowship *(koinōnia)* is to involve them in fellowship. Involvement here means participation.[15] The best way to discover the meaning, the power, and the joy of faith is to be exposed to experiences of faith. The best way to learn the meaning of prayer is to pray. The teacher's evangelistic task is to help people recognize and celebrate the reality of God in their lives. Many people have been led to Christ through their participation in small groups. The effectiveness of what some people call small-group evangelism can apply as much to a Sunday school class as to any other group experience.

5. Include

Closely related to involving people is the conscious effort to include them: that is, to make them feel part of the church family. For teachers, this means keeping tabs on the members of their classes. It means not just making them feel welcome when they come, but letting them know they are missed when they don't come. This applies to church members and their children as well as to visitors. The dropout syndrome appears in Sunday school attenders just as in Sunday church worshipers: first an absentee, then an irregular, then a stay-away, then a dropout. The longer a teacher waits to check on an absentee, the easier it is for the person to become an irregular, and it is a short step from being an irregular to becoming a stay-away. "Why come, if no one really cares whether I come or not?" The psychology of the dropout syndrome is remarkably consistent. At each stage people give different reasons for not coming. The closer they come to dropping out, the more they tend to shift the blame to others and to voice their disenchantment with the church. Personal visits and telephone calls from the teacher are a good antidote to the dropout syndrome. Sending sympathy, thank-you, and congratulatory notes and cards, recognizing birthdays and anniversaries, calling attention to special achievements of class members, and attending and supporting important events in their lives are other ways of making people feel included and important.

6. Inspire

The teacher is a channel, not the Source of inspiration; an instrument in the faith development of others, not the Prime Mover. Yet the teacher can prime the pump for the Holy Spirit by sharing her or his own faith and encouraging others in the class to do the same, by asking sensitive faith questions and responding supportively, positively, and encouragingly to every evidence of growth in people's lives.

For the pastor-evangelist the teaching of teachers can be one of the most satisfying aspects of ministry. It is certainly one of the most important, for teachers are indispensable colleagues in the work of an evangelist.

We have been talking not about curriculum materials and teaching methods but about evangelism in the church school. There is nothing complicated about these rules, yet how many teachers are practicing them? For the pastor-evangelist, doing the work of an evangelist as a teacher includes equipping others to follow these simple rules. They are easily remembered; just tell the teachers, when it comes to evangelism in the church school, the "I"s have it!

PART FOUR

**The Pastor-Evangelist
as Discipler**

14

Biblical Insights

Most pastors understand themselves to be engaged in the task of equipping the saints for the work of ministry (Eph. 4:12). Teaching and training are part of that task. I have felt it necessary to make a distinction between teaching a subject and training people. As a young pastor I soon became aware of the difference between teaching stewardship, for example, and training people to *be* stewards. As a professor of evangelism I have had to make the same distinction, for there is a huge difference between talking about evangelism and doing evangelism. I have never been content with merely theoretical discussions about matters so essential to the Christian life. I want my students not just to know what evangelism is; I want them to be eager and able to do the work of an evangelist. Knowing the meaning of evangelism is one thing; *being* an evangelist is something else. Teaching subjects is much less demanding on the teacher than training people. Teaching is fun; training is draining! Maybe that's why I always feel so wrung out after conducting an evangelism seminar. The very urgency of the task is part of the burden of training people to do the work of evangelism.

Many pastors describe their ministry primarily in terms of equipping. I deliberately chose not to name Part Four "The Pastor-Evangelist as Equipper" because the word connotes something different from what is meant by the word "discipler." Equipping is preparing people for tasks; discipling is relating people to Jesus. We are not just equipping people to work in the church; we are making disciples of Christ. Although much of what pastors do in their other professional roles is related to the task of making disciples, the specific and purposeful task of discipling deserves to be considered as a unique area of ministry in and of itself.

A brief word study will help us understand the distinction. The Greek word for disciple is *mathētēs.* In the ancient Greek world a *mathētēs* was a pupil engaged in learning from a person of superior knowledge. The *mathētēs* was totally dependent upon and under the authority of the teacher, or master. Thus the relationship involved far more than a teacher's instruction of a pupil. Similarly, in the New Testament "*mathētēs* always implies the existence of a personal attachment which shapes the whole life of the one described as *mathētēs.* "[1]

The word is used 262 times in the New Testament, but only in the Gospels, where it refers mostly to those who attached themselves to Jesus (especially the Twelve), and in Acts, where it is applied to Christians generally.[2] The relationship between Jesus and his disciples *(mathētai)* centered on the person of Jesus (Matt. 16:15; Mark 8:29; Luke 9:20), who gave the relationship its form and content (for example, Matt. 16:24; 28:20; Luke 5:32; John 8:31; 13:34–35; 14:6; 15:8, 14; 6:35–51; 10:11–14; 11:25–26; and many more).[3]

In contrast to the rabbi-disciple relationship, which was based on the pupil's respect for the rabbi's knowledge of the Torah, the key element in the disciples' relationship to Jesus was their faith in *him* (for example, Luke 22:32; John 1:12; 14:1, 11; Acts 16:31; 20:21; Rom. 3:21–22; 10:9; Gal. 3:25–26). In contrast to the teacher-disciple relationship of the Greeks, which was based on the learner's allegiance to the *ideas* of the master, Jesus bound his *mathētai* to himself.

So we hear Jesus calling, "Come to me, all who labor and are heavy laden, and I will give you rest. Take my yoke upon you, and learn from me. . . . For my yoke is easy, and my burden is light" (Matt. 11:28–30). The word "yoke" (*zeugos* in Greek) is a symbol of absolute dependence, but the yoke that binds one to Jesus is different from all other yokes. Whereas it normally represents an oppressive burden, Jesus offers himself as a refreshing contrast to the burdensome legalism of the scribes and the Pharisees (see also Mark 8:34; John 15:5; 17:20–24).

Yet those who would follow Jesus must count the cost and understand the demands of discipleship. He expected his disciples to renounce everything for his sake (for example, Matt. 6:24; Mark 10:21), to accept his authority unconditionally (for example, Matt. 10:37–38), to share his suffering (for example, Matt. 10:16–22; 20:22–23; Mark 8:31; John 15:18; 17:14), and to carry on his work (for example, John 14:12; 17:18; Matt. 28:18–20).

The last-mentioned text is Matthew's version of the Great Commission, the first part of which could be viewed by the pastor-evangelist as Jesus' charge to be a discipler: "Go therefore and make disciples of all nations." The Greek verb is *mathēteuō*. In the New Testament it is used twice in the passive form, where it means "to be trained" (Matt. 13:52) or "to be a disciple" (Matt. 27:57), and twice in the active form, as a transitive verb meaning "to make disciples" (Matt. 28:19; Acts 14:21).

What has been said so far about the nature of Christian discipleship defines our role as disciplers. The pastor-evangelist seeks to bring people into that totally dependent, intimately personal relationship with Jesus Christ. Since no one can come into that relationship except by the power of the Holy Spirit (John 6:44, 65; Rom. 8:9, 16–17; 1 Cor. 12:3), the pastor-evangelist's role as discipler is instrumental. Claiming people as disciples is Christ's work; challenging and training people to be Christ's disciples is the work of the pastor-evangelist. The teacher imparts knowledge about Jesus; the trainer equips the saints to serve Jesus. The discipler helps people to know what it means to be totally identified with Jesus, totally dependent upon Jesus, and totally obedient to Jesus.

Trainers equip people for tasks; disciplers equip people to disciple other people. Disciplers are the church's duplicating department. As head of the department, the pastor-evangelist is concerned with five principal areas of discipleship: stewardship, evangelism, worship, service, and leadership.

15

Stewardship

Perhaps the most inclusive area of discipleship is stewardship. In fact, discipleship can be described in terms of stewardship, which, broadly defined, is the faithful management of the whole created order and all of life in grateful recognition that God, who is the source of all good things and who has redeemed us through Jesus Christ, has entrusted to us that responsibility. Thus evangelism can be described as the stewardship of the gospel, for as Paul reminded the Corinthians, God has entrusted to us the message of reconciliation (2 Cor. 5:18–19). Evangelism and stewardship go hand in hand. They have been the two key emphases in my own role as a discipler.

The Hebrew term for steward is *'asher 'al bayith*, literally, "he who is over the house." In the Old Testament there are references to "the steward of his [Joseph's] house" (Gen. 43:16, 19; 44:1, 4). Isaiah 22:15 reads, "Come, go to this steward, to Shebna, who is over the household." In Daniel 1:11, 16, there are references to the steward whom the chief of the eunuchs had appointed over Daniel, Hananiah, Mishael, and Azariah. Moses is God's servant, "entrusted with all my house" (Num. 12:7).

The Greek word for steward is *oikonomos,* from *oikos* (house) and *nemein* (to manage). It occurs ten times in the New Testament. The word *oikonomia* is translated as "stewardship" four times in the RSV. A Greek synonym for *oikonomos* is *epitropos,* which refers to someone to whom something is committed, hence a guardian or tutor (Gal. 4:2) or a steward (Matt. 20:8; Luke 8:3).

A perusal of the pertinent biblical texts reveals the surprising fact that the words "steward" and "stewardship" are not used in reference to giving money. What one does with one's material possessions is certainly an important aspect of discipleship, but Christian stewardship is much more than that. The pastor-evangelist as discipler

will try to broaden people's understanding and practice of stewardship, which involves all of life. Human beings were created to be
God's stewards (Gen. 1:26–30; 2:15–19), but that relationship was
broken by human sin. As Christians we believe that relationship has
been restored through the redemption of the world by Jesus Christ,
who was God's perfect steward, never for an instant departing from
all that had been entrusted to him. It is Jesus, with his unswerving
obedience to the will of God, his unique revelation of the nature of
God, his faithful proclamation of the kingdom of God, his supreme
demonstration of the love of God, his perfect example of the life in
God, who shows us what it means to be a steward.

"This is how one should regard us," wrote Paul, "as servants of
Christ and stewards of the mysteries of God" (1 Cor. 4:1). Disciples of Christ are those who have entered into Christ's stewardship.
They understand that God is the creator (Gen. 1:1), owner (Ps.
24:1), and giver of all things (1 Chron. 29:14). All that we have, all
that we are, we have and are by the grace of God, who gives to all
"life and breath and everything" (Acts 17:25). We are trustees of
God's gifts. We own nothing, "for we brought nothing into the
world, and we cannot take anything out of the world" (1 Tim. 6:7).
We manage everything (Ps. 8:6).

In acknowledgment of our stewardship of all of God's gifts, we
Christians give back to God through the church a portion of our
material possessions. For that reason our financial stewardship is the
most tangible, visible, and practical measure of our spiritual commitment and growth. Nothing happens to a person's giving until something happens to the person. So it was said of the mission-minded
Macedonians, "First they gave themselves to the Lord" (2 Cor. 8:5).
If we truly give our hearts to God, it will always be reflected in our
giving. What we give to the church is an expression of our gratitude
for all that God has given us, of our trust in God's providential grace,
and of our obligation to be God's faithful stewards.

Stewardship includes what we give of what we have, what we do
with what we keep, and what we plan for what we leave. In a
monetary economy, we give money to the church as a part of our
financial stewardship, which is not limited to what we give to the
church. Financial stewardship includes how we get the money we
make and how we spend the money we keep, as well as what we give
of the money we have.

The basic motive for giving is grateful obligation. I used to say
gratitude, but it has to be more than that. It is gratitude plus a sense
of obligation. Too many people thank God for their possessions
without being stewards of them. The faithful steward asks with the
psalmist, "What shall I render to the LORD for all his bounty to me?"

(Ps. 116:12). We also give in obedience to Christ's commandment to love God and our neighbor with all our heart, soul, mind, and strength (Matt. 22:37; Mark 12:30; Luke 10:27; cf. Deut. 6:4).

The pastor-evangelist as discipler challenges believers to put God first in their giving (Prov. 3:9; Matt. 6:33), to give in proportion to their means (Gen. 28:22; 2 Cor. 8:3), to give sacrificially (2 Sam. 24:24; Mark 12:41–44), and to give systematically (Num. 28:1; 1 Cor. 16:1–2).

The discipler will also remind them that they are accountable to God for their stewardship, as the wasteful steward was in Jesus' parable (Luke 16:2). They are accountable for their words (Matt. 12:36–37) as well as for their deeds (1 Peter 1:17). Nonbelievers, too, will be held accountable for their life-style (1 Peter 4:3–5). The whole world is accountable for keeping the law (Rom. 3:19) and everyone will give account of himself or herself to God (Rom. 14:12). In terms of material possessions, everyone is accountable, no matter how little or how much one has (Matt. 25:14–30; Luke 19:12–27), but more will be expected of those to whom more has been given, such as teachers (James 3:1).

"As each has received a gift," Peter enjoined his readers, "employ it for one another, as good stewards of God's varied grace" (1 Peter 4:10). It has already been pointed out, in reference to discipling people for the church's ministry of evangelism, that one very important aspect of discipling people is helping them to discover and employ their gifts in the service of Christ.[4] I am using the word "gift" in an inclusive sense to signify that all human mental and physical abilities are gifts of God.[5]

Disciples learn to celebrate one another's gifts and to share their own gifts in a spirit of gift giving. There is no place for arrogance or boasting in the fellowship of Christ. As Paul so forthrightly put it, "What have you that you did not receive? If then you received it, why do you boast as if it were not a gift?" (1 Cor. 4:7).

Where if not in the church should people be able to discover their gifts? If a church is large enough to have a stewardship committee, the discipler works with the members of the committee to facilitate the process.[6] A little imagination undergirded with lots of prayer is all they need to uncover all kinds of useful talents for the work of the kingdom. I immediately think of a remarkable octogenarian named Owen Young, a modern Job, whose eyes and nose had been eaten away by cancer. One of his legs had been amputated at the crotch, and the other was sore-ridden.

Owen's face resembled that of Lon Chaney made up as the Phantom of the Opera, but his radiant spirit was beautiful. With the aid of a hearing device, he had partial hearing in one ear. He lived in a one-room abandoned storefront, for which he paid $25 a month out of the $71 a month he received as a pension. That was his only income when we first discovered him. His only communication with the outside world was his old box radio and a circular dial telephone, which he used to call the numbers he had memorized. After discovering Owen, our congregation took him under its wing, providing for his weekly food order from a nearby grocery store, cleaning up his room, and tending to his personal needs. A day never passed without his receiving a visit or telephone call from someone in the church, and those who ministered to Owen were the ones most richly blessed. Every visit with Owen was a faith-sharing experience.

After about three and a half years, Owen told me on one of my calls that he wanted to join our church. I was hesitant at first, since Owen was a Roman Catholic. When I reminded him of that fact, he said, "I have nothing against the Catholic Church, but no one from my parish ever visits me. Your congregation has become my family, and I'd like to become a member if you'll have me." If we'd have him! A special meeting of the Session was held in Owen's one-room apartment for the purpose of receiving him into the church with the current new members class. I wore my robe and we gave him a Bible, as was our custom with those who joined on reaffirmation or confession of faith. His personal faith testimony was inspired, and Owen himself was moved to tears he had not the eyes to shed.

This background is needed in order to appreciate fully what followed. Owen was prepared for membership. He took his vows with great seriousness. Out of his meager income he pledged two dollars a week to the church, one for benevolences and one for current operating expenses, as our members were being asked to do. Moreover, he made a three-year pledge of $300 to the church's renovation fund. When I suggested it might be too much for him, he rebuked me severely. Talk about sacrificial giving!

But that is not end of the story. Owen had been listening to tapes of the sermons and he knew all about our emphasis on personal stewardship, including the stewardship of time and talent, as well as treasure (the three famous "T"s). He insisted that I suggest something he could do for the church. As an answer to my desperate prayer for an idea, God inspired me to suggest that Owen take the names and numbers of five of our elderly shut-ins, whom he would call every day to visit and pray with on the phone. Owen was delighted with that suggestion. He memorized the names and numbers as I told him about each of the persons, whom I then alerted that Owen would be calling.

Owen continued that ministry until his death. Several months later I was calling on one of his former telephone companions, a woman in her nineties who was terminally ill. Miss Lou had no close relatives and was a sweet but lonely person. As I sat by her hospital bed shortly before she died, she whispered softly, "Oh, Mr. Armstrong, if only I could have seen Mr. Young face to face, so I could tell him how much his calls meant to me. He made my life worthwhile."

One more point needs to be made about discipling stewards: It takes one to make one. The pastor-evangelist must set the believers an example in stewardship. I cannot urge others to be what I myself am not sincerely striving to be. I cannot challenge people to give sacrificially if I myself am not even a tither. Tithing is not a legalistic requirement, but it represents the principle of proportionate giving, and for many people it is a starting point for sacrificial giving. For some it may still be a goal to shoot for, but in either case the pastor-evangelist as discipler should be setting an example, not just in terms of giving but also in terms of willingness to share one's own struggle to be a faithful steward. The stewardship of so many Christians is stymied by the totally false notion that "It's nobody's business what I give to the church." Jesus' disciples should know better!

Discipling people to be stewards is not accomplished by haranguing or scolding them from the pulpit or by pleading for money. It is best achieved by teaching people what Christian stewardship is and showing them how faithful stewards live.

16

Evangelism

For the pastor-evangelist, the role of discipler must include equipping others to do the work of an evangelist. To outline an evangelism program for the local church, including a curriculum for training church members, is beyond the scope of this book.[7] What needs to be examined here is the pastor's personal ministry of discipling lay evangelists.

Some of the pastor's discipling efforts will be carefully planned and highly structured, while some will take place in the context of his or her preaching ministry. The latter will especially include motivating people, which the pastor-evangelist as preacher and teacher is uniquely able to do. From the pulpit he or she will be encouraging the congregation to invite their friends and neighbors to church, extending a warm welcome to visitors in worship and urging the members to do the same, celebrating the work of various groups and individuals in the church's ministry of evangelism, sharing inspiring illustrations of the church's ministry in the community, celebrating significant events in the life of the church, and sharing the love and joy of God's people. All this is part of the work of an evangelist, for it reinforces the faith of the saints and gives unchurched visitors an experience of what it means to belong to the body of Christ.

The pastor-evangelist as discipler will be constantly trying to heighten the evangelistic sensitivity of the members of the choir, the church school classes, the youth groups, the men's and women's organizations, and every other organization of the church, to make them aware of and responsive to the strangers in their midst. Greeters and ushers will be trained how to identify, welcome, and introduce strangers. People with the gift of hospitality will be enlisted as fellowship builders during the social times before and after worship. The ministry of hospitality has to be intentionalized.

Training classes will have to be held for those who agree to serve as evangelistic callers. If the pastor does not feel qualified to offer such training, there are always evangelism seminars and workshops being offered for pastors and laypersons. I consider the equipping of church members for the work of evangelism to be one of the most important duties of the pastor as evangelist. How can any pastor shirk that responsibility?

Creating the Climate

The pastor, more than anyone else, is responsible for creating a favorable climate for evangelism in the local church. There is a direct correlation between the pastor's level of commitment to evangelism and that of the congregation. If evangelism is not a priority for the pastor, it will hardly become a priority for the congregation as a whole. Instead, the few individuals who may delight in telling others about Jesus are more likely to be criticized by their fellow members or perhaps even labeled fanatics. Feeling the lack of support, would-be evangelists often become discouraged or disillusioned, and some even leave the church for greener evangelism pastures.

Sermons, articles in the church newsletter (if there is one), notices in the Sunday church bulletin, seminars and classes on faith sharing, conversations, and every other means of teaching people the meaning and importance of evangelism will help to dissipate the negative images that many people have about the dreaded "E" word.

But a favorable atmosphere requires more than just an acceptance of the legitimacy of evangelism. It is a climate in which there also breathes a spirit of acceptance, a genuine interest in people, a comfort with and appreciation of individual differences, an openness to dialogue, and a commitment to mutual caring. The pastor can help to create such an atmosphere by reflecting these qualities. The pastor's love of people will foster their love for each other. The pastor's friendliness engenders friendliness in the congregation, and a friendly atmosphere is an essential ingredient in the church's ministry of evangelism.

It is vitally important that the official board of the church assume "ownership" of this emphasis. Before the pastor tries to launch an evangelism rocket, he or she had better make sure the board is on board! Otherwise, the pastor is in for a lonely voyage, and the mission may soon be aborted. The pastor and the officers together define the church's mission priorities, which they then spell out in a mission statement, reflecting the needs of people both inside and outside the walls of the church building. Having studied the biblical mandate for evangelism, and having been introduced to a style of evangelism that is incarnational, holistic, and service-oriented, the board members will be much more ready to give top priority to the ministry of evangelism.

The next task is to transmit this commitment to the congregation, so that the entire membership will affirm the importance of evangelism and accept their individual responsibilities as witnesses for Christ. As the Constitution of my own denomination declares, "The church is called to be Christ's faithful evangelist."[8] Not every church member is gifted as an evangelist, however that word is defined, but there is something every member can do to help the church fulfill its corporate ministry of evangelism.

The pastor-evangelist's task as discipler is to help people to discover, celebrate, develop, and employ their gifts in the church's evangelistic ministry. Those who offer their services as baby-sitters for the children of a young couple wanting to attend a new members class are doing their part, just as much as those who are out ringing doorbells and inviting people to church. So are the people who provide refreshments for the callers or transportation for people who need a ride to church, or who serve as new member sponsors, greeters, ushers, church school teachers, choir members, youth leaders, church officers, and hospital visitors or in any other capacity that facilitates the church's mission and ministry.

In fact, *every* member can help the church do the work of evangelism just by fulfilling the duties of church membership, including being faithful in worship, stewardship, study, and prayer. There are also things some members can do that others cannot do, such as sing in the choir or teach a Bible class. The latter are the kinds of tasks for which some people are specially gifted or trained, or for which they may knowingly or unknowingly have a particular aptitude. There are in every congregation people who can be equipped to do interpersonal evangelism. They need to be identified, recruited, and trained for the church's vital ministry of visitation. They are the special trainees of the pastor-evangelist as discipler, who inspires, motivates, and equips them to *be* disciples and to *make* disciples.

As people discover their gifts and realize that they can make a contribution to the work of evangelism, even if they would never feel comfortable calling on prospective members, the whole atmosphere of the church is dramatically changed. But it does not just happen. All these things must be "intentionalized." For the pastor-evangelist, it takes much time and energy, a great deal of patience, and tremendous commitment. It takes time to bring the board on board. It takes time to motivate the congregation. It takes time to discover people's gifts. Beyond all that there remains the all-important task of equipping people for their various tasks.

Discipling the Saints as Witnesses

The pastor's evangelistic task as discipler is not limited to helping people discover their gifts and training evangelistic callers. There is the equally important task of discipling the saints to be faithful witnesses. Not everyone can be an evangelist, but every Christian is a witness. The question is not, Shall I be a witness? but, What kind of witness am I? Witnesses are those who testify to what they have seen or heard and believe to be true. The pastor-evangelist wants people to be able to bear witness to Jesus Christ, to share their faith comfortably, cordially, and convincingly. Discipling includes training people to do that.

People can learn to share their faith. But as I am constantly telling people in training seminars, "You can't share a faith if you don't have a faith to share!" One of the tasks of the discipler, therefore, is to help people to discover, articulate, and communicate the ways God has been at work in their lives.[9] This can be a threatening experience for some people, who may never have examined their own faith assumptions or taken seriously the givenness of faith. Once they understand and accept their total dependence on God for the faith to believe in Jesus Christ, they can then share the personal experiences which for them are confirming evidence of their faith assumptions (convictions). The most common reaction of lay people to faith-sharing seminars I have conducted is the sense of being relieved of a great burden, as they discover they do not have to try to argue people into the kingdom. Instead, they learn to listen, to ask sensitive questions, to plug in to the other person's faith experience, and to share their own faith story when the other person is ready to hear it.

It is especially important that church officers, Sunday school teachers, youth advisers, and other lay leaders be trained to share their faith. They need to be discipled so they can disciple others. Thus they are the prime prospects for and the primary responsibility of the pastor-evangelist as a discipler of faithful witnesses.

So, too, are prospective church members, whose formal discipleship training begins in the new members preparation class. I, among others, prefer to call them inquirers classes, in the hope of attracting seeking agnostics and others who simply want to explore the possibility of joining the church. Invitations to attend the class, therefore, are not limited to those who are already committed Christians or who have already decided to join. The evangelistic goal of the discipler with respect to such persons is getting them *ready* to join, not getting them *when* they're ready to join.

What a marvelous opportunity the inquirers class experience can be for faith sharing! The pastor-evangelist will help candidates understand that joining the church entails a decision to become Christ's faithful disciple. They need to think deeply about what that commitment means, so that when and if they decide to join the church, they can take their membership vows with integrity. New members, by the way, often make the best witnesses, because they are enthusiastic about the church and about their faith. Knowing that to be the case, the pastor-evangelist will want to strike while the iron is hot and press them into service.

For churches that practice infant baptism, another context for discipling people to be evangelists is the prebaptism class for the parents of children to be baptized. Along with the meaning of the sacrament and its relationship to the whole sweep of covenant theology, the concept of prevenient grace, the role of the congregation, the biblical doctrines of sin, forgiveness, atonement, and many other pertinent matters pertaining to baptism, the pastor-evangelist can instruct parents regarding their crucial role in the evangelization of their children. The instruction that is given during the actual baptism is important both for the parents and for the rest of the congregation, but there is much more time for in-depth instruction in a prebaptism class, assuming there is such a class! The pastor-evangelist will see that there is and insist that parents attend.[10] That is why I have always favored scheduling baptisms on certain Sundays throughout the year. Otherwise, it is much more difficult to fit the prebaptism classes into the schedule.

It should be evident that there is no more productive aspect of the work of an evangelist than discipling other disciples to do the work of an evangelist. There is always room for more in the duplicating department!

17

Worship

In the New Testament there are several Greek words for worship, each with its own special emphasis. The verb most frequently used is *proskyneō*, meaning "to bow" or "to do obeisance." Its equivalent in Hebrew is *hishtahawah*, meaning "to prostrate oneself before." The Greek word *latreuō*, which literally means "to serve," always in reference to a divine object (hence "to worship"), corresponds to the Hebrew word *abad*, "to serve." The Greek word *eusebeō* (to show piety toward) is translated as "worship" only in Acts 17:23. The noun *eusebeia* (piety, godliness) in the New Testament refers to one's conduct in relation to God, one's manner of life. It has nothing to do with any legalistic observance of ritual or acts of congregational worship. "Nor is it a virtue, though it may be pursued like an ideal and it may also be practised."[11] Two other Greek words are *sebō*, meaning "to honor," and *leitourgeō*, meaning "to serve" or "to minister." The transliteration of the corresponding noun *leitourgia* is our English word "liturgy."

In the Old Testament the worship of God was closely connected to the service of God, whose anthropologically conceived wants were served by sacrificial offerings and obedience to the divine will. Two developments occurred with the passage of time. One was the ritualization of worship, represented by the increasingly complicated application of the Levitical code. At the same time, there was a growing awareness of the importance of the spiritual attitude of the worshipers, who were commanded to serve (worship) God with all their heart and with all their soul (Deut. 11:13). The prophets picked up this theme, at times even in opposition to the ceremonial observances (Micah 6:6–8). The burnt offerings of the unjust and the unrighteous were not acceptable to God:

> I hate, I despise your feasts,
>> and I take no delight in your solemn assemblies.
> Even though you offer me your burnt offerings and cereal offerings,
>> I will not accept them,
> and the peace offerings of your fatted beasts
>> I will not look upon.
> Take away from me the noise of your songs;
>> to the melody of your harps I will not listen.
> But let justice roll down like waters,
>> and righteousness like an ever-flowing stream.
>> Amos 5:21–24

The ceremonial practice of worship maintained its vitality, nevertheless, because for the Hebrews it was a matter of obeying what God had commanded. Worship for the Israelites was a national affair, for which the temple at Jerusalem was the only legitimate sanctuary. The emergence of synagogues came after the exile, because the Jews of the diaspora needed their own places of worship. The synagogues were places of instruction, where prayers were substituted for ritual sacrifices. Many Jews made pilgrimages to Jerusalem for the major festivals.

By the time of Jesus, the ritualistic aspect of Jewish worship was often overemphasized at the expense of true spirituality. Jesus condemned not ceremonial worship per se but the hypocrisy of those whose legalistic practice of it was contradicted by their own life-style. He himself observed the feasts (Matt. 26:17–19; Mark 14:12–16; Luke 22:7–13) and honored the authority of the priesthood (Luke 17:14). But for Jesus, worship was serving God with heart, soul, mind, and strength. How one related to one's neighbor was the measure of the integrity of one's worship.

The early Christians gathered in one another's homes to study, sing, and give thanks (Col. 3:16; Eph. 5:19–20), to pray (Acts 12:12), and to share the Lord's Supper (1 Cor. 11:20–26). The first day of the week was apparently a principal day of worship in the early church in celebration of the resurrection (Rev. 1:10; Acts 20:7; 1 Cor. 16:2). Some Christians continued to observe the Sabbath, but early in the second century the Lord's day became the primary day of worship, as it has remained ever since.

In light of this biblical perspective, discipling people to be faithful worshipers is not a legalistic enterprise. True piety is not measured by one's participation in congregational acts of worship or in the observance of a particular form of liturgy. Worship is meant to be the natural response of believers to the Creator, Redeemer, and Sustainer of all life. It is an experience they share with other believers who have been called into the same fellowship with God, a fellowship made possible through the reconciling work of Christ.

Yet disciples are called to be faithful worshipers (John 4:23–24; Heb. 10:25; Rom. 12:1). Participation in worship is not a proof but an expectation of discipleship. Worship is the stewardship of the gift of faith. It includes both corporate worship and private devotions. Regarding corporate worship, the task of the pastor-evangelist as discipler is not just to exhort people to be more regular as church attenders but to help them to be more involved as worship participants. That means training lay people to assist in worship leadership and teaching others how to worship more meaningfully. Much of the discipler's teaching will take place in the context of worship. The congregation will receive in-the-pew training, taking place in varying degrees every Sunday.

If there is a worship committee, the pastor-evangelist will regularly be thinking with them about the order, form, and content of the worship services.[12] In the process, the pastor as worship leader will be discipling the members of the committee regarding their own worship responsibilities, including their involvement in discipling the rest of the congregation. Articles in the church newsletter, congregational mailings, pamphlets in the narthex on various aspects of worship, explanatory notices in Sunday bulletins, interpretative comments during worship, and occasional sermons on the meaning and practice of worship are some of the ways of discipling people to be more faithful worshipers.

If people know why things are done the way they are, their worship experience will be more meaningful. If they know how the hymns are selected and see how they tie in with the theme of the service, they will sing them more appreciatively.[13] If they are taught the history and significance of the liturgy, they are more likely to sense the holiness of beauty as well as the beauty of holiness. If they understand that worship is a privilege as well as a responsibility, an opportunity as well as an obligation, a response of thanksgiving and praise as well as of personal confession and need, they will identify with the psalmist when he exclaimed, "I will give thanks to the LORD with my whole heart, in the company of the upright, in the congregation" (Ps. 111:1); "I was glad when they said to me, 'Let us go to the house of the LORD!' " (Ps. 122:1).

Disciples understand that attending corporate worship regularly is not to prove one's piety or to fulfill a legalistic requirement. It is for one's edification, inspiration, and participation in the corporate celebration of God's majesty, glory, goodness, power, justice, righteousness, grace, mercy, truth, and love. They also know that the better prepared one is for worship, the more meaningful one's experience of worship will be. Reading and meditating on the lectionary passages in advance, praying for the worship leader and the congregation, and asking for the Holy Spirit to be mightily present in the pulpit and in the pews will have a powerful effect on one's worship experience. Think what the impact would be if the entire congregation, as well as the worship leader, were doing the same! Disciples know that the more they put into worship, the more they get out of it.

They know, too, that church hopping is not the same as worshiping faithfully with one's own congregation, if for no other reason than the lack of continuity that results from hearing a different preacher every Sunday. Church hoppers do not have the benefit of a carefully crafted sermon series or the holistic presentation of the gospel as it is presented progressively in the planned preaching ministry of one pastor. They get a bit of the gospel here and a bit there, but listening to random sermons is never a guaranteed way to hear the whole gospel.

Worship and education are inseparably related aspects of the discipling process. Worship gives impetus to education, and education gives meaning to worship. Christian education can be worshipful, but Christian worship is always educational. Teaching people to worship is an educational task. Relating people to the Christ in whose name they gather for worship is a discipling task. That task cannot be accomplished in a one-hour-a-week worship service. A disciplined daily devotional life is an essential ingredient of faithful discipleship. This is the private (individual) as opposed to corporate (congregational) dimension of worship. People need encouragement and help with their private devotions. Meditation, prayer, and Bible study are the essential elements of the devotional life. One effective way to help people is to encourage them to read good Christian literature, including in this case devotional literature. They can read a classic like Harry Emerson Fosdick's book *The Meaning of Prayer* or C. S. Lewis's *Screwtape Letters* as part of their daily devotions. I have a friend who gives dozens of books away every year. It is his way of helping to disciple people. The pastor's library is often the church's best library, and the pastor-evangelist as discipler will make it a lending library.

The same means used for discipling the congregation as corporate worshipers can be employed to instruct them regarding their private devotions. Sermons on the various spiritual disciplines, for example, can be immensely helpful. People like practical, how-to sermons relating to the Christian life and their own faith pilgrimage. Try a sermon series on topics like "How to Pray," "How to Read the Bible," "How to Worship," "How to Meditate," "How to Witness," "How to Give." I predict you will have an enthusiastic response.

Children need training, too. The communicants class is, as the word implies and as has been the historical practice, a time of preparation for admission to the sacrament of Holy Communion. It is part of their discipleship training.[14] Young people need to be taught the meaning of the sacraments, the seasons of the Christian year, the important symbols of the faith, the reason for the various elements of worship, and so on. Their training is not limited to the communicants class. They too should be part of the in-the-pew training. If your service includes a children's sermon, make it count. It is part of the discipling process. Let it be a time of joyful learning for them. If there is no children's sermon, do not ignore their presence in the service. Rather, make sure they are included in other ways; for example, invite them to participate in the leadership of various parts of the worship service. Preparing them for their participation presents another ideal opportunity for the pastor-evangelist as discipler.

In *The Pastor-Evangelist in Worship* I have covered at length the pastor's role as worship leader. The focus in this present section has been on the pastor's role as a discipler of faithful worshipers. Once again, the pastor-evangelist's own devotional life and leadership style in worship will be the most important elements in discipling others. We cannot inspire people to do what we ourselves are not disciplined enough to do.

18

Service

We have seen that in reference to the worship of God, our English word "service" is a synonym for "worship." It may help to explain our use of somewhat redundant expressions like "the worship service" and "the service of worship." To worship God is indeed to serve God, but the Mosaic law made it clear that the service of God was tied directly to the treatment of one's fellow human beings. This is the powerful message of Jesus' parable of the sheep and the goats, as it has come to be called (Matt. 25:31–46). Discipleship, therefore, includes service. The pastor-evangelist as discipler will help people to understand what it means to be a servant of Jesus Christ and will equip them for service, not just in the church but in the world (John 17:18).

The different Greek and Hebrew word groups for our English words "service," "servant," and "to serve" make distinctions that are hidden by the use of the three related English words. Note the different emphases in the following Greek verbs:

douleuō	To serve as a slave (Mark 10:45)
latreuō	To serve for wages (Matt. 4:10)
diakoneō	To serve at table (1 Tim. 3:10)
leitourgeō	To serve the state or church (Heb. 10:11)
therapeuō	To serve as a healer (Acts 17:25)
hypēreteō	To serve as a rower (Acts 13:36)
paredreuō	To serve as one sitting by constantly (1 Cor. 9:13)
prosechō	To serve attentively (Heb. 7:13)

All these words are translated in the RSV by the single verb "to serve." It is obvious that one must examine the context in order to understand the subtle distinctions implied by the use of the different Greek words for this complex concept of service.

The literal meaning of the word *doulos* is "slave," and it is translated as such 38 times in the New Testament, 84 times as "servant."[15] It refers to service that is not a matter of choice and implies complete dependence upon and total commitment to the owner or master *(kyrios)*. That explains Jesus' saying in the Sermon on the Mount, "You cannot serve [as a slave] God and mammon" (Matt. 6:24), and Paul's statement, "Do you not know that if you yield yourselves to any one as obedient slaves, you are slaves of the one whom you obey, either of sin, which leads to death, or of obedience, which leads to righteousness?" (Rom. 6:16).

Although slavery represented bondage, servility, and restriction, we are called to be *douloi* (slaves) of Jesus Christ, as the apostles referred to themselves: for example, "Paul, *doulos* of Jesus Christ" (Rom. 1:1); "Paul and Timothy, *douloi* of Christ Jesus" (Phil. 1:1); "James, a *doulos* of God and of the Lord Jesus Christ" (James 1:1); "Simon Peter, a *doulos* and apostle of Jesus Christ" (2 Peter 1:1).

To be the *doulos* of Christ is to be freed from bondage to sin (Rom. 6:22), to impurity and iniquity (Rom. 6:19), to passions and pleasures (Titus 3:3), to the law itself (Rom. 7:4–6), and to anyone (1 Cor. 7:23) or anything (Gal. 4:3, 8) less than God. Yet because we are slaves of Christ, we are free through love to serve *(douleuō)* one another (Gal. 5:13). Jesus is never referred to directly as the *doulos* of God,[16] but he was said to have "emptied himself, taking the form of a *doulos*" (Phil. 2:7), and he put himself in the position of a *doulos* when he knelt and washed his disciples' feet, one of the duties of a slave. In so doing he demonstrated to his disciples the nature of his own ministry and that of the service to which they were called, and he gave them an example of the self-effacing attitude that should mark those who would be his *douloi*. The incident "thus constitutes the permanent basis of the obligation of mutual service, and of service in and for the community, which is laid on all Christians."[17]

Another important word for "servant" is *diakonos,* which in the KJV is usually translated "minister." A *diakonos* is one who renders service. The English transliteration is "deacon." It is the word Jesus used when he said, "Whoever would be great among you must be your servant" (Matt. 20:26; Mark 10:43). "The Son of man came," Jesus said, "not to be served but to serve *(diakoneō)*" (Matt. 20:28; Mark 10:45); "I am among you as one who serves" (Luke 22:27).

Thus Jesus set the pattern for discipleship. To be his disciple is to take the role of a servant. "Whoever serves me must follow me, and where I am, there shall my servant be also" (John 12:26). Although the original meaning of *diakoneō* and related words had to do with serving tables, and the words are sometimes used in that connection in the New Testament (for example, Luke 10:40; 12:37; 17:8; John 12:2; Acts 6:2), the word came to be used in a much broader sense. In Jesus' parable of the sheep and the goats, *diakoneō* includes feeding the hungry, clothing the naked, and ministering to the sick and those in prison (Matt. 25:34–45). Paul speaks of "varieties of service" *(diakonia)*, just as there are varieties of spiritual gifts (1 Cor. 12:5).

Paul also spoke of himself as "a minister *(leitourgos)* of Christ Jesus to the Gentiles in the priestly service of the gospel of God" (Rom. 15:16). The Greek word is used of one who fulfills a public office (Rom. 13:6) or a priestly ministry (Heb. 8:2). The related noun *leitourgia* refers to public or religious service. The subtleties of the distinctions in the Greek words for "service" can be seen in Paul's interesting expression in 2 Corinthians 9:12: *hē diakonia tēs leitourgias tautēs,* which in English could be translated "the service of this ministry" or "the ministry of this service." To avoid the redundancy the RSV has "the rendering of this service."

This relatively brief word study does not do justice to the richness and complexities of the biblical concept of service. It is sufficient, however, to make the point that to be a disciple of Christ is to be a servant of Christ, and that to be a servant of Christ is to be a servant of humanity. In that sense there is no distinction between laity and clergy. Both are involved in ministry (service). Both are part of the priesthood of all believers. There are functional distinctions to which some are called and set apart as clergypersons. Their ordination by the church gives them special authority to preach the Word and administer the sacraments. Others are commissioned or set apart by ordination to various lay ministries. Many have not been commissioned to any special service, but all are part of the church's ministry by reason of their call to be Christ's servants. This is the implication of Peter's oft-quoted words, "You are a chosen race, *a royal priesthood,* a holy nation, God's own people" (1 Peter 2:9a, emphasis mine). The priesthood of all believers means not that we are all ministers of the Word and sacrament but that we are all ministers of Christ to, for, and with each other; not that we are all clergypersons, but that we are all servants of Jesus Christ.

The task of the pastor-evangelist as discipler, therefore, is to enlist, train, and motivate people for service in the church and in the world. Here again, the need is to help people to discover their gifts, as well as the varieties of service there are to be performed. The personal stewardship of time and talent is what is involved here, as well as the church's corporate stewardship of its spiritual, material, physical, and human resources. The church serves its Lord by ministering to the needs of people within and without its walls.

Discipleship is service in the spirit of, by the grace of, and in obedience to Christ. That is the difference between secular service and Christian discipleship. The distinction is not between what is secular and what is sacred. Since worship means service, secular acts of mercy are sacred. The distinction is rather between secular humanism and Christian discipleship, between the secular worker's self-motivation, self-direction, and self-evaluation and the disciple's total dependence upon Jesus Christ.

The pastor-evangelist will use every medium and means to mobilize people for service. A special committee or task force can do a thorough demographic study of the community and of the church's resources, so that the church's mission and ministry can be geared to the needs of the congregation and the community. A conscious effort will be made to address and relate to issues such as world peace, hunger, race relations, the rights of minorities and women, the problems of urbanization, pollution, crime, political corruption, pornography, drugs, and the like. Discipling includes broadening people's awareness of and increasing their concern for the world about them, and translating that concern into meaningful involvement. There are many ways to help disciple people for service, such as special offerings for hunger and other causes, informative programs that dispel ignorance and fear, bulletin board displays that capture people's interest, and inspirational sermons that move people to give themselves and their resources to worthy causes in the name of the Christ who sends his disciples into the world, even as he was sent (John 20:21).

Some people are not aware that they have anything to contribute in the service of humanity. They have to be shown how and where their time, talent, and treasure can be put to use in meeting the needs of people all around them. You may be surprised by people's responses to your appeals for service. After church one Sunday a young doctor informed me that during the sermon he had felt a call of God to take a six-month leave of absence in order to contribute his services to a mission hospital in Africa. A few months later he and his wife were on their way overseas.

At another Sunday morning service I informed the congregation during the announcements that I would be speaking that afternoon at a potentially explosive rally in support of a controversial race-related cause. I explained my position and my reasons for participating and asked not for their agreement but for their understanding and prayers. To my amazement and joy, a large number of our church members showed up for the rally to lend their support, even though being there was terribly threatening for some of them.

The responsible stewardship of persons requires that we not abuse their sincere desire to serve by involving them in meaningless busywork. Some activities in the church should be allowed to die a decent death. There should not be so much going on all the time that attending church functions becomes a substitute for service. That point was brought home to me at a session meeting early in my ministry when, during the standing committee reports, the chair of the Church and Society Committee reported, "I've been so busy in the church, I haven't had time for society. No report!" He was not trying to be funny.

The pastor-evangelist as discipler helps people and the church to order their priorities and keep things in perspective. That takes plenty of prayer and many faith-sharing conversations, as people begin to ask, What is Christ calling me to do? What does it mean to be a servant of Jesus Christ, and how can I be of service in the church and in the world? That is the stuff disciples are made of. How great a privilege and joy it is for the pastor-evangelist to be in the role of discipler with people who are asking questions like these!

19

Leadership

Much of Jesus' teaching was leadership training. He trained the Twelve and gave them authority to carry on his work (Matt. 10:1). He called on all believers to be his witnesses to the ends of the earth. The apostles discipled others to be leaders in the churches they established. Paul reminded the Corinthian church members that they were given various gifts for their common good and that they were all part of the body of Christ with important functions to perform (1 Cor. 12:4–26). He mentioned several offices to which God appoints people in the church, including apostles, prophets, teachers, workers of miracles, healers, helpers, administrators, and speakers in various kinds of tongues (1 Cor. 12:27–30). The persons who served in these various ways were all lay leaders, not clergy. In the early churches there were elders *(presbyteroi),* of whom some served as bishops *(episkopoi,* "overseers"). The latter gradually assumed preeminence, until eventually each church had one bishop, who was the leader of the church, and a professional priesthood came into being. The separation between clergy and laity continued until the Protestant Reformation, with its resounding affirmation of the priesthood of all believers.

In keeping with that doctrine, it can be unequivocally stated that leadership development is just as essential today as it was in the early church. One of the most important tasks of the pastor-evangelist is discipling people for the responsibilities of Christian leadership, broadly understood as the rightful exercise of authority and influence. Not every disciple is called to be a charismatic, up-front kind of leader, but all disciples are called to accept responsibilities for the accomplishment of tasks, to participate in the decision-making processes of the church, to influence others (by example, persuasion, and suggestion), to take stands on moral issues, to exercise their rights of conscience, to serve in positions of responsibility when asked, and to utilize their God-given gifts in creative and constructive ways. These are all forms of leadership.

Not every disciple can champion an unpopular cause and win others to it, but any disciple with normal intelligence should be able to serve as a member of a church committee and, with training, perhaps even as a church officer. Not everyone can be an effective youth leader, but any disciple can be trained to assist in the leadership of worship. Not every church member has the ability to head the "every member canvass," but every church member can set an example by participating enthusiastically and encouraging others to do the same. Not every member can moderate a congregational meeting efficiently, but every member can express an opinion and vote responsibly.

People's spheres of influence will vary, but to the extent that they are motivating or helping another person to move in a direction in which he or she might not otherwise be heading, they are exercising a degree of leadership. Leaders are their own persons. Nobody owns them. They make up their own minds. They listen to their consciences. They can be wrong. They can be evil. (Hitler was a leader.) But disciples know that their leadership is subject to the higher authority of Jesus Christ. Disciples are always followers of Christ as well as leaders of others. They are worthy to be followed only as they follow Christ.[18] Christian leadership is servant leadership. It is exercised not by coercion but by persuasion, not by exaction but by example, not by force but by faith.

Christian leadership is also shared leadership, because it is exercised by boards and committees within the community of faith. There is no room for dictators in the body of Christ. Disciples know that the Holy Spirit is at work wherever two or three are gathered in Christ's name (Matt. 18:20). Because Christian leadership is shared, more people are able to participate than would be the case if leadership were exercised by only a few individuals. They can be equipped to serve in all sorts of ways that involve them in the shared responsibilities of leadership.

One important aspect of leadership development is church officer training. Before leadership can be developed, however, potential leaders must be discovered. Depending on the polity of the church, an individual or a committee will be charged with the responsibility of nominating individuals for the various boards of the church. In most Protestant churches the congregation will then vote on the nominees and any others who are nominated from the floor.

Again, depending on the polity of the denomination, the pastor-evangelist can be very much involved in this process, being constantly on the lookout for potential officers, watching how people comfort themselves and how they interrelate, looking for people who are independent in their thinking but interdependent in their style, people who are not stubborn, domineering, or overaggressive. As pastor and thus an ex officio member-without-vote of the church nominating committee, I exercised my own leadership not by appointing but by approving, not by insisting but by suggesting, not by advocating but by endorsing, not by dictating but by discussing. I bent over backward to avoid appearing as if I were trying to "stack the supreme court."

Yet I had both the right and the responsibility to give input, and I did so by helping the committee to focus first on the qualities they were looking for in their church officers. Here is where the pastor-evangelist as discipler can help the committee members grow in their own leadership abilities, as they set standards, order their priorities, and clarify their expectations and goals. So they talk about the *kinds* of persons before they discuss the *names* of persons. The pastor's role requires the utmost tact and diplomacy, as from time to time the pastor will have to draw upon pastoral information that cannot be shared with the committee but can be a reason for not considering a particular individual at that time.

Persons who are asked to stand for nomination often want to talk over their decision with their pastor. This presents another wonderful opportunity for the pastor-evangelist to disciple the disciples, as together they discuss the responsibilities of the office and their own qualifications for it. The pastor-evangelist will help the nominees to consider their call as lay ministers, to examine their own priorities and personal stewardship, and to seek the will of God for their lives, as they make their decisions in the context of prayer and faith.

The conscientious pastor-evangelist will be involved in a three-level sequence of church officer training. It begins with the pastoral counseling many people receive when they are considering their nomination. The second level is whatever formal training (for example, a class or a church officer retreat) is provided for newly elected officers. Beyond those two levels, there should be continuing education for all church officers throughout their tenure in office. These three important dimensions of the discipling process call for the pastor-evangelist to work closely with the people who are his or her closest companions and colleagues in ministry. They need and deserve their pastor's special attention, and that takes much time and person-to-person contact.

Discipling lay leaders includes helping them to discover their gifts and supporting them in the use of these gifts, both within and without the walls of the church. Some will have gifts for leadership in evangelism, or stewardship, or worship, or many other different kinds of service. Some will have administrative skills, or planning skills, or communications skills. Some will have the gift of artistic creativity, or the gift of literary expression, or the gift of hospitality. Some can be mobilizers, some unifiers, some organizers, some visualizers. Some may have an aptitude for teaching, or visiting, or financial management. Others can be trained to take on responsibilities they never dreamed they could handle, such as working with young people, or older people, or handicapped people, or disturbed people. The pastor-evangelist as discipler will be the catalyst in getting people excited about helping one another to discover and use their gifts in the service of Christ.

The discipler will also seek to motivate church members to be leaders in their communities, where the need and the possibilities are unlimited. Organizations are always looking for leaders, people who are willing to take on responsibilities for various aspects of their programs. My father, who was a fantastic teacher and coach, used to tell his students, "Any one of you who wants to be can become a leader. All you have to do is offer your services." Dad disagreed completely with the old saying, "Never volunteer!"

Everywhere and anywhere Christians are involved with people, they have the opportunity to exercise leadership: in their civic, social, or service clubs, their political or charitable organizations, their neighborhood or alumni associations, their sororities or fraternities, their educational or athletic connections, their business or professional groups—in whatever activity or cause with which they are or could be involved. The discipler helps them to remember that they are Christ's persons wherever they may be, always seeking to know and to do his will, bearing witness in word and deed to the truth as God gives them grace to see it.

Disciplining people also includes helping them to know when and how to make their witness, so that they do not dishonor the name of Christ by arrogantly, insensitively, or rudely imposing their faith on others. Some Christian witnesses have misused Paul's words about not being ashamed of the gospel (Rom. 1:16) to justify their own discourteous behavior. Disciples should learn from the example of Jesus, who never forced himself on anyone.

Church members live and work among people with different beliefs, values, principles, and priorities. As disciples they want to bear witness to their Lord in a way that will attract other people to him, not repel them. They do that best by example, by being Christ's persons, exemplifying fairness, justice, honesty, kindness, compassion, courtesy, and goodwill in their relations with others. They may not succeed in converting the PTA to Christ, but they will be heard with respect if their words and deeds are consistent.

A distinction should be made here between leadership and authority. All leaders have a certain degree of authority, which may be conferred upon them by virtue of the office they hold, the responsibilities they are given, or the sanctions attendant on their position. There is a kind of leadership, however, that claims its own authority simply because of the leader's personal charisma or force of personality. Jesus was that kind of leader, one of whom it was said, "He taught them as one who had authority *(exousia),* and not as the scribes" (Mark 1:22).[19] His authority was unique because it was the authority of God. "For I have not spoken on my own authority," he said; "the Father who sent me has himself given me commandment what to say and what to speak" (John 12:49). Jesus' authority was not based on any academic credentials or recognized standing as a rabbi. He spoke with authority because of who and what he was.

The authority of charismatic leaders is not acquired by appointment. It is different, for example, from that of military personnel. Military officers have authority according to and on account of their rank. They may or may not be charismatic leaders, but their commission gives them the authority to give orders to those beneath them in rank. Police officers, fire fighters, business executives, doctors, judges, college professors, and mayors have authority, though some of them may never have been leaders before they achieved their professional or vocational status.

Not everyone can be a charismatic leader. That kind of leadership is a natural ability, not a teachable skill. It is a mistake to assume that electing someone to be a deacon or an elder will automatically transform that person into a dynamic mover and shaker. The person will have the authority conferred upon those who are set apart as elders and deacons and will exercise the leadership that is the function of those offices.

Charismatic leadership, as the term implies, is a gift.[20] It cannot be delegated. It can only be demonstrated. Authority, on the other hand, can be delegated or conferred. A person can be in a position of authority without having the personal charisma of a born leader. That is as true in the church as it is in government, business, athletics, or any other sphere of life. Handing me a baton does not make me an orchestra leader. Charismatic leaders are born, not made. Leadership based on natural ability (God-given gifts) cannot be conferred on people. This is an important distinction to keep in mind, lest people be given responsibilities for which they are not qualified.

The broader understanding of leadership for which I am appealing helps people to avoid that common administrative pitfall by letting them see that there are different areas and kinds of leadership, not to mention different styles. Part of the gift-discovery task is to channel persons into areas where their particular kinds of leadership can be effective. The pastor-evangelist as discipler can be a catalyst in that process, helping people to help each other discover, develop, and use their gifts.

We have looked at five key areas of discipleship. The role of the discipler is to bring people into relationship with the one who bids his disciples to take his yoke upon them and learn from him. For the pastor-evangelist as discipler, therefore, doing the work of an evangelist means yoking people to Christ in the spreading of the good news of the kingdom, in the stewardship of all life, in the worship of God, in the service of humanity, and in the exercise of Christian leadership in the church and in the world.

PART FIVE

The Pastor-Evangelist
as Administrator

20

Understanding the Pastor's Administrative Role

Among the many professional hats a pastor wears, the one most often donned is the hat bearing the label "administration." Depending on what one includes under the heading, pastors might spend anywhere from 50 to 70 percent of their time on administrative duties. It behooves us, therefore, to consider what it means to do the work of an evangelist as an administrator.

In chapter 11 we looked at the pastor's evangelistic teaching opportunities in the boardroom, which was used as the generic symbol for every place church boards and committees meet. That discussion would have fit here just as well, since working with the committees and organizations of the church is an important part of the pastor's administrative ministry. There is much more to church administration than attending meetings, however, and for that reason there is more to be said about the pastor-evangelist as administrator.

Biblical Precepts for Administration

The Bible provides a solid base for affirming the indispensable role of the administrator in the effective fulfillment of the mission of God's people. Except for the wise advice of his father-in-law, Jethro, Moses would probably have burned himself out in a hurry. He was trying to do everything all by himself. Jethro urged the harried leader to appoint rulers of thousands, hundreds, fifties, and tens to share the administrative burden. The rulers judged the people at all times; only the hard cases were brought to Moses (Ex. 18:13–27). Thus the principle of delegating responsibility with commensurate authority was put into practice, and Moses became a much more efficient administrator.

Although the churches in New Testament times did not have to deal with the complexities of church administration as we understand it today, they did many things that would fall under that category, such as choosing officers (Acts 14:23) and delegates (Acts 15:22), raising money (2 Corinthians 8 and 9), receiving new members (Acts 11:24), sending out missionaries (Acts 13:2–3), supporting mission causes (Acts 11:29–30; 1 Cor. 16:1–3), disciplining members (2 Cor. 13:1–2), settling disputes (Acts 15:1–21), drafting policy statements (Acts 15:22–29), having church suppers (Jude 12, "love feasts" gone awry!), ministering to the sick (James 5:14), the needy (Gal. 2:10; James 1:27), and those in prison (Heb. 13:3), providing for the worship (Col. 3:16) and education (2 Tim. 2:2; Titus 1:9) of the faithful, and relating to the often hostile world about them (2 Cor. 10:3–4; Phil. 2:15).[1]

No wonder Paul included administrators among the offices appointed by God in the church! Somebody had to coordinate and manage all those activities. The word Paul used *(kybernēseis)* is a descriptive noun, not a title. Those who performed the administrative functions may have been the elders *(presbyteroi)* or bishops *(episkopoi)*. The two words at first "did not imply any distinction, let alone antithesis."[2] In time it was the bishops who became the chief administrators, their office being preeminent in the Roman and Eastern churches.

In addition to providing a basis for the importance of the role of administrator, the Bible also offers insights on the nature of that role. The word "administrator" occurs only once and in the plural in the RSV, as a translation of the Greek noun *kybernēseis,* which Paul uses in a metaphorical sense as one of the offices of the church listed in 1 Cor. 12:28: "And God has appointed in the church first apostles, second prophets, third teachers, then workers of miracles, then healers, helpers, *administrators,* speakers in various kinds of tongues" (emphasis mine). The literal meaning of the Greek word is "steering" or "pilotage." The KJV has a more accurate but awkward translation, using the nonparallel term "governments." The related Greek word *kybernētēs* occurs twice: in Revelation 18:17, where it is translated "shipmaster" in both the RVS and the KJV; and in Acts 27:11, where the RSV has "captain" and the KJV has "master."

The corresponding Greek verb means "to steer a ship." The use of nautical terms is instructive for our understanding of Paul's view of this particular gift of grace. "The reference can only be to the specific gifts which qualify a Christian to be a helmsman to his (or her) congregation, i.e., a true director of its order and therewith of its life."[3]

The pastor, then, is at the helm, steering the church ship. The metaphor would seem to justify defining church administration as the executive management of the affairs of the church: "executive" because the pastor as administrator is the chief executive officer of the local church. Even though many of the administrative duties are delegated to volunteers and, in larger churches, to other staff members, the administrative buck stops at the pastor's desk.

The pastor is much more than a manager, however. He or she is also the spiritual leader of the congregation. Pastors are not just boatswain's mates following orders. They do more than carry out someone else's instructions or program. They help define the program. They are policy makers as well as program implementers.

The Bible helps us define the nature of pastoral leadership. The Greek word *diakonia,* the basic meaning of which is "ministry" or "service," is twice translated as "administration" in the KJV: 1 Corinthians 12:5 reads, "And there are differences of administrations, but the same Lord"; 2 Corinthians 9:12 refers to "the administration of this service." The RSV has the word "service" in both places. Paul uses the passive form of the corresponding Greek verb *(diakoneō)* in referring to "this grace, which is administered by us" and to "this abundance which is administered by us" (2 Cor. 8:19, 20, KJV).[4] Would it not be fair to say that the linking of the word "administration" with the concept of service suggests that pastoral administration calls for *servant* leadership?

Another biblical insight comes from the use of the two related Greek words *oikonomia* and *oikonomos.* The first word has two principal meanings in the New Testament: (1) "the office of household administration and the discharge of this office," and (2) "plan of salvation, administration of salvation or order of salvation."[5] It is the same word that is translated four times in the RSV by the word "stewardship." The second word, *oikonomos,* appears ten times in the New Testament, and is translated eight times in the KJV and the RSV as "steward." In Jesus' parables in Luke 12 and 16 the steward is a servant who manages the master's household or estate (see chapter 15). Paul applies the word metaphorically to Christian ministers, who are "servants of Christ and stewards of the mysteries of God. Moreover, it is required of stewards that they be found trustworthy" (1 Cor. 4:1–2). "A bishop, as God's steward, must be blameless" (Titus 1:7). The apostle Peter extends the application to all Christians: "As each has received a gift, employ it for one another, as good stewards of God's varied grace" (1 Peter 4:10).

Pastors as church administrators, therefore, are to be faithful stewards of all that has been entrusted to them, including the temporal affairs of the church and the spiritual welfare of the people. What is required of stewards is trustworthiness. In short, faithful pastoral administration is characterized by trustworthy management and servant leadership.

Manager or Leader?

The distinction between a manager and a leader is critical to our discussion because of the influence of modern management theory. In his insightful book *Wheel Within the Wheel: Confronting the Management Crisis of the Pluralistic Church,* which remains one of the outstanding contributions to the field of church administration, Richard G. Hutcheson, Jr., presents a penetrating analysis of that distinction. Drawing on an article by Abraham Zaleznik in the *Harvard Business Review,*[6] Hutcheson finds a remarkable congruence between Zaleznik's concept of leader and "the church's concept of minister as one responsible not so much to the organization as to God."[7]

Managers and leaders differ, according to Zaleznik, in their attitudes toward goals, in the conception of work, in their sense of self, and in their relations with others. Managers tend to be impersonal, if not passive, about goals. Leaders actively shape them; they change the way people think about things. Managers view work as an enabling process, using their skills to bargain and negotiate, with rewards, punishments, and coercion, if necessary. Leaders do the opposite, developing new ideas and approaches that motivate and excite people.[8]

"Managers see themselves as conservers and regulators of an existing order with which they identify and from which they gain rewards. Leaders, says Zaleznik, may work in organizations but they never belong to them. Their sense of who they are does not depend upon membership, or work roles."[9] Instead of being shaped by it, leaders help to shape the organization.

It is in their relations with others that Hutcheson sees the most significant difference. Managers deal with people as one element to be managed (manipulated?) in the achievement of goals. "For the manager of a church organization . . . personnel are *means to an end:* the achievement of the congregation's goals. For the leader, people *are* the end." Church members respond more to leaders than to managers; they often refuse to be "managed."

"In real life," concludes Hutcheson, "the distinction between leader and manager is not so clear-cut. It is probable that all really effective managers have some leadership qualities. . . . It is undoubtedly possible for leadership and managerial skills to be combined in the same person. *But the two are different roles.* Management of a church organization is not the same thing as congregational leadership" (emphasis added).[10]

I have quoted at length from Richard Hutcheson's book because of the significance of his role distinction for our consideration of the pastor-evangelist as administrator. It is clear that doing the work of an evangelist is a function of leadership ability rather than management skills. To view oneself primarily as a manager is not conducive to sharing faith or to bearing witness. Managers tend to be more task oriented than people oriented. The challenge for the pastor-evangelist as administrator is to be both.

Church Administration and Secular Management Theory

As with pastoral counseling, so with church administration, pastors can learn from secular theorists and practitioners. Many books have been written propounding different management theories, but the church need not sell out to them. Most management theories are atheological at best and antitheological at worst. Secular categories and humanistic worldviews should not displace the biblical/theological assumptions, doctrines, and values of our Christian faith. If some of the techniques and instruments of Organizational Development, or Management by Objectives, or any other secular management system or theory are to be used, let them first be baptized: that is, let them be adapted to the context and made consistent with the beliefs of the Christian community.

The key to faithful administration is to remember that Jesus Christ is the Lord of the church. He is the one for whom we manage and the Leader (with a capital L!) in whose name we lead. In all our planning, goal setting, budgeting, strategizing, implementing, communicating, motivating, managing, and evaluating, our task as pastors is to listen to, learn from, and follow the Holy Spirit. We follow in order to lead. The Holy Spirit is the "wheel within the wheel," to use Richard Hutcheson's descriptive metaphor. Let us never think we are the big wheel. Pastors are important wheels, yes; but we are little wheels. The Big Wheel is the Holy Spirit.

Having given that caveat, I shall quickly add an important qualifier regarding pastoral leadership. Despite the numerous studies that attempt to categorize various management styles, it should be apparent to any observer of pastors that leadership is a highly individualistic phenomenon. The leadership style of the pastor of an urban black congregation may differ radically from that of the pastor in a suburban white congregation, because of the difference in the amount of authority each is accorded. In the parish ministry courses I have taught, African-American students have continually reminded me that black pastors of black congregations usually have a much greater degree of authority and that their leadership therefore tends to be more authoritarian in style. They exert more power and influence in their churches and in their communities than does the average white pastor. There are exceptions on both sides, to be sure.

Cultural, racial, theological, and ecclesiastical influences, not to mention personality factors and other individual characteristics, all help to shape the pastor's leadership style. I would not presume, therefore, to advocate a particular style of leadership, let alone impose it on anyone else. The purpose of this study is rather to identify principles that are valid for *any* pastor who is serious about doing the work of an evangelist. Whether one operates, for example, on a Theory X or a Theory Y assumption of leadership, to use Douglas McGregor's categories,[11] one can still ask the question, How can I do the work of an evangelist as an administrator?

21

Looking at Church Administration Evangelistically

The diversity of the questions pastors and congregations face reflects the broad scope of church administration. Should the congregation contribute to and participate in this or that worthwhile community project? Should the church make a voluntary contribution in lieu of taxes to the township or county for police and fire protection, trash collection, and other services received? Should the church make its facilities available to this or that outside organization and, if so, on what terms? Is the church paying its employees fairly? Should an incompetent but desperately needy employee be dismissed in the interest of efficient church management or retained out of a sense of compassion? How does the church evaluate its employees' work and by what criteria? How and when should the church pay its creditors? How should the church decide which benevolent causes to support, how much to give them, and when to pay the grants? Should the church renovate the sanctuary or increase its mission giving by what it would cost to do the renovation? Is the official board making it too hard for people to join the church by requiring them to attend a six-week membership preparation class?

Should the church mortgage this property? Take a stand on that public issue? Buy a bus? Sell the rectory? Advertise its services in the local newspaper? Sponsor a series of revivalistic open-air services? Hire a youth minister? Raffle tickets for prizes to raise money for the building campaign? Encourage people to include the church in their wills? Charge its members for weddings in the sanctuary? Take out a "key person" insurance policy on the pastor? Use its endowment income for current operating expenses? Own stock in tobacco or beer or weapons manufacturing companies? Have two services instead of one on Sunday mornings? Discontinue the Wednesday night service for lack of attendance? Replace the stained-glass windows in the sanctuary with translucent glass? Keep the sanctuary open at all times, or locked except for worship services? Adopt this or that curriculum? Take these persons off the rolls? Allow those persons to serve Communion? Do such and such? Appoint so-and-so? Et cetera, et cetera, and so forth!

These kinds of administrative decisions, which pastors, church officers, committees, congregations, and individual members face constantly, are often a challenge to their Christian conscience and a test of their openness to the Holy Spirit. Such decisions are moments of opportunity for the pastor-evangelist as administrator to lead both by example and by exhortation and persuasion.

Administration and Evangelism

Our focal question is, How does a pastor do the work of an evangelist in his or her administrative role? In view of the variety and scope of the pastor's administrative duties, perhaps the most sensible way to address the question is to examine the different aspects of church administration through an evangelistic lens. The larger the congregation, the more complex the administrative structure is likely to be and the more expansive the program. Oddly enough, the pastor's personal management responsibilities will probably be broader and more varied in a small church than in a larger one. In the large church the pastor functions more as the chief executive officer (CEO), delegating responsibilities to other staff members, whose duties and functions are specialized to varying degrees, depending on the size of the church. In a small church, however, the pastor is more of a generalist, having to assume many of the administrative responsibilities that can be delegated in a large church.

Whether in a large church or a small church, the pastor will be working with people, and as the spiritual leader of the congregation, as well as the administrator or managing director of the overall program of the church, he or she will have many opportunities to do the work of an evangelist. Here are some.

Staff Relationships

The pastor's relationships with other staff members, if there are any, are of first importance to the church's ministry and mission. The focal question applies as much to the pastor's relations with other professional staff members as it does to the pastor's relations with anyone else. Poor staff relationships, from my observation point, are the most common problem in larger churches. Too many assistant and associate pastors and lay professionals are unhappy with the head of staff, and too many senior ministers are unhappy with their associates. The perils of professionalism, the temptations of prestige and power, the prima donna syndrome, disparities of income (psychic as well as financial) and material benefits, differences in theology, life-style, or work habits—these are the kinds of hazards that foment personal insecurity, pride, and jealousy and erode and destroy staff relationships.

Doing the work of an evangelist does not mean trying to impose one's theology or life-style on your colleagues. Rather, it means being the kind of person your colleagues can come to with their problems and needs, someone who cares, listens, understands. Assistant and associate pastors can be that kind of person for each other and for the senior minister, and a pastor can be that kind of person without abrogating his or her role as head of staff.

It also means encouraging your colleagues to share their faith and being willing to share your faith with them. An able administrator knows that shared goals, adequate incentives, clear job descriptions, good communications, and mutual loyalty and trust are essential to good staff relationships. The pastor-evangelist as administrator views these conditions from a theological perspective and works for them under the constraint of his or her personal commitment to Jesus Christ. So the principle of delegating authority commensurate with responsibility is not just a matter of good administration; it is what faith demands. Likewise, my personal practice of "public praise, private reprimand" was not a rule I learned from secular management theory; it was an expression of my Christian concern for my colleagues. Again, working for creative and constructive solutions to conflict is not a technique I acquired at an Organization Development seminar; it is an expression of my commitment to the Christian doctrine of reconciliation.

As an administrator, the pastor-evangelist bears witness to colleagues and other employees more by example than by words. One witnesses not by what one says one will do, but by how one gives credit, accepts blame, shows concern, shares authority, responds to suggestions, reacts to criticism, expresses appreciation, fulfills commitments, makes decisions, rights wrongs, cooperates, coordinates and communicates with others, and everything else one does.

The purpose of faith sharing among ministerial colleagues is not conversion but faith *building,* mutual reinforcement. There may be times, however, when a colleague's faith is at low ebb. Even (maybe especially) ministers have their faith struggles. Over the years I have heard ministers say more times than I ever would have suspected before I became a minister, "I'm losing my faith!" Doing the work of an evangelist has never seemed more important and necessary to me than at times like these. If my own faith ever sinks that low, I hope someone will do that for me.

What has been said about staff relationships applies to lay employees as well as ordained persons. Opportunities to do the work of an evangelist are far more likely with lay employees, who may not be church members or even Christians. Not everyone who is employed by a church necessarily belongs to that church—or to any church. Even if employees do belong, they are not necessarily strong believers. Church employees have the same kinds of doubts and fears, problems and pains, worries and frustrations, weaknesses and shortcomings as other people. The pastor-evangelist is therefore available to all church employees who need and would welcome the pastor's interest and support in their faith struggles and personal problems. They will often seek out and initiate a faith-sharing conversation with a pastor whom they perceive to be a sensitive, caring man or woman of God.

Volunteers

In terms of the pastor's administrative style, the same general principles apply when working with volunteers as when working with professional staff (if there are paid personnel). There are, however, some special considerations regarding volunteers that have a bearing on the pastor's work as an evangelist. As administrator, the pastor does not have the same sanctions in dealing with volunteers as with employees, who can be fired by the church. Volunteers have to be motivated differently and monitored more closely. They have to see their work as really important. Clear instructions are essential. Their only compensation is the satisfaction of a job well done and the praise and recognition they receive for doing it. If at all possible, they should be allowed to serve when and where they have offered to serve. People are annoyed, and justifiably so, when they respond to an appeal for volunteers and then are never put to work. It happens too often in too many churches. It is important, too, that volunteers not be overworked or made to work too long. Some people feel as if they have been appointed for life. Volunteers can burn out too! Above all, they need to be trained for and supported in whatever task they have accepted.

In relating to volunteers, the pastor-evangelist has many opportunities to do the work of an evangelist. As the head of staff, the pastor has a special interest in and concern for those who help in the office, or the kitchen, or on the grounds, or somewhere else around the church. As a good administrator, the pastor-evangelist will want to help them see how their work ties in with and is vital to the ministry and mission of the church. A word of thanks, or praise, or encouragement, or instruction is much appreciated by those who often feel they have a special claim on the pastor because of their greater access. Like everyone else, they have their troubles and their faith questions, which they are usually not reluctant to share with a pastor who will listen. Such faith sharing does not take a lengthy counseling session, perhaps only a brief exchange in the hallway. It involves keeping in touch, being available, expressing concern, building faith. If such a relationship is maintained, when there *are* problems, the pastor is more likely to know it.

Church Boards, Committees, and Organizations

The point has already been made that every church meeting is a teaching opportunity. Each presents its own possibilities for faith sharing. The pastor-evangelist is constantly trying to set the business of the church within the context of faith, articulating the theological issues, sensitively reminding everyone present to ask, What is Christ challenging us to do or to be in this situation? Most important, every meeting is undergirded with prayer, which is itself a powerful witness.

The pastor-evangelist is aware of people's feelings, always reading their faces and body language, alert to clues of need, or struggle, or growth, or anger. If a concern seems appropriate and important enough, sometimes it is best to pursue the matter right then and there. It thus becomes a learning experience for everyone. If it is something of a sensitive or delicate nature, it may be prudent to deal with it later on a one-to-one basis.

I remember trying to reason with one irate elder until two o'clock in the morning after a particularly heated discussion in a session meeting. The conversation was so intense that neither of us noticed the time. But our spouses did! His wife knew where he was, because we were sitting in their kitchen. But Margie had no idea where I was. She was very upset with me, although relieved when I finally came home safely. After trying unsuccessfully to reach me by telephone at the church, she had been about to call the police, fearing I had encountered foul play on the way home.

I certainly do not recommend upsetting one's spouse, but I do believe in seeking to be reconciled, if at all possible, with an angry church officer. One should at least try. Every conflict presents an opportunity for reconciliation, every issue offers a possibility for Christian compromise, every shared pain is a moment for compassionate ministry, every shared joy is a moment for mutual celebration, every financial decision is a test of stewardship, and all are opportunities for faith sharing.

Sometimes a pastor has to take an unpopular position and may even stand alone. There are times when one cannot and should not compromise. To take such a position is to do the work of an evangelist, because of the powerful effect of such a witness, on some if not on everybody. When one is striving to be faithful, one usually does not have to stand alone.

That was the case in the Oak Lane Presbyterian Church when I offered to resign as pastor if the Session decided, because of the opposition of a vocal minority, that we should cease our efforts to evangelize the black families who were rapidly moving into our community. We were at the time an all-white church. It was a tense moment. One by one each elder around the table declared himself or herself. When all had spoken, it was unanimous. We would continue to reach out to *all* our neighbors, black and white alike, regardless of who or how many of our present members left the church. "We would do everything possible in a spirit of love and compassion to persuade those who felt differently, but as a Session it was our duty to take our stand for Christ as God gave us grace to see it. And there was no doubt in this case. If we lost two-thirds of our membership, that was a risk we had to take. We realized that we might have to die as a church in order to be born again as a church. But if that's what God wanted, we were ready. The Session was unanimous."[12]

So, in a budget meeting, the pastor-evangelist helps the finance committee order its priorities in keeping with the stated mission of the church and the principles of Christian stewardship. With the board of trustees, the pastor-evangelist asks if the policy for the use of the church building conforms with the church's commitment to community outreach. In a meeting of the stewardship committee, the pastor-evangelist shares her or his own struggle to be a faithful steward, as an encouragement to others to do the same. The pastor need not and should not attend every meeting of every committee. There are many ways to keep in touch and in tune with the work of the church and to show one's interest and support. But whenever the pastor *is* present as people meet to do the work of the church, she or he can always be ready to do the work of an evangelist. Thus every meeting can be a meeting that matters.

That applies to congregational meetings, too. These are marvelous opportunities for the pastor-evangelist as administrator, who has the opportunity to inspire and motivate the flock toward noble goals and worthy ends. The congregation, as well as the various committees, needs to learn to look at the business of the church through the eyes of faith and to think theologically about the various issues that are discussed. This is a teaching responsibility for the pastor in his or her administrative role.

Suppliers, Service People, and Transients

The pastor-evangelist as administrator relates to persons who supply the church with various goods and services, people who do business with the church and with whom the church does business. Volunteers are not necessarily around when somebody comes to read a meter, deliver a package, ask about using the social room for a reception, or whatever. In small churches the pastor may be the only person in the building much of the time.

It is important to remember that those strictly business contacts may be the closest some persons ever get to a minister or to a church. Doing the work of an evangelist means being alert and ready to respond to hints of need, curiosity, or interest. Unfortunately, it is easy for pastors to be too busy, too preoccupied with other matters, to be concerned with these "outsiders," and when one is not concerned one is not likely to be sensitive to the needs of such persons.

If, however, one is serious about doing the work of an evangelist, one cannot be callous to the suppliers, salespersons, workers, and others who are continually passing in and out of the church building. To ignore the persons on our very doorstep puts the lie to our evangelistic concern for the world around us. And what a sad commentary on our evangelism if nothing about us or about the church is attractive enough to arouse their curiosity, or appealing enough to evoke their interest, or compassionate enough to invite their confidence.

A word should be said about the transients who wander into the church office seeking some kind of help, usually a handout. Many churches have established procedures for assisting such persons. They can be given vouchers for food or gasoline, or provided temporary shelter, or given work to do around the church, or referred to an appropriate social agency, or offered help in finding a home and permanent employment. Whatever the policy, it can be administered either in a perfunctory manner or with evangelistic sensitivity. The pastor-evangelist realizes that transients do not come into the church wanting to be evangelized. They come for a handout. In order to get it, they may endure some overeager pastor's attempt to evangelize them, but their heart is not in it. Evangelistic sensitivity does not mean forcing the gospel on some poor wretch who has been reduced to begging for survival. Rather, it means seeking to break through the defensive barriers and dividing walls of hostility and to relate on a deeper level to another human being in need. It means treating transients as *persons,* even though you know you have to take their story with a huge grain of salt. It means not just telling them but showing them the good news by *being* good news to them.[13]

Social Events

Some people downplay the importance of bazaars, fairs, sports outings, picnics, and other church social events, especially when they are held for fund-raising purposes. I admit there are some dangers connected with such activities.

1. They can be a source of conflict. Feelings can be hurt. Misunderstandings can arise. The green-eyed monster, jealousy, is hiding in every church kitchen, waiting to claim its victims. The result is conflict.

2. They can be a barrier to or a substitute for financial stewardship. Church members can spend more energy raising money from others than raising their own giving. When people feel that working for a Christmas bazaar is more important than becoming better givers, fund raising has become a substitute for personal stewardship. When the church finance committee has to think of fund-raising projects to balance the budget instead of challenging the congregation to practice sacrificial, proportionate, systematic giving, those activities have become a substitute for corporate stewardship.

3. They can be a detour from worship. Some people think they can satisfy all righteousness by being involved in a social event. They will smugly claim, "I get more out of working for the bazaar than I do out of going to church!" Maybe they do, but is that any justification for not worshiping God? The fellowship activities and social events of the church are valuable and important, but not as a substitute for corporate worship or a detour from the obligation to grow spiritually.

4. They can be the activity tail that wags the program dog. Instead of a program that emphasizes spiritual growth and outreach, social events can involve the congregation in busywork that is neither edifying nor outward-looking in its intent, especially when the measure of the participants' success is the degree to which they exceed last year's income.

So there are inherent risks in such activities. But there are benefits as well, when the events are viewed through evangelistic glasses.

1. Yes, they can be a source of conflict, but to many people these kinds of activities afford a sense of belonging to the church family. This is not to suggest that such activities should be more important than worship for anyone. People can worship, however, without feeling themselves to be part of the family of faith, especially if no one speaks to them or makes them feel welcome. It should not and need not be that way, but for some people it is. In the process of working for a church supper they may find a sense of belonging, because they are relating to other members of the church and feel as if they are contributing something.

2. It is true that fund-raising activities can be a substitute for stewardship, but they do not have to be. They can be a supplement rather than a substitute. The organizations themselves can practice corporate stewardship of the funds they raise, while continually

reminding their members of their stewardship obligations regarding their material possessions and personal resources.

3. It is true that social events can be a detour from worship for some people but, again, they do not have to be. On the contrary, they can be an exciting encouragement to worship, as friendships are formed and the persons involved discover the joy of belonging to a *worshiping* community. At Second Presbyterian Church in Indianapolis, all the workers for the Christmas bazaar would gather for a brief devotional period just before the doors were opened to the public. That little worship service put everyone in the right spirit and set the tone for the day. It also helped build a feeling of fellowship among the participants which in itself is an aid to Sunday worship. Part of the joy of worship is seeing and being with Christian friends on the Lord's day.

4. Yes, social events can be the activity tail that wags the program dog, and they may have to be at times. But as such, they may be doing more than anything else to challenge the congregation to demonstrate to themselves and to the world that the love of Jesus Christ transcends all barriers. Indeed, in the Oak Lane Church it was in their fellowship activities that the members discovered and appreciated their oneness in Christ, as blacks and whites became socially comfortable with one another. That happened *after* they had been worshiping together. The real test of their oneness was not their willingness to worship together; the worship context was not threatening to anyone. It was when they began to work and socialize together in and out of one another's homes, in connection with the fellowship activities of the church, that they became a church family.

Knowing all this, the pastor-evangelist sees these events as opportunities to do the work of an evangelist. Bazaars and other such activities attract people from the community, many of whom are unchurched. They are times for welcoming, mingling, engaging, inviting, introducing, all of which can be doorways to subsequent faith-sharing conversations. Need it be mentioned that the pastor should not be the only one doing the work of an evangelist on such occasions? It is to be hoped that others will have been trained to circulate among, seek out, and relate to unchurched visitors. Our focus, however, is still on the *pastor* as evangelist.

Office Management

Many of the pastor's administrative duties fall under the category of office management. Depending on the size of the church, this can include working with other employed or volunteer office personnel, or it can mean having to do everything oneself, including correspondence, record keeping, filing, scheduling, ordering and storing supplies, answering the telephone, preparing the church bulletin, planning and producing congregational mailings and the church newsletter (if there is one), completing denominational reports, and so on. One might legitimately ask, What have such duties to do with the pastor's work of evangelism? One cannot evangelize a typewriter or a telephone! True, but one can use a typewriter for the work of evangelism. A personal letter can be an immensely effective medium for evangelism, as well as for pastoral care.[14] So can a telephone call, as has already been discussed in chapter 2. Some churches list a number people can call for a recorded prayer ("dial-a-prayer") or brief message. Many who call may not be members of a church or even believers, but the fact that they dial the number indicates they are probably seekers or at least persons in need of help. The pastor-evangelist, therefore, will word the prayers and messages with evangelistic sensitivity.

The pastor's column in the church newsletter can be treated merely as space for advertising and promoting forthcoming events, or it can be used as a marvelous medium for communicating the gospel, sharing faith, and addressing people's deepest questions. The church bulletin can also be a much more evangelistically sensitive instrument than are many I have seen.[15]

If the church can afford it, sermons can be duplicated and mailed to homebound people, service personnel, students away at college, and others. Some pastors make them available to the entire congregation. One Yale student wrote to tell me that she had shared one of my sermons with her nonbelieving college roommate. It was a sermon I had preached more than ten years earlier, when she was just a little girl. Some churches record the worship services and make tapes available to shut-ins and people in nursing homes.

These are the kinds of things the pastor-evangelist as administrator will think about as she or he goes about the daily routine of the office. These illustrations can be reminders that a pastor can be doing the work of an evangelist even when sitting alone behind a desk.

Public Relations

Among the pastor's administrative responsibilities are matters pertaining to public relations. This work may be assigned to a committee or church member, or it may be one more hat the pastor has to wear. Does the church advertise its Sunday services and other events? If so, the pastor-evangelist will see that it is done with evangelistic sensitivity, which includes listing sermon topics that will attract people's interest. I hope some sermons are not as pedantic and dull as their titles!

Few pastors have a journalistic background. They may never have been taught, therefore, how to write a press release. Yet this is something many pastors have to do from time to time. Most secular newspapers will not accept material that is deliberately and obviously evangelistic in tone and content. They will publish newsworthy articles, and even inspirational human interest stories, if they are couched in appropriate language. The pastor-evangelist knows how to get the message across indirectly.

Many radio stations and some television stations offer free air time to churches and other organizations for public service announcements. The evangelistically minded church will avail itself of such opportunities, and the pastor-evangelist will see that the announcements are sensitively and winsomely worded, keeping in mind the diverse nature of the radio audience. The appeal should be to the unchurched people who may be listening. What would trigger their interest about this or that event? What information is most relevant for them, and how should it be stated? A radio or television station might also offer to broadcast a worship service, but the discussion of that topic does not rightly fall within the scope of this section.[16]

A form of advertising that does belong here is what could loosely be called "displays." The most important form of display advertising is the outdoor sign on the church lawn. It should be clearly visible to passing motorists, perpendicular (not parallel) to the street, informative but not too "busy," and current (next Sunday's sermon topic, not last Sunday's!). The topic should be one that makes a passerby want to come in and hear what you have to say. Thought should be given also to the bulletin boards inside the building, where visitors may be attracted by pictures and news of church members, information about the mission causes supported by the church, news of upcoming events, who's who, what's what, and where's where.

Directional signs should be strategically placed on the main roadways leading to the church, and directories and floor plans provided inside the building to help strangers find their way around. Pew rack materials and other handouts should be periodically reviewed and updated. Do the visitor cards invite the right kinds of information for pastoral follow-up? Is there a pamphlet describing how to join the church? Are the pastor's office hours and telephone numbers indicated? The pastor-evangelist as administrator sees that these kinds of things are not overlooked.

In addition to publicity, promotion, and advertising, public relations, as the term implies, includes maintaining good relations with the various elements of the public at large. The pastor as administrator wants the church to be highly regarded in the community. It is important to establish close ties with the local police and fire departments, neighborhood associations, local school authorities, public officials, hospitals, funeral directors, nursing homes, neighboring

churches and synagogues, service agencies, community organizations, and special need groups such as Parents Anonymous, Compassionate Friends, Alchoholics Anonymous, and Parents Without
Partners. Representatives of these organizations and groups will
often refer people who need pastoral help to the churches they know
and respect, and they themselves may call on the church for various
kinds of help, including the use of the church's facilities. The last
possibility is a reason for the church to have a farsighted policy on
the use of the building, one that is consistent with the church's
mission statement.

Buildings and Grounds

Let us hope there is either a sexton or a dedicated volunteer who
sees that the church is kept in good physical condition. Larger
churches will have a buildings and grounds committee, which is
always one of the busiest committees in the church. The pastor
should not have to function as a sexton, but after living in a manse
next door to the church for ten years, I can testify that proximity
may give a pastor no choice but to serve as the unofficial assistant
sexton and night watchman. Many were the nights I had to go to the
church with a robe over my pajamas, to turn out a light or lock the
doors. On more than one Sunday morning I had to shovel snow off
the walkways. I figured that sort of thing came with the territory.

But it was not the best use of my time. A pastor is called to do
the work of an evangelist, not the work of a sexton, as important as
that is. As administrator the pastor-evangelist can help those who are
responsible for the upkeep of the property to understand why their
work is important to the mission of the church. An ill-kept building
speaks volumes to visitors. It can be a very humble, simple building,
but if it is spick-and-span, visitors will think, These people love their
church! A dirty sanctuary, with cracks in the ceiling and paint
peeling off the walls, sends the opposite message.

The pastor-evangelist can also help those responsible for the decor
of the sanctuary to think about the symbolism of the architecture.
Do the carved symbols, the antependia, the stained-glass windows,
the design of the chancel, and the general layout of the sanctuary
express the tradition and theology of the church? Should the pulpit
be central? Or the Communion table? Or the altar? Where and how
should the cross be displayed, and what kind of cross should it be?
If there is an organ, where should it be placed, and where should the
choir be seated? What liturgical colors will be used for which Sundays or seasons of the year, and why? These kinds of questions need
to be thought about, decided upon, communicated, and interpreted
to the members of the congregation, so they can appreciate how the

architecture of the church bears witness to the faith they profess. The total impact of the worship service will thus be enhanced for church members and visitors alike.

Many more aspects of church administration could be mentioned. These should be sufficient, however, to make the point that in the role of administrator the pastor has ample opportunity to do the work of an evangelist. It should also be perfectly clear by now that being a pastor-evangelist is not an occasional activity or a function one performs now and then, like preaching. A pastor may not always be *doing* evangelism, but a pastor is always an evangelist. Being a pastor-evangelist means approaching every task, everything one does, with evangelistic sensitivity.

PART SIX

**The Pastor-Evangelist
as Public Figure**

22

Being a Public Figure

There are those who point with great chagrin to what they are convinced is the eroding influence of the clergy in most Western societies. Theology, they say, is no longer the queen of the sciences, and theologians are thought to have nothing to contribute to any serious discussion of world issues. Gone are the days of the great princes of the pulpit, whose Sunday morning commentaries on life were reviewed in the secular press. Gone are the days when the pastor was the most influential leader in small-town America.

The popularity of television evangelists has only aggravated the general public's indifference if not antipathy toward clergypersons, whose opinions are neither sought nor listened to by the movers and shakers of industry, business, politics, education, science, or any other secular sphere. Except among their dwindling captive audiences, the opinions of most clergy are consigned by the rest of the world to the trash heap of irrelevancy.

So goes the argument. I, for one, disagree. That is not to say there is no truth whatsoever to the negative assessment. Things have changed. The world has changed. But a pastor is still very much a public figure, if for no other reason than his or her relationship to a significant institution in the community. The position, as well as the nature of the profession itself, is conducive to public recognition. Pastors are important to their congregations, who in turn make their pastors known to others.

Whether positively or negatively, pastors are talked about, listened to, questioned, and quoted. This happens more often in small towns than in large cities, where the degree of public exposure may not be proportionately so great as in a smaller community. Nevertheless, even in metropolitan areas, pastors are public figures. They are asked to speak here and there, depending on their particular skills, interests, and expertise. Members of their congregations belong to civic and service clubs, which are always looking for speakers, or to organizations that have banquets or meetings and need a professional "invoker" or "blesser." Church members teach in schools that need someone to give a commencement address, or a baccalaureate prayer, or a talk to a school assembly. So it goes, and pastors find themselves accepting various invitations that take them outside the parish into the wider community, into situations where they are indeed public figures.

They may become involved, moreover, in community affairs, serve on the local school board, or on the town council, or with the volunteer fire department; become president of the PTA of the local junior high school, or chaplain to the local police department, or a member of the mayor's task force on housing. They may take on one or more responsibilities out of an endless number of possibilities, all of which give them public exposure and may project them into a position of even greater prominence in the community.

That being the case, the focal question for this discussion is, What does it mean to do the work of an evangelist as a public figure? To be an effective ambassador for Christ when you are perceived as a public figure requires a high degree of evangelistic sensitivity, for the risk of negative reaction is great. The challenge for the pastor-evangelist as public figure in a pluralistic society is to be a faithful witness with an ecumenical spirit. Each pastor must find his or her own style for meeting that challenge. However you approach the task, it is helpful to keep in mind three important implications of your being a public figure.

Your Presence Is Conspicuous

As a pastor you cannot travel incognito. You are by no means anonymous. You cannot hide in a crowd. When you go to the local high school basketball game, your church members spot you and say, "There's our pastor!"

Your presence at community functions, furthermore, carries weight. It may be viewed by others as an endorsement or a protest, a blessing or a burden, depending on the event and what you are doing there. In any case, because you are who you are and what you are, your presence is conspicuous. How you bear witness in a given situation depends on whether you support or oppose what is going on.

Doing the work of an evangelist as a public figure may require disassociating yourself from or taking a stand against what is happening at the moment. Some years ago I was invited to give the invocation and benediction at a testimonial luncheon for a well-known baseball player, who happened to have been a personal friend when we were both with the Orioles. The meal was followed by a high-priced entertainment program, beginning with several selections by a famous blind pianist. He was followed by a well-known comedian, whose jokes got filthier as he went along. As I had already been introduced and was wearing a clerical collar, many of the twelve hundred people present, including women and children, were glancing at me to see how I was reacting. My distaste and anger were mirrored in my facial expression. I deliberately avoided even the semblance of a smile. Finally I got up from my place at the long speakers' table, made my way to the master of ceremonies, who was seated next to the microphone where the comedian was speaking, and whispered that I was leaving. The emcee, who was also a good friend, was shocked. With a look of dismay he replied, "But you can't leave, Dick—you have to give the benediction!"

"I'm sorry, John," I replied, "but I am not going to bless this kind of filth, nor am I going to sanction it with my presence."

My friend's expression immediately changed. "I understand, Dick. We'll just skip the benediction, and I'll explain to Bob"—the guest of honor—"that you had to leave."

With that I walked off the dais, and I am sure most everyone in that banquet hall, including the comedian, noticed my departure. My empty chair remained as a visible but silent protest to the inexcusably obscene performance of that entertainer. That incident, by the way, led to a fantastic faith-sharing conversation a few days later with John, who thanked me sincerely for the impact my action that day had had on his life. "Because of what you did, Dick, I've gotten back in touch with God."

On another occasion I was asked to give an invocation at a Saints and Sinners Luncheon, where the governor of the state was to be honored in the unique style of that organization. Knowing that many of the guests would be exposed to the preluncheon activities in the so-called sideshows, which I learned were as revolting as a pornographic movie, I wondered how in the world I could invoke God's blessing on such a gathering, even though the luncheon itself was on a much higher plane. What they needed was not a prayer of invocation but a prayer of confession! For the sake of all the decent folks and the honored guests there, I wanted to honor my commitment to pray, but without compromising my own integrity. I also believe a prayer should be a prayer, not a sermon. After addressing and thanking God; I continued with these words: "Wilt thou be our unseen guest at these tables, not because we are worthy of thy favor, for we are more sinners than saints, but because thy presence hallows every occasion. And wilt thou bless us not just with the things of this world but with the desire and the strength to live better lives, with *cleaner* thoughts, and kinder words, and worthier deeds, for thy name's sake. Amen."

It was couched in appropriate language, but I am sure the message was clear to all who knew about the sideshows. After I sat down, the governor leaned over to me and said, "Your prayer was right on target, Mr. Armstrong. I hope everyone was listening!"

That was the way I chose to make my witness on that occasion. I felt I could not and should not ignore what had been going on, so my prayer was the medium for my message. It was addressed to God, of course, but everyone got the point.

Your Life-style Is Crucial

Being conspicuous makes your life-style all the more significant. If you err, it is news. If you break the law, it is a public scandal. If you use profanity, or utter an obscenity, you are more subject to criticism than the average person whose vocabulary is sprinkled with such language. If you are too loud, or too belligerent, or too opinionated, or too garrulous, or too anything else, you are likely to evoke the criticism of people who think, A minister shouldn't act like that![1]

That is why Timothy is told to "set the believers an example in speech and conduct, in love, in faith, in purity" (1 Tim. 4:12) and bishops are exhorted to be above reproach from believers and nonbelievers alike (3:1–7). It is wise, therefore, to avoid even the appearance of wrongdoing, for mean-spirited people love to cast aspersions upon people in "high" places, especially clergy. The reputation of many a minister has been sullied by misrepresentation and distortion, hearsay and rumor. Such treatment is unfair and dishonest, but it can happen to any of us. Much of the time we are not even aware of it. Nor can we do anything about it, if we are aware, except to show by the way we live that the rumor is unfounded. In most instances it is better to absorb criticism than to give it credence by defending oneself. The best defense against gossip is the impeccability of one's character and the integrity of one's life-style.

Like that of other public figures, your behavior is observed and evaluated. Your family relationships, your community involvements, your social graces or lack thereof, your conduct as a citizen and neighbor, how you drive a car, behave at a party, compete in sports, discuss politics, relate to the person who delivers your mail, or empties your trash, or pumps your gas—in all these things public figures, especially ministers, are fair game for critics.

The reality of this fact was brought home to me even before I became a minister. A few days after the announcement of my resignation as public relations director of the Baltimore Orioles in order to study for the ministry appeared in the newspapers, I was playing in a softball game. After what I thought was a particularly inept call by the umpire, I said some rather unpleasant things to the gentleman behind the plate. To my surprise and embarrassment, he offered no retort to me but commented in a voice loud enough to be heard by everyone on and off the field, "He sure doesn't act like a minister!" I learned the hard way that evening that I could not behave the way I used to and get away with it, even though at that stage of my development it was to me just part of the game. All of a sudden people expected more of me, now that I was going to become a minister.

And it works both ways. The summer following my first year of seminary, I paid a visit to Memorial Stadium in Baltimore, where I had worked. While enjoying a good visit with some of the coaches and players in the locker room, I was startled when someone said, "Watch your language, you guys. You don't want the Reverend to hear that kind of talk!" All of a sudden I was "the Reverend"! Never before had any of those same men ever watched their language around me. The one who made the comment was completely serious, but I was as amused as I was surprised by the new respect accorded me simply because I was now a seminary student. With a grin on my face, I replied, "It's not whether I *hear* it, but whether you *say* it that matters to God." They all laughed, but I could tell they got the message.

You can complain about the double standard by which pastors are judged, but you cannot escape its consequences. You can resent it, but you cannot deny it. Living under the burden of a double standard is an occupational hazard for us ministers, as is always being asked to say grace at public banquets. Our resentment is unwarranted, however. If we do not practice what we preach, our words will have an empty sound. We have seen the disastrous effects of the transgressions and extravagances of some of the television evangelists. I do not think we can win the world for Christ by imitating the world. We are witnesses for Christ, ambassadors who have been commissioned to represent Jesus in word and deed.

Pastors are constantly under the scrutiny of people who hear us preach or who know that we preach. How we behave in public had better conform to what we preach in the pulpit.

> The proof of the pudding for prophets of old
>   was whether things happened as they had foretold.
> The proof of the pudding for preachers today
>   is whether their actions confirm what they say.
> For prophets and preachers who speak in God's name
>   the call to be faithful is ever the same.

The proof of *that* pudding was then and is still:
one's words *and* one's deeds must conform to God's will!

The point is, Never forget you are a minister. The people around you won't. Your life-style, therefore, is crucial.

Your Role Is Constructive

As a pastor-evangelist you have a constructive role to play in the community. You will often find yourself in the role of mediator, a role in which you want to be seen as a fair-minded arbiter, one who builds bridges and *is* a bridge between people. You will sometimes find yourself championing worthy causes, which you will want to represent reasonably, fairly, and honestly. You may also become involved in worthwhile community enterprises, which test your willingness to work cheerfully, cooperatively, and ecumenically with others. You want always to be an upholder of justice and a seeker after truth, a guardian of the public welfare and a voice of conscience in the community.

In your own volunteer work and community service, therefore, you gain people's confidence by the way you participate in the affairs and discussions of the groups and organizations to which you belong. It is the nature and style of your interpersonal relations that pave the way for doing the work of an evangelist. Indeed, living the gospel in the community is part of your evangelism. For the pastor-evangelist, being a public figure implies as much.

23

Public Praying and Public Speaking

One can strive to be open-minded and ecumenical in spirit without compromising one's own faith convictions. The pastor-evangelist is always an apologist for the cause of Christ, but one can be that and still be sensitive to the beliefs and feelings of others.

Public Prayers

Take, for example, the matter of praying at public functions. When I know there are people of other faiths present, I do not give a Trinitarian benediction or end a prayer with the words "in Jesus' name we pray." I feel it is inappropriate to do so when many people whom I am representing in prayer are *not* praying in Jesus' name. Would it not be more appropriate to end with something like "to the glory of thy holy name, Amen" or "forever and ever, Amen" or some other inclusive expression? Instead of offending Jews by giving an apostolic benediction at a high school baccalaureate, why not use the Aaronic benediction, which Christians and Jews alike can relate to?

> The LORD bless you and keep you:
> The LORD make his face to shine upon you,
>   and be gracious to you:
> The LORD lift up his countenance upon you,
>   and give you peace.
>
> Numbers 6:24–26

There are those who argue that to avoid using Christ's name is to compromise the Christian gospel. They quote Paul's letter to the Romans, in which the apostle declared that he was not ashamed of the gospel (Rom. 1:16). Why, then, should we be ashamed? Paul knew, furthermore, that to preach about a crucified Messiah was "a stumbling block to Jews and folly to Gentiles" (1 Cor. 1:23). Jesus himself offended many people with his teachings. Knowing that, say these critics of compromise, why should any Christian witness hesitate to pray in the name of Christ just because there are non-Christians present?

I served for several years on the board of directors of the National Conference of Christians and Jews (Indiana region). My Jewish colleagues on the board knew of my interest and involvement in evangelism and respected my right to do the work of an evangelist, because they knew I respected their religious convictions and that I was sensitive to their feelings about the way I expressed mine. When I offered a prayer at one of our luncheons or meetings, I did not feel that I compromised my own beliefs by trying to be sensitive to the group in whose behalf I was praying. I do not believe in forcing my faith down anyone's throat. To do so *would* be compromising my own beliefs. You don't win people to Christ by flaunting your beliefs, or by imposing your faith on others, or by verbally coercing people to agree with your convictions. On *my* turf I pray in the name of Christ; on *their* turf I pray in the spirit of Christ, who never forced himself on anyone.

Does that mean you should never mention God in public because there may be an atheist in the audience? Not at all. If you have been invited to give an invocation, for example, the invitation itself is your authorization to address God. To whom else would you pray? In that situation I would be less worried about offending an atheist than about insulting adherents of other faiths in whose behalf I have been asked to pray. In fact, I am always thinking about how to word a prayer in a way that might trigger a response in the heart of any unbelievers in the audience. I choose, therefore, to use a common God language, with which all believers can identify, and through which some unbelievers may be reached.

I feel it is as inappropriate to use Trinitarian language in a pluralistic setting as it would be to put "In Christ we trust" on our national currency. There are some who resent even the words "In God we trust," but they have not yet been able to persuade Congress to remove the motto from our coins. If someone were to lobby for the words to be changed to "In Christ we trust," I would oppose any such legislation simply because it is not true. Some of us, but by no means all of us, trust in Christ!

While trying to be sensitive, it is always appropriate for us to "contextualize" our public prayers: that is, to make them relevant to the situation. That is far more meaningful for the participants than our having an all-purpose invocation to suit any assembly, a generic blessing for all breakfasts, lunches, and dinners, and a general closing prayer for every meeting. Doing the work of an evangelist as a public figure requires a sense of the occasion. Sometimes it is possible to express our prayers in the idiom of the group for whom we have been asked to pray. When we do, they are much more likely to hear, reflect upon, and remember our prayers. (For some examples see Appendixes A–C.)

It is well to remember that the longer the prayer, the less the retention. For pity's sake, keep it short! People have a very limited attention span for public prayers, as we have been visually reminded when watching presidential conventions and inaugurations on television. Why is it that so many ministers on these occasions offer such interminably long prayers? People are fidgeting, looking around, glancing at their watches, chatting with the person next to them, and doing everything but listening, while the invoker drones on and on. I suspect even God is annoyed by long-winded prayers, which drive away the very people God wants to reach.

Public Speaking and Preaching

Preaching and speaking in pluralistic settings are quite different from praying. When I am the one voicing a prayer for a group of people, I feel I should be identifying with them and speaking for them. When I am preaching, I am speaking *to* them, not *for* them. The two agendas are not at all the same. When I am speaking in a pluralistic setting, I want to do so with evangelistic sensitivity, always seeking to make a case for God and trying to present and represent Jesus Christ to the people to whom I am speaking. I identify who I am and "where I am coming from." I know I cannot *prove* God, but I am determined to make as reasonable a case for God as I possibly can. I feel I can do that best by coming clean at the start—I confess my faith assumptions and then acknowledge that my faith is a gift for which I can take no credit at all.

Not long after returning to Philadelphia as a pastor, having lived there before as a baseball executive, I was a guest on a late-night radio talk show.[2] A self-professed evangelical who had heard the live broadcast called the next day to express his concern about my "failure to bear witness to Jesus Christ." I explained that my talk-show host was an agnostic Jew and rather cynical to boot, that the program was being broadcast from a nightclub, with a live audience in addition to the radio audience, that we had talked much of the time about God and about my own call into the ministry from my career as a major-league baseball front-office executive, and that I had indeed borne witness to Christ in what I felt was an appropriate manner for the audience and the occasion. The telephone caller was unconvinced. "You should preach Christ crucified and not worry about offending people. If they're offended, that's their problem."

The criticism needs to be taken seriously. Was I being ashamed of the gospel by not proclaiming Christ more forcibly that night? I honestly think not. To have come on too strong would not only have annoyed my host and invited the scorn of the nightclubbers, it would also have been a betrayal of the purpose of my being invited there. The program was not a forum for proclamation. I chose instead to share my faith and to find points of contact with my inquisitive host, the questioners in the live audience, and the people who called in. Even though my host claimed to be an unbeliever, he had no objection to my talking about God or to my faith expressions about Jesus, which I prefaced with expressions like, "As a Christian, I believe. . . ." I did not want to make dogmatic statements as if they were self-evident to my unbelieving host.

Subsequent reflection on this issue has led me to conclude that a distinction has to be made between the offense of the gospel and the offensiveness of the witness. Paul's words should not be used to justify our own rudeness, arrogance, or hypocrisy. The gospel is indeed a stumbling block to some and folly to others, but that is their problem, not ours. All too often, however, what offends people is not the gospel but the way it is presented, not the evangel but the evangelist. The problem with people like the evangelical gentleman on the telephone is that they have not taken seriously the givenness of their own faith. They think that what they believe is true simply because they believe it. They state their beliefs as if they were self-evidently true to someone who does not share their faith assumptions. They speak dogmatically instead of confessionally, and that is what turns people off.

The confusion regarding the offense of the gospel and the offensiveness of the witness is due partly to the failure to distinguish between *authority* and *integrity*. The scriptures have their own self-authenticating authority. The measure of our authority as witnesses is our conformity to the Word of God. The authority is in the message, not the messenger. The integrity of the witness has nothing to do with the authority of the scriptures, but it has much to do with the credibility of the witness. Our integrity as witnesses has to do with the sincerity of our convictions and the genuineness of our faith, as evidenced in the way we live our lives. If people reject the authority of the scriptures they will answer to God, but if they reject the message because of our hypocrisy or insensitivity, then *we* will have to answer to God.

The pastor-evangelist as a public figure comes into contact with people of other faiths and no faith. The public is not a captive audience like the congregation on Sunday morning. One's ideas have to prove their worth in the marketplace of truth. As one who lived and worked in the secular world before going into the ministry, I want to be able to relate to secular people and people of other faiths.

I don't have to deny who I am in order to do that. I want to be both a witness and an apologist for Christ. I know I can't prove my faith, but I can *confess* it. I am talking about a style, not a method. I listen for points of contact and agreement. When I've earned the right to be heard, I don't state my faith as if what I believe is self-evident to a non-Christian. That is what I mean by confessing my faith; it is speaking as one who is aware of the *givenness* of one's faith.

If I am speaking on a religious theme to an audience that includes people of other faiths, I confess my assumptions at the outset, then move on from there to those elements of faith we hold in common. When speaking in a synagogue, I love to show how the Jewish Bible and our New Testament fit together, how we Christians cannot understand the New Testament without their Bible (which we call the Old Testament); how the New Testament was written by Jews, for Jews (mostly), and about a Jew; how the earliest Christians were Jews, and to understand Christian theology one has to understand Hebrew theology.

I might preach on an Old Testament passage, making the point the Bible makes and then presenting, as a statement of faith, my own Christian perspective on the passage, or what it means to me as a Christian. If I do the latter, I do so as one endeavoring to make a case for the reasonableness and attractiveness of the gospel, not as one who thinks the truth of the gospel is self-evident to my Jewish listeners. There is a time and place for powerful proclamation, but I believe our proclamation should not be presumptuous. The gospel should be presented with the humility becoming a person who understands that faith is a gift, not a possession.

If I am performing a particular function at a secular event of some kind, I do not want to betray or violate the expectations of those who invited me. At the same time, I feel I must be true to myself. I do not feel that I can or should deny who I am. I seek, therefore, a common ground where I can make my witness, which under those circumstances will usually be more subtle or low key. For several years I served as chaplain of the Pennsylvania Sports Hall of Fame, in which capacity I had the responsibility of delivering the charge to the newly elected inductees at the annual banquet. In that rather secular setting, it would have been insensitive and irresponsible for me to act as if all fifteen hundred people present were Christians. I made sure, however, that my charges always included the name of God and often a quote from the Bible or a reference to Jesus or his teachings. I am convinced that this low-key approach was far more effective than an aggressive attempt to evangelize that boisterous audience would have been. (One of those charges is included as Appendix D.)

The pastor-evangelist is always aware of the context in which she or he is functioning. This is when actions speak much louder than words. I learned that when I was serving a parish in a predominantly Jewish community. I did not wear my Christianity on my sleeve or display it on the bumper of our car. I tried to the best of my ability and by God's grace to live it. At the annual meeting of the board of directors of our local civic association, some of the members were expressing concern about what would happen to residential property values if black families should move into the neighborhood. It was the typical reaction of those who put property rights above human rights. Our neighborhood was the last bastion of segregation in the city of Philadelphia.

I submitted a resolution calling on the board to make a strong public stand for open housing and extending a welcome to all persons regardless of race, nationality, or creed. I followed my motion with an impassioned plea for the board to exercise its leadership in the community by taking a clear stand for justice and human rights. As I was speaking, a member of a neighboring church was overheard to remark, "We have ways to get rid of him!"

A heated discussion ensued, at the end of which I stood up for my closing statement as the mover to the resolution and said, "I do not see how anyone can in good conscience oppose the spirit of this resolution. If it is not passed, I shall tender my resignation from this board and publicly announce my reasons." The motion passed. Segregation had been officially renounced. In time the area became and remains today a genuinely integrated community.

After that meeting one of the directors came up to me and said, "Mr. Armstrong, I'm a Jew, but if I ever decide to become a Christian, I'd like to join your church, because I admire the stand you and your congregation have taken on race relations."

The commitment of our congregation to being an inclusive church in a racially changing community helped set the tone and the pace for our neighbors in Oak Lane, with the result that the desegregation of the area proceeded without the ugly violence and racial conflict that occurred in other parts of Philadelphia and in many other cities during those turbulent years. Ours was a proactive role rather than the reactive role that so often characterizes the church in a changing community.

Probably because I was the pastor of an integrated congregation, I was invited to be the speaker at a community memorial service held in a local schoolyard on April 5, 1968, for Dr. Martin Luther King, Jr., following his assassination. In all my years as a minister that assignment stands out in my memory as still, for me, the most convincing example of the challenge of relating to a mixed audience under extremely difficult and emotional circumstances. The large gathering of blacks and whites included people of different religions and no religion. In church the previous morning I had paid tribute to Dr. King as a servant of Christ. Now, because I was speaking in a secular setting as the representative of a pluralistic aggregation of people who were there to share their common grief in the wake of a national tragedy, I paid tribute to him simply as a great man. My black neighbors, some of whom were filled with anger, all of whom were grief-stricken, expressed their appreciation. They understood. And they knew I cared.

I did not feel it would be appropriate for me to exclude half of the audience by an insensitive use of Christian terminology. My Jewish neighbors appreciated that and told me so. They knew I was a Christian minister, and they certainly knew Dr. King was. But because I was trying to express *their* feelings as well as my own, they were able to identify with my remarks, instead of being turned off by them and distracted from the main point of our being there.

I have related this incident to illustrate my own belief in the need to try to be sensitive in our public appearances when there are non-Christians present. (The brief address I gave on that occasion is included as Appendix E.)

As a public figure, probably more than in any other role, the pastor-evangelist is an ambassador for Jesus Christ. As Christ's representatives in the community, we will be observed as spokespersons for and interpreters of the Christian faith and as examples of the Christian life. It is crucial that in both our words and our deeds we reflect the love of Christ. If in our actions we behave indiscreetly, indecently, or unethically, we dishonor the name of Christ and betray the cause of his church. If in our public speaking we lock people out by the insensitive use of Christian jargon, we may be doing the work of an evangelical while failing as an evangelist.

Concluding Thoughts

The personal relationships and professional roles that I have dealt with in the three books on the theme of the pastor-evangelist have been arbitrarily identified and discussed as those which define the life of a parish minister. The fact that some people have asked me if I have in mind yet another book dealing with certain other areas of ministry, such as new church development, youth ministry, and institutional chaplaincies, suggests that I need to make the distinction between what I call a professional role and an area of responsibility. I think of worship leadership, preaching, teaching, visiting, counseling, administering, discipling, and relating to the wider public as activities in which all pastors are engaged, fulfilling their professional roles as a pastor.

Youth ministry, on the other hand, is a specific area of responsibility. That is why there is no section entitled "The Pastor-Evangelist as Youth Minister" or "The Pastor-Evangelist as New Church Developer." Whatever their specific areas of responsibility may be, those engaged in parish ministry function from time to time in the above-named professional roles. The content of these three volumes is as relevant for a youth minister or new church development pastor as it is for anyone else. The evangelistic principles are broadly applicable, since they are related not to one's job description but to one's ministerial functions.

So the question can be asked of the youth minister who preaches occasionally, assists in worship leadership, teaches confirmation classes, visits parishioners, counsels people of various ages, administers a youth program, makes disciples, and appears at local high school athletic and social events, as it can be asked of any other minister of the Word and sacrament, What does it mean to do the work of an evangelist?

I have wrestled long and hard with this question. I have taught courses, conducted hundreds of seminars and workshops, and written books on the subject, and the more I have thought about it the more aware I have become of the complexities of its theological, practical, and ethical implications. That makes it difficult for anyone to pretend to speak as a final authority on doing the work of an evangelist, especially when one's theology insists that the ultimate converter of human hearts is God alone. The role of the evangelist is important and necessary, but only instrumental. To focus on the evangelist is not to deny or diminish the role of the Holy Spirit, but to explore and understand the role of the instrument.

The experiential, personal approach I have adopted in this book involves the risk of vulnerability. To expose one's own evangelistic intentions and practice to the critique of one's peers is threatening, especially when one is well aware of one's limitations. The risk is worth it, nevertheless, if others can identify with the risk taker's experience and apply whatever lessons can be drawn from that experience to their own struggle to do the work of an evangelist.

One thing is certain: We are not likely to take the biblical mandate seriously, let alone fulfill it, unless our own faith in Jesus Christ is intact. The importance of the pastor's personal faith has been discussed at length in the preceding two books, but it bears emphasizing. So does the importance of prayer, which is absolutely indispensable to the ministry of evangelism. There is a direct correlation between the pastor's devotional life and her or his commitment to and effectiveness in doing the work of an evangelist.

Although I have not dealt with these matters as a separate subtopic in this book, what I have stated in the preceding paragraph is implicit throughout and should be obvious to the reader. One's ministerial practice inevitably, although not always consistently, reflects one's theology, even as one's theology informs one's pastoral style. Admitting that one's methodology and theology are not always concordant, my own effort to do the work of an evangelist has been predicated on my desire to take seriously the injunction to Timothy and to be faithful to the Great Commission (Matt. 28:19; Mark 16:15; Luke 24:47–48). The question for me as a minister of the gospel is not *whether* to do the work of an evangelist but *how* to do it.

The question deserves a serious and thoughtful answer, for to be an evangelist in a pluralistic world, where conflicting ideologies, other religions, and secular values are competing for human minds and hearts, and where cultural barriers impede the acceptance of the gospel, is not an easy task. Busy pastors may be tempted to ignore or even deny their own evangelistic role or, what is more likely, to assume they are fulfilling it because, they say, "Everything I do is evangelism, and besides, my job is to equip others to do it."

My total disagreement with such a rationale for denying one's personal responsibility was the main reason for my writing this book and its two companions. Another reason was my observation that the biggest bottleneck to evangelism in many local churches, especially the so-called mainline churches, is the pastor, without whose leadership, support, involvement, and example the congregation is not likely to fulfill its own ministry of evangelism.

My prayer is that those who read these three volumes will not only be challenged to do the work of an evangelist but will be motivated to encourage others to do the same.

Appendix A

Invocation Delivered at the Economic Club of Indianapolis, Indiana

Almighty God, we have seen the business you have given us to be busy with, and we know that it is your gift to us that we should eat, and drink, and take pleasure in all our toil. We are grateful for these blessings, and we acknowledge our responsibility to be stewards of all you have entrusted to us.

Recognizing the limitations of our human wisdom, we pray that our efforts to solve the economic problems of these difficult days may be marked by growth in faith and full employment of love, high production of works, and an economy of words.

Deliver us from the inflation of ego, and from the depression of despair.

Give us the courage to take the high risk of investing in the cause of freedom and the willingness to pay the price of justice.

Then may we take stock of ourselves and have the honesty to assume the losses of our past mistakes.

In that spirit, O God, we ask your special blessing on this gathering, that we may listen and learn, and so depart a little wiser than we were, for your sake and for ours.

Amen.

Appendix B

Invocation Delivered at a Dinner Meeting
of the Indiana State Chamber of Commerce

Amid the complexities of commerce and the pressures of our daily lives, we humbly bow before you, O God. Aware of our interdependence, make us mindful of our dependence upon you as the ultimate source of life and hope.

> Help us who manufacture things to remember that the hand that made us is divine.
>
> Help us who buy and sell to remember that your gifts are free for the asking.
>
> Help us whose decisions affect the welfare and direct the course of society to acknowledge that our earthly affairs must find their meaning and purpose in your divine economy.

So inspire us, gracious God, to be faithful stewards of all your bounties, that we may not just work to live but live to work. Then may our thanks be worthy and our gratitude sincere, for food that nourishes our bodies, for fellowship that warms our hearts, and for faith that stirs up our souls to nobler effort and higher goals, for your kingdom's sake.

Amen.

Appendix C

Invocation Delivered
at an Interfaith Memorial Service
Princeton University Chapel

Almighty God,

    whose wisdom and power are displayed in the works of thy creation,
    whose justice and mercy are revealed in thy Word,
    and whose goodness and love are known to all who believe in thee,

we gather this afternoon to remember before thee our classmates who have departed from this earth. May thy presence be felt among us, thy truth be known to us, thy will be done in us, and thy love expressed through us, so that their names may be honored and thy name may be glorified. For thine alone is the kingdom, and the power, and the glory, forever and ever.
    Amen.

Appendix D

Charge to the Newly Inducted Members of the Pennsylvania Sports Hall of Fame

Gentlemen, we salute you for the great honor which has been bestowed upon you tonight. Our commonwealth, like many of her sister states, has seen fit to recognize her sons and daughters who have distinguished themselves in the ever-widening world of athletics. The civic-minded citizens who founded and have supported the Pennsylvania Sports Hall of Fame have made possible this appropriate way of enshrining your names among the immortals already so honored.

Like the other celebrated members of this elite company, you too have basked in the sunlight of success. You have savored the sweet taste of public esteem. You have nobly earned and justly deserve the plaudits of those who admire and respect the quality of excellence.

The tribute you have received tonight is eloquent testimony to your achievements. But these are behind you now, and this trophy is of a different kind from others you have received. It is not just another laurel wreath to grace the brow of a competitor for a record set or a victory won. It is not a harbinger of triumphs yet to come. It points not to the future but to the past. May it give you, therefore, a sense of perspective, of privilege, and of responsibility.

First, a sense of perspective. May it be for you a reminder that one may never linger long on the stage of renown. There are always others waiting in the wings to take your place, and those who have stood beneath the floodlights of fame must one day slip quietly into the mists of memory, there to join the other heroes of yesteryear. "Time, like an ever-rolling stream, Bears all its sons away; They fly forgotten, as a dream Dies at the opening day."

May this tribute give you a sense of perspective. May it give you, too, a sense of privilege. May it be a reminder of the priceless privilege that has been yours to live in a land where men and women may compete in freedom and be judged with fairness, where ability is recognized and rewarded, and where people have the time and means to enjoy the luxury of spectator sports. May it remind you that life itself is a precious gift that should never be taken for granted. Nor should you fail to be grateful to your Creator for the talents with which you have been endowed.

A sense of perspective, a sense of privilege, and, finally, may this tribute give you a sense of responsibility. You have used your talents well. You have been acclaimed for your feats of glory in athletics. But the greatest victories of life are yet to be won, for the toughest competitor you will ever face is yourself. This is the challenge that remains when you have hung up your jersey and put away your spikes.

So live that when the game of life is over and—if I may paraphrase the late great Grantland Rice—the final score is entered in the eternal record book, the Master Coach will say of you, "Well done, thou good and faithful servant. Thou hast been faithful over a little; I will set you over much. Enter into the joy of your Master."

Congratulations, and God bless you!

Appendix E

Address Delivered at Memorial Rally for Dr. Martin Luther King, Jr. Philadelphia, Pennsylvania

Martin Luther King, Jr., is dead—like the late President Kennedy, a victim of an assassin's bullet. This too was a shot heard round the world, a shot that has ricocheted into the hearts of decent folks in every land.

The meaning of this tragedy has been and will be expressed by far more eloquent tongues than mine. The shock, the injustice, the terrible cruelty of such an utterly senseless murder leaves our nation with a sorrow that is deep and difficult to bear. The capture of the assassin can hardly compensate for the pain and anguish that we feel, nor fill the void that is in the hearts of four children who have lost their father, and a wife who has lost her husband.

The untimely death of this man, whose courage, whose wisdom, whose creative ability and dynamic leadership have been an inspiration to freedom-loving people everywhere, is a stunning loss to the entire world. His life has been snuffed out at the very peak of its usefulness. Yet already he had been acclaimed for his contributions to humanity. Winner of the cherished Nobel Peace Prize, he had received the plaudits of those in high places as well as the praise of those of humble estate. Although it is not for us to assess his greatness, I am confident that history will record his name among the moral and spiritual giants of our age.

It will be for you and me, and for our children, to decide whether or not he has lived and died in vain. The cause for which he gave his life was the cause of justice and freedom for all people. If we believe in what he lived and died for, then we will do all in our power to further that cause. It is not by flowery words and impressive eulogy that we show the genuineness of our grief for this champion of justice, but by deeds of virtue and sacrifice.

His was a sacrifice made for all people, not just for one race of humankind. It is our common loss, by virtue of our common humanity. So let not his death be used as an excuse for violence and bloodshed, nor for pillaging and plunder. That would be a denial of everything he stood for. As one who has far more reason for bitterness than most of us, Jacqueline Kennedy, sharing the grief of Coretta Scott King, said this morning, "Let the assassination of Dr. King make room in people's hearts for love, not for hate."

I pray that men, women, and children of goodwill everywhere may see that Martin Luther King's ideals are not betrayed, that our nation will not be torn asunder by hatred and revenge, and that together we will work for justice and freedom for all humanity, until the day when neither violent nor nonviolent protest will be needed, because America will have become what she was destined to be: one nation, under God, with liberty and justice for all!

Notes

Preface

1. To name just a few books my seminary students found helpful: *Today's Pastor in Tomorrow's World,* rev. ed. by Carnegie Samuel Calian (Philadelphia: Westminster Press, 1982); *Growth in Ministry* edited by Thomas E. Kadel (Philadelphia: Fortress Press, 1980); *The Ministry in Historical Perspectives* edited by H. Richard Niebuhr and Daniel Day Williams (New York: Harper & Brothers, 1956); *The New Testament Image of the Ministry* by W. T. Purkiser (Kansas City, Mo.: Beacon Hill Press, 1969); *Freedom for Ministry* by Richard J. Neuhaus (New York: Harper & Row, 1979); and *Creative Ministry* by Henri J. M. Nouwen (Garden City, N.Y.: Doubleday & Co., 1971).

2. Douglas Webster's book *What Is Evangelism?* (London: Highway Press, 1961) and David M. Stowe's *Ecumenicity and Evangelism* (Grand Rapids: Wm. B. Eerdmans Publishing Co., 1970) have stood the test of time. So has Michael Green's *Evangelism in the Early Church* (Grand Rapids: Wm. B. Eerdmans Publishing Co., 1970). For differing perspectives see the following representative works. Anglican: *Turning to Christ* by Urban T. Holmes (New York: Seabury Press, 1981) and *The Open Secret* by J. E. L. Newbigin (Grand Rapids: Wm. B. Eerdmans Publishing Co., 1978); Presbyterian: *Rethinking Evangelism* by Ben Campbell Johnson (Atlanta: John Knox Press, 1983) and *The Church as Evangelist* by George E. Sweazey (New York: Harper & Row, 1978); Baptist: *Introduction to Evangelism* by Delos Miles (Nashville: Broadman Press, 1983); Methodist: *The New Evangelism* by Alan Walker (Nashville: Abingdon Press, 1975) and *The Contagious Congregation* by George G. Hunter (Nashville: Abingdon Press, 1979).

3. The "five points for faith sharing" and the principles relating to the use of the telephone are re-presented in chapter 2, for example. Some other

ideas have been reworked or expanded. For the most part, however, where the subject matter has been dealt with in my earlier writings, appropriate references are given. The theological principles and evangelistic style represented in all three of the books are, I hope, consistent.

4. See my book *The Pastor-Evangelist in Worship* (Philadelphia: Westminster Press, 1986), Appendix A, "The Integrity of Evangelism," pp. 161–173.

Introduction

1. Or as seminary professors, or church administrators, or pastoral counselors, or whatever!

2. This definition appeared first in my book *The Pastor-Evangelist in Worship*, pp. 124–125. In chapter 2 of *The Pastor as Evangelist* (Philadelphia: Westminster Press, 1984) I list twenty or more definitions from a variety of sources.

3. Tom Allan's book *The Face of My Parish* (New York: Harper & Brothers, 1957) is the inspiring story of the North Kelvinside Church of Glasgow, Scotland, describing what happened when members of the congregation embarked on a "mission of friendship" to their surrounding community.

4. An account of the revitalization of Oak Lane Presbyterian Church is contained in my book *The Oak Lane Story* (New York: Division of Evangelism, Board of National Missions, United Presbyterian Church U.S.A., 1971).

5. The order of the phrasing has been changed slightly from the way it first appeared on p. 53 of my *Service Evangelism* (Philadelphia: Westminster Press, 1979). It seems appropriate to put "listening to them" before "identifying with them."

6. The paradoxical nature of faith and its implications for evangelism are covered more fully in *Service Evangelism,* chapter 2, "The Case for Faith Sharing," and in *The Pastor as Evangelist,* chapter 4, "The Pastor's Personal Faith."

7. Any attempt to categorize the various ministerial functions or professional roles of a pastor is bound to be arbitrary. Some easily identifiable roles, such as preacher or counselor, will undoubtedly be on everyone's list. Others will vary with the list maker. For a thorough summary of the biblical images and concepts of ministry and the functional roles of a minister, I highly recommend W. T. Purkiser's excellent book, *The New Testament Image of the Ministry* (Kansas City, Mo.: Beacon Hill Press, 1969).

Part One
The Pastor-Evangelist as Visitor

1. In *The Pastor as Evangelist* I used a "horizontal" approach in discussing the pastor's personal relationships and the various factors that shape the context for pastoral evangelism.

2. In his widely used text *Basic Types of Pastoral Care and Counseling: Resources for the Ministry of Healing and Growth,* rev. and enl. ed. (Nashville: Abingdon Press, 1984), p. 26, Howard Clinebell identifies and describes five functions of pastoral care: healing, sustaining, guiding, reconciling, and nurturing.

3. One reason the inclusive nature of pastoral care is often overlooked may be the unfortunate (in my view) linking of the term with counseling. People speak of "pastoral care and counseling" as one expression, as if they were separate and equal functions. They are not; pastoral care *includes* counseling.

4. *Webster's New International Dictionary,* 2d ed., Unabridged (Springfield, Mass.: G. & C. Merriam Co., 1941). Some of the other pertinent definitions given are as follows: Calling on in friendship or courtesy; going or coming to see in an official capacity in order to examine or correct abuses; staying with a person as a temporary guest; coming to or upon with a particular action or purpose understood or specified (that is, to comfort, reward, benefit or bless; or to afflict, punish, or avenge, going to see as a physician; attending a person). The intransitive verb "to visit" can be used to mean "to call, to sojourn, to frequent, or to chat" (colloquial, as in visiting on the telephone).

5. The Greek word for visitation is *episkopē.* The related Greek word *episkopos* means "a superintendent, guardian, or overseer." Paul uses it as the technical term for the office of bishop (Phil. 1:1; 1 Tim. 3:2; Titus 1:7). The root meaning of the word suggests that whatever else bishops do, they should be first and foremost visitors. Any priest would agree that a visitation by the bishop was not necessarily always a blessing.

6. Hermann Wolfgang Beyer in Gerhard Kittel, ed., *Theological Dictionary of the New Testament,* vol. 2, trans. Geoffrey W. Bromiley (Grand Rapids: Wm. B. Eerdmans Publishing Co., 1964), p. 603. The author comments further: "James adopts both the best in Jewish ethics and the demand of Jesus for practical love to our neighbors when he says in 1:27, 'Pure religion before God and the Father is this, To visit the fatherless and widows in their affliction' " (p. 604).

7. Cf. Stephen's comment about Moses in Acts 7:23: " 'When he was forty years old, it came into his heart to visit his brethren, the sons of Israel.' "

8. For example, *erchomai* (to come to, 1 Cor. 16:5, 12); *proserchomai* (to approach, Acts 10:28); *eiserchomai* (to enter or go into, Acts 16:40; 28:8); *historeō* (to inquire into or observe, Gal. 1:18).

9. Friedrich Buchsel in *Theological Dictionary of the New Testament,* vol. 3 (1966), p. 396.

10. Commenting on Hebrews 14:14–15, Beyer writes (loc cit. note 6), "It is worth noting that *episkopein* here expresses an attitude which displays the responsibility of the community for the eternal salvation of all its members, and that what later became the specific task of the one, of the leader, is thus represented as a matter for the whole congregation. The congregation as a whole is understood to have as such an essential episcopal ministry and office" (p. 604).

11. Charles L. Goodell, *Pastoral and Personal Evangelism* (New York: Fleming H. Revell Co., 1907), p. 83. Dr. Goodell, who later served as Secretary of the Commission on Evangelism and Life Service of the former Federal Council of the Churches of Christ in America, called for ministers of the gospel to be "pastor-evangelists."

12. For further comments on the turf factor, see *The Pastor as Evangelist,* pp. 98–99 and 116–117.

13. The experience is described in my book *The Oak Lane Story,* which is out of print but available in many seminary and church libraries.

14. See *The Pastor as Evangelist,* pp. 145–146.

15. One of the strengths of James Kennedy's "Evangelism Explosion" is its emphasis on training by modeling. Those who have been trained duplicate themselves by training others.

16. See *The Pastor as Evangelist,* chapter 11, and *Service Evangelism,* chapters 5 and 6.

17. Rebecca Manley Pippert, in her book *Out of the Saltshaker and Into the World: Evangelism as a Way of Life* (Downers Grove, Ill.: Inter-Varsity Press, 1979), describes three models for intentionally turning a conversation to spiritual matters. All three methods involve the use of questions, but the presupposition of each is that the witness does the "sharing." The questions are intended to pave the way for what the witness has to say, rather than to free the other person to share her or his experience of God.

18. For additional thoughts on suiting the approach to the person, see *The Pastor as Evangelist,* pp. 166–169. The chart on page 169 graphically underscores how many different possibilities there are and how important it is for the witness to *listen,* in order to know where the other person is coming from.

19. The distinction between listening skills and good listening is discussed more fully in *Service Evangelism,* rev. ed. (Philadelphia: Westminster Press, 1983), pp. 90–95, 114, 200. In no way is the distinction intended to disparage the importance of listening skills, which are certainly essential to good listening. There are many resources for learning to listen, including especially those offered by LEAD Consultants. See John S. Savage, *The Apathetic and Bored Church Member* (Pittsford, N.Y.: LEAD Consultants, 1976), chapter 5. Savage, Director of LEAD Consultants, offers a 40-hour workshop (Lab I) on listening skills. For those who wish to become certified

to teach the Savage method, an additional 50 hours of training are required (Lab II). With Dr. Savage's permission I have incorporated some of the LEAD materials in the *Faithful Witnesses* (Philadelphia: Geneva Press, 1987) evangelism training course (*Participant's Book,* pp. 21–35; *Leader's Guide,* pp. 24–32). As listening skills, though extremely important, are only one component in the larger task of equipping people for the work of evangelism, I have had to find quicker ways of helping people to understand what it means to be a good listener and to develop their listening skills.

20. For a fuller discussion of the "Five Points for Faith Sharing," see *Faithful Witnesses—Participant's Book,* pp. 44–46.

21. See *Faithful Witnesses—Participant's Book,* p. 22, for diagrams of seating arrangements. See also *Service Evangelism,* pp. 85–87.

22. See *The Pastor as Evangelist,* chapter 8, which deals with the number of persons involved in a faith-sharing conversation as an important factor shaping the context for evangelism.

23. Ibid.

24. For some suggestions, including exercises, on faith sharing see *Faithful Witnesses—Leader's Guide,* pp. 41–49, and *Faithful Witnesses—Participant's Book,* pp. 42–51. See also the helpful book by E. Eddie Fox and George E. Morris entitled *Faith-Sharing: Dynamic Christian Witnessing by Invitation* (Nashville: Discipleship Resources, World Methodist Council, 1986).

25. A biblical/theological rationale for faith sharing is presented in *Service Evangelism,* chapter 2. The relationship between faith sharing and evangelism is discussed in *The Pastor as Evangelist,* pp. 38–40.

26. A very practical resource for those wishing to explore other dimensions of this topic is Arthur H. Becker's little book, *The Compassionate Visitor: Resources for Ministering to People Who Are Ill* (Minneapolis: Augsburg Publishing House, 1985).

27. Cf. Matt. 8:16; 12:15; 14:14; 15:30; 19:2; 21:14; Mark 1:34; 3:10; Luke 4:40; 5:15; 6:17–19.

28. For further discussion of the evangelistic implications of the problems of aging, see *The Pastor as Evangelist,* pp. 125–132.

29. I have referred to the turf factor in chapter 2.

30. To ensure the anonymity of those involved I am using fictitious names.

Part Two
The Pastor-Evangelist as Counselor

1. E. Brooks Holifield traces the historical development of pastoral counseling in his book, *A History of Pastoral Care in America* (Nashville: Abingdon Press, 1983).

2. Carroll A. Wise, *Pastoral Counseling, Its Theory and Practice* (New York: Harper & Brothers, 1951), p. 68. Dr. Wise intended this to be a

descriptive statement rather than a definition, since earlier in the book he declared that his purpose was not to define the term but to clarify the process (p. 4).

3. Seward Hiltner's writings, including especially his books *Pastoral Counseling* (Nashville: Abingdon Press, 1949) and *Preface to Pastoral Theology* (Nashville: Abingdon Press, 1958), were a major force in the shift from moralistic exhortation and advice giving in counseling to moral clarification and self-understanding. Verbal persuasion gave way to the nondirective, client-centered approaches advocated by Carl Rogers (*Client-Centered Therapy;* Boston: Houghton Mifflin Co., 1951) and others. More recently some writers in the field are calling for more directive counseling, for example, William Glasser, *Reality Therapy* (New York: Harper & Row, 1976), in an authentic moral context, for example, Don S. Browning, *The Moral Context of Pastoral Care* (Philadelphia: Westminster Press, 1976).

4. Howard J. Clinebell, *Basic Types of Pastoral Care and Counseling: Resources for the Ministry of Healing and Growth,* rev. and enl. ed. (Nashville: Abingdon Press, 1984), p. 26.

5. Seward Hiltner viewed spiritual direction as part of the guiding activity of the pastor.

6. Donald Capps, in his book *Biblical Approaches to Pastoral Counseling* (Philadelphia: Westminster Press, 1981), discusses the use of the Psalms, Proverbs, and parables in pastoral care and counseling. See also William B. Oglesby, Jr., *Biblical Themes for Pastoral Care* (Nashville: Abingdon Press, 1980). Wayne Oates addressed the topic thirty years earlier in his book *The Bible in Pastoral Care* (Philadelphia: Westminster Press, 1953).

7. In his book *Outside Looking In* (Toronto: United Church Publishing House, United Church of Canada, 1987), Gordon Turner offers Acts 8:26–40, the story of Philip and the Ethiopian eunuch, as a model for pastoral care and evangelism (p. 59). Turner sees Philip as exemplifying what Carl Rogers identifies as the five tenets of human conversation: acceptance, understanding, reflection, clarification, and integration (p. 73). Having established a pastoral base, Philip starts at the Ethiopian's point of need, that is, the passage he has been reading (p. 75), becomes a mutual searcher, as he is invited to join the Ethiopian in the chariot (p. 81), probably engages in some existential sharing of faith stories with his host (p. 90), and undoubtedly uses the power of suggestion to encourage the eunuch in the direction he appears to be moving (p. 96). Although Turner relies heavily on speculation in his use of this particular passage to illustrate his own model of pastoral conversation, he makes a reasonable case for using Philip as a model for pastoral care and evangelism. If Turner's hypothetical dialogue were actually part of the text, perhaps we could even use the incident as a (not *the*) model for pastoral counseling!

8. "Martha, Martha, you are anxious and troubled about many things; one thing is needful. Mary has chosen the good portion" (Luke 10:41–42).

9. "O woman, what have you to do with me? My hour has not yet come" (John 2:4).

10. "Get behind me, Satan! For you are not on the side of God" (Mark 8:33; Matt. 16:23).

11. "Woe to you, scribes and Pharisees, hypocrites!" (Matt. 23:13, 15, 23, 25, 27, 29).

12. "For you have had five husbands, and he whom you now have is not your husband" (John 4:18).

13. "Truly, I say to you, this very night, before the cock crows twice, you will deny me three times" (Mark 14:30; cf. Matt. 26:34; Luke 22:34).

14. "You son of the devil, you enemy of all righteousness, full of all deceit and villainy" (Acts 13:10).

15. "King Agrippa, do you believe the prophets? I know that you believe" (Acts 26:27).

16. "Confrontation is an indispensable skill in much pastoral counseling, involving the sensitive use of the minister's authority. . . . The central goal of confronting anyone is to enable *self-confrontation*—i.e., to help them (sic) face the behavior that hurts themselves and/or others and to feel the guilt that therefore is appropriate" (Howard Clinebell, *Basic Types of Pastoral Care and Counseling,* p. 142).

17. Ibid., pp. 142–149.

18. The Greek word *paraklētos* occurs five times in the New Testament and only in the Johannine writings. It is used of the Holy Spirit four times (John 14:16; 14:26; 15:26; 16:7), and once of Jesus (1 John 2:1), where it is translated as "advocate" ("but if any one does sin, we have an advocate with the Father, Jesus Christ the righteous").

19. "The only thing one can say for certain," writes Johannes Behm in the *Theological Dictionary of the New Testament,* vol. 5 (1968), "is that the sense of 'comforter,' favoured by, e.g., Wycliffe, Luther and the A.V. in John's Gospel, does not fit any of the NT passages. Neither Jesus nor the Spirit is described as a 'comforter' " (p. 804). "As regards the translation of *paraklētos* in John, the history of the word and concept shows that in the course of religious history subsidiary senses were interwoven into the primary sense of 'advocate,' so that no single word can provide an adequate rendering" (p. 814). Of the subsidiary meanings, Behm opts for "supporter" or "helper," though he concludes that "the basic concept and sustaining religious idea is that of 'advocate' " (p. 814).

20. Paul W. Pruyser, in his book *The Minister as Diagnostician* (Philadelphia: Westminster Press, 1976), discusses the biblical themes that help counselors to approach their task theologically.

21. See the Westminster Shorter Catechism, Question 14: "What is sin? Answer: Sin is any want of conformity unto, or transgression of, the law of God."

22. A glance at the indexes of many books on counseling will prove the

point. Theological terms such as sin, redemption, the Holy Spirit are not listed.

23. Karl Menninger, *Whatever Became of Sin?* (New York: Hawthorn Books, 1973). The contents of this book were first presented by Dr. Menninger at Princeton Theological Seminary as the Stone Lectures, which I was privileged to hear.

24. Dr. Vincent M. Bilotta III speaking to a group of Air Force chaplains at Scott Air Force Base, January 8, 1975.

25. Halford E. Luccock, *Communicating the Gospel,* The Lyman Beecher Lectures on Preaching, 1953 (New York: Harper & Brothers, 1954), p. 84.

26. It is encouraging to note that the pastoral counseling profession itself has become aware of the displacement of the spiritual dimension by psychological categories and constructs, and has cautioned pastors to be consistent with their theological presuppositions. Howard Clinebell, for example, in a chapter entitled "Facilitating Spiritual Wholeness: The Heart of Pastoral Care and Counseling" *(Basic Types of Pastoral Care and Counseling),* writes: "Pastors are called to be enablers of spiritual wholeness throughout the life cycle. . . . Enabling spiritual healing and growth is the core task in all pastoral care and counseling (p. 103). . . . It is important for the pastoral counselor to stay open to the energy of God's transforming love during counseling sessions" (p. 130).

27. R. D. Rosen labeled the more extreme forms of jargonism "psychobabble," in his provocative book by that title (New York: Atheneum Publishers, 1977).

28. Distinctions have been made between various styles of listening in counseling. There is active listening (Carl Jung), passive listening (Carl Rogers), directive listening (William Glasser), and so on. I am not sure it is always easy to distinguish between them. Insofar as the designations are valid, in actual practice I find myself using all three styles, depending on the situation and the conversational need at the moment.

29. I found Wayne E. Oates's book *Where to Go for Help* (Philadelphia: Westminster Press, 1957), a very useful reference, when I was starting out as a pastor. See the revised and enlarged edition by Wayne E. Oates and Kirk H. Neely (Philadelphia: Westminster Press, 1972). See also William B. Oglesby, Jr., *Referral in Pastoral Counseling,* rev. ed. (Nashville: Abingdon Press, 1978).

30. For extensive bibliographical suggestions for various types of counseling, see Howard Clinebell's *Basic Types of Pastoral Care and Counseling.* He includes lists of recommended readings and resources at the end of each chapter in which the different types of counseling are discussed.

31. Early in my ministry I made good use of Granger Westberg's helpful booklet *Premarital Counseling* (Office of Publication and Distribution of the National Council of the Churches of Christ in the U.S.A., 1958). Howard Clinebell's book *Growth Counseling for Marriage Enrichment* (Philadel-

phia: Fortress Press, 1975) offers useful suggestions for "pre-marriage and the early years" (the book's subtitle).

32. Three books that have stood the test of time for me are Dean Johnson's *Marriage Counseling: Theory and Practice* (Englewood Cliffs, N.J.: Prentice-Hall, 1961); Charles William Stewart's *The Minister as Marriage Counselor* (Nashville: Abingdon Press, 1961); and Howard and Charlotte Clinebell's *The Intimate Marriage* (New York: Harper & Row, 1970).

33. The Garden Grove Community Church of Garden Grove, California, has had one of the largest programs in the United States for singles and formerly married persons. The director of that program in 1976 published a book offering practical guidance for persons facing divorce. See Jim Smoke, *Growing Through Divorce* (Irvine, Calif.: Harvest House, 1976). See also Stewart's *The Minister as Marriage Counselor,* chapter 9, "Divorce and Post-Divorce."

34. In the traditional Presbyterian service, the parents were asked to respond to the following questions: "In presenting your child for baptism, do you confess your faith in Jesus Christ as your Lord and Saviour; and do you promise, in dependence on the grace of God, to bring up your Child in the nurture and admonition of the Lord?" (*The Book of Common Worship,* p. 122). The Presbyterian Church (U.S.A.), like most other denominations, has been updating its liturgical language, but many pastors prefer the traditional forms.

35. See *The Pastor as Evangelist,* chapter 8, for a discussion of the impact of the numerical factor in interpersonal witnessing.

36. Some years ago I was introduced to the Successful Pastoral Counseling series, edited by Russell L. Dicks. Among the many helpful volumes covering different aspects and types of pastoral care and counseling is Ernest E. Bruder's book, *Ministering to Deeply Troubled People* (Englewood Cliffs, N.J.: Prentice-Hall, 1963).

37. For a psychological study of the emotional stages of terminal illness, see Elisabeth Kübler-Ross's influential book *On Death and Dying* (New York: Macmillan Co., 1969). See also Granger E. Westberg, *Good Grief* (Philadelphia: Fortress Press, 1976); Jack S. Miller, *The Healing Power of Grief* (New York: Seabury Press, 1978); and Glen W. Davidson, *Living with Dying* (Minneapolis: Augsburg Publishing House, 1975).

38. I have dealt more fully with the pastor-evangelist's ministry to the bereaved in *The Pastor as Evangelist* and *The Pastor-Evangelist in Worship.* Consult the index of each of these books for the relevant sections.

39. I am not referring here to those unfortunate people who are chronically unemployed—street people, transients, migrants, illegal aliens, the homeless. Their problems are quite different and must be addressed at the causative level, not just symptomatically. They are a result and manifestation of the systemic evils of society, and the church must use its corporate power and influence to address and help correct those evils.

40. Among the professional experts to whom we should be prepared to refer people are those qualified to help them with matters pertaining to financial management and estate planning, including perhaps a reputable tax attorney, a certified public accountant, an insurance agent, and someone who knows about various kinds of deferred gifts (such as an institutional development officer or fund raiser). The pastor-evangelist should never pretend to be an expert in these highly technical areas. In larger churches there may be persons in the congregation with these kinds of expertise.

41. As of this writing there have been some encouraging breakthroughs in medical research that give hope for an eventual discovery of both a cure for and an immunization against AIDS.

42. For a discussion of the content of the gospel, see *The Pastor-Evangelist in Worship,* pp. 123–148; see also *Faithful Witnesses—Leader's Guide,* chapters 7–9, and *Faithful Witnesses—Participant's Book,* pp. 52–54.

Part Three
The Pastor-Evangelist as Teacher

1. Douglas W. Johnson, *Report on a Survey of Pastors' Involvement in Christian Education* (Institute for Church Development, 1980).

2. The verb "to educate" (from the Latin *educo, educere,* "to lead out," and *educo, educare,* "to bring up") occurs only once in the RSV, where it is used to translate the Greek verb *paideuō.* Here Paul refers to himself as being "educated ("taught," KJV) according to the strict manner of the law of our fathers" (Acts 22:3). Elsewhere the Greek word is translated variously as chasten, chastise, correct, discipline, instruct, punish, train, and learn (passive), never as teach. Does Christian education include all of the above?

3. See, for example, W. T. Purkiser's *The New Testament Image of the Ministry* (Kansas City, Mo.: Beacon Hill Press, 1969), chapter 2.

4. See Matt. 4:23; 9:35; 11:1; Acts 5:42; 15:35; 28:31; 1 Tim. 5:17.

5. "The goal of proclamation in the hearers," wrote Gerhard Friedrich, "is faith rather than understanding" (*Theological Dictionary of the New Testament,* vol. 3, p. 712).

6. Ibid., p. 713.

7. Ibid. Friedrich points out that we are never told that John the Baptist taught. He was first and foremost a *kēryx.*

8. Ibid.

9. See Part One of *The Pastor-Evangelist in Worship* for an inclusive treatment of the pastor's role as worship leader.

10. Some clergypersons have been called to multiple-staff churches as ministers of administration.

11. For a discussion of the nature of evangelistic preaching, see *The Pastor-Evangelist in Worship,* pp. 85–88, 109–122.

12. Parker J. Palmer, *To Know as We Are Known: A Spirituality of Education* (New York: Harper & Row, 1983).

13. Educational theory, curriculum development, teaching methodologies for different age groups, and other such matters relating to Christian education are not discussed here. The focus is on the pastor-evangelist as teacher. The evangelistic principles being discussed are applicable at all age levels. For suggestions relating specifically to the evangelization of different age groups (children, youth, young adults, middle-aged and older adults), see *The Pastor as Evangelist,* chapter 7.

14. For those interested in exploring faith development theory, see James W. Fowler's *Stages of Faith: The Psychology of Human Development and the Quest for Meaning* (New York: Harper & Row, 1981); *Becoming Adult, Becoming Christian* (San Francisco: Harper & Row, 1984); and *Faith Development and Pastoral Care* (Fortress Press, 1987). The work of Jean Piaget, Erik Erikson, Lawrence Kohlberg, and many others has been influential in the exploration of faith development. V. Bailey Gillespie's book *Religious Conversion and Personal Identity* (Birmingham, Ala.: Religious Education Press, 1979) is a helpful introduction to the psychology of religious conversion and an overview of those who have contributed to the discussions in the field. Fowler's writings have been critiqued by James E. Loder, Craig R. Dykstra, and others. See Craig Dykstra and Sharon Parks, eds., *Faith Development and Fowler* (Birmingham, Ala.: Religious Education Press, 1986). For a feminist view of faith development theory, see Carol Gilligan's book *In a Different Voice: Psychological Theory and Women's Development* (Cambridge, Mass.: Harvard University Press, 1982).

Ann Elizabeth Proctor McElligott, an Episcopal priest, has developed an evangelism training curriculum for the Evangelism Working Group, Division of Church and Society, of the National Council of the Churches of Christ in the U.S.A. (copyrighted 1986), incorporating the insights of faith development theory. She writes in the *Leader's Guide,* p. 3, "Faith Development Theory can be a valuable tool for the evangelist. It provides a means of examining one's own faith journey, a way of talking with others about their religious experience, and a means of understanding these stories within a common framework of developmental stages." Some teachers of evangelism have made use of Abraham Maslow's hierarchy of needs in their evangelistic training programs.

15. One of the English words used to translate the Greek word *koinōnia* is "participation."

Part Four
The Pastor-Evangelist as Discipler

1. K. H. Rengstorf, in *Theological Dictionary of the New Testament,* vol. 4 (1967), p. 441.

2. There are references also to the disciples of John the Baptist (Matt. 9:14; 11:2; Mark 2:18; Luke 5:33; 7:18–19; 11:1; John 1:35, 37; 3:25); the Pharisees (Matt. 22:16; Mark 2:18; Luke 5:33); Moses (John 9:28); and Paul (Acts 9:25).

3. Again, the texts listed are merely representative of many others that could be cited, including all of the "I am's" of Jesus and his statements about why he had come.

4. A wonderful stewardship illustration from the Old Testament is the story of the building of the tabernacle, when the people of Israel gave their time, talent, and treasure to the project (see Ex. 35:22; 36:1).

5. The Greek word *charisma,* which occurs, with one exception (1 Peter 4:10), only in the letters written by or attributed to Paul, means "a gift of grace" or "a free gift." The so-called spiritual gifts *(charismata)* are listed in Romans 12:6–8 (prophecy, service, teaching, exhortation, contributing, aiding, and acts of mercy), 1 Corinthians 12:9–10 (faith, healing, working miracles, prophecy, distinguishing between spirits, speaking in tongues, and interpreting tongues), 1 Corinthians 12:28 (apostles, prophets, teachers, miracle workers, healers, helpers, administrators, and speakers in tongues) and 1 Corinthians 12:29–30 (apostles, prophets, teachers, miracle workers, healers, speakers in various tongues, interpreters of tongues). Although there is some overlapping, the lists are not identical, and therefore none of them is definitive. Three of the other Greek words for "gift" are *dōrea,* which in the New Testament always refers to the gift of God or of Christ to people (e.g., John 4:10; Eph. 4:7); *dōron,* which is used for people's gifts to each other, gifts of money in the temple, and in one instance God's gifts to humankind (Eph. 2:8); and *dōma,* which is used four times as a synonym for *dōron* (e.g., Matt. 7:11). The English rendering of Ephesians 4:11 ("And his gifts were that some should be apostles") is an idiomatic translation of the verb form *edōken* (from *didōmi,* to give). In attempting to identify all the spiritual gifts, one of my students listed "martyrdom," adding that it was a gift that could be used only once!

6. The stewardship committee may be the place the pastor-evangelist as discipler needs to start. The members of the committee need to be discipled as stewards so that they can help disciple others. They ought to be concerned with much more than just fund raising!

7. The *Faithful Witnesses* materials are such a curriculum. Included in the *Leader's Guide* is an outline of a visitation evangelism program for the local church. There is also a list of other evangelism resource materials for congregations. See also my *Service Evangelism* and *The Church as Evangelist* (New York: Harper & Row, 1978) for discussions of the church's corporate ministry of evangelism.

8. *Book of Order,* Presbyterian Church (U.S.A), G-3.0300.

9. The 16-week *Faithful Witnesses* course is designed to do that. A shorter training model is the P.R.O.O.F. seminar, which uses a 15-hour

format to help people to learn to share their faith. See *Service Evangelism,* chapters 7 and 8.

10. According to Presbyterian polity the session is responsible for prebaptism instruction, but the pastor is usually the one who does the instructing.

11. Werner Foerster, in *Theological Dictionary of the New Testament,* vol. 7 (1971), p. 183.

12. See *The Pastor-Evangelist in Worship,* pp. 17–18, for a list of the kinds of questions with which the worship committee needs to wrestle.

13. Ibid., pp. 30–37. The music of worship, including the criteria for selecting hymns, is discussed.

14. Communicant members are those who are entitled to participate in the sacrament.

15. The closest Hebrew word is *'ebed* (servant), which in the Old Testament is seldom used in a derogatory sense. Worshipers of God were God's servants *('abadim),* of whom David and Moses are notable examples. The concept reaches its highest expression in the Suffering Servant passages of Isaiah, where the *'ebed* fulfills the mission of the Lord by suffering and dying for the sins of the world (see especially Isaiah 53).

16. The Greek word *pais,* which literally means "child," is often used in the Septuagint to translate the Hebrew word *'ebed* (servant). It appears much less frequently in the New Testament than does *doulos.* Jesus is called the "servant *(pais)* of God" five times in the New Testament. The word is used as a title of respect.

17. K. H. Rengstorf, in the *Theological Dictionary of the New Testament,* vol. 2, p. 278.

18. In the Form and Order for the Ordination of Ruling Elders in the Presbyterian *Book of Common Worship* the members of the congregation are charged to render the elders "all due obedience, co-operation, and support, and [to] follow them so far as you see them follow Christ" (p. 249).

19. The Greek word *exousia* denotes the ability or power to perform an action, the right to do something, or the right over something. It is often synonymous with the Greek word *dynamis* (power). In the New Testament *exousia* is used in reference to the power of God over nature and the spiritual world, and of the power or freedom given to Jesus and by him to his disciples. It includes both the right and the power to act. As such it always reflects the authority of God; nothing takes place apart from God's *exousia,* which cannot be grabbed, only granted. Thus Jesus claimed: "All *exousia* in heaven and on earth has been *given* to me" (Matt. 28:18, emphasis mine). The *exousia* which Jesus grants "cannot be used arbitrarily; in its application the apostle is bound to the Lord" (Werner Foerster in *Theological Dictionary of the New Testament,* vol. 2, p. 570).

20. The Greek word *charisma* means "a gift of grace."

Part Five
The Pastor-Evangelist as Administrator

1. The texts cited are simply illustrative of many, many others that could be listed.

2. Hermann Wolfgang Beyer in *Theological Dictionary of the New Testament,* vol. 2, pp. 615–616.

3. Hermann Wolfgang Beyer in *Theological Dictionary of the New Testament,* vol. 3, p. 1036. Writes Beyer: "No society can exist without some order and direction. It is the grace of God to give gifts which equip for government. . . . The early Church soon came to like the picture of the Church as a ship and Christ as the Helmsman" (ibid.).

4. The corresponding RSV translations are "this gracious work which we are carrying on" and "this liberal gift which we are administering" (2 Cor. 8:19, 20).

5. Otto Michel in *Theological Dictionary of the New Testament,* vol. 5, pp. 151–152.

6. Abraham Zaleznik, "Managers and Leaders: Are They Different?" *Harvard Business Review* 55, no. 3 (May–June), 1977.

7. Richard G. Hutcheson, Jr., *Wheel Within the Wheel: Confronting the Management Crisis of the Pluralistic Church* (Atlanta: John Knox Press, 1979), p. 168.

8. Ibid., p. 165.

9. Ibid., p. 166.

10. Ibid., p. 167.

11. According to Douglas McGregor, Theory X leaders operate on the assumption that people function well only if offered a carrot or threatened with a stick, whereas Theory Y leaders assume people will work better if they help to determine the objectives and perceive them to be worthwhile.

12. My book *The Oak Lane Story,* p. 37.

13. In *The Pastor as Evangelist,* pp. 105–107, the subject of relating to transients is covered more fully.

14. See *The Pastor as Evangelist,* pp. 141–145.

15. In *The Pastor-Evangelist in Worship,* pp. 26–30 and 174–177, there is a checklist for evaluating a church bulletin as an evangelistic instrument.

16. See *The Pastor as Evangelist,* pp. 146–149.

Part Six
The Pastor-Evangelist as Public Figure

1. Heaven forbid that we should ever allow ourselves to be advertised the way one clergyman did recently. The flyers announcing his speaking appearance referred to him as "God's Messiah from Lahaska, Pennsylvania" and "God's gift to Trenton, the world, and the universe"!

2. Some pointers for the use of radio and television as mediums for evangelism are offered in *The Pastor as Evangelist,* pp. 146–149.

Index

Notes

Notes

Notes

Notes

Notes

Notes

Notes